To inspire others
a gift from one heart
to another.

Doug Petersen

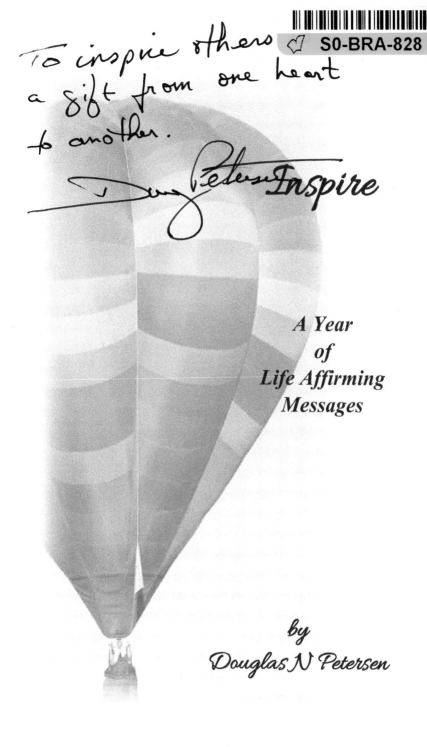

Inspire

*A Year
of
Life Affirming
Messages*

*by
Douglas N Petersen*

Inspire: A Year Of Life Affirming Messages, by Douglas N Petersen.

ISBN 978-1-62137-266-0 (soft cover); 978-1-62137-267-7(ebook)

Library of Congress Control Number: 2013907532

Published 2013 by Virtualbookworm.com Publishing Inc., P.O. Box 9949. College Station, TX 77842, US.

Front cover photograph by Steve Bower.
Cover design by Kassi Cooper.

Printed in the United States of America.

Introduction

For those who are familiar with my work know this is the fifth book in a series where I share inspirational and life affirming messages. Each one was written randomly, and usually spontaneously, with no recurring theme from one to the next except for focusing on personal values.

Some of you may know a little of my story with some of the challenges I have faced and perhaps some can relate to similar situations. The pages that follow are as much for me as they may be for you. Just because we grow up and become a responsible adult doesn't mean we will not face more challenges in life. We will for sure. The three hundred and sixty-nine messages contained in this book are meant to be a reminder, we're not alone. We're not the only one going through this part of a similar journey. The words on each page are meant to be a simple reminder that there is a solution, and most of the time is within us already. The solution is many times refocusing on our personal values, or how can we serve others as they travel on their path.

In these messages, I make many references to 'our journey' or 'the path' we are traveling. This journey is our life and the end of our journey, our destination, is when we leave this world, and perhaps move on to another one. Are all the answers to every situation we will face in life in this book? They are most certainly not. However, if just one page of this book makes a small difference in your life, and makes your day just a little better, I have fulfilled my purpose in this journey of mine.

My life's purpose is to mentor and inspire an awakening in others, through care and compassion, a self-awareness of their personal values and self-worth.

I share these messages not only in the books I publish, but also through a free email newsletter, various social media sites, and my personal blog page. I virtually attempt to reach out to thousands with an inspiration of hope and awareness of the differences we make in the lives of so many. Thank you for being part of my journey. Let's travel together, One Day At A Time.

Douglas N. Petersen

Table of Contents

January

January 1

A new day is born, as the sun slowly makes its presence on the eastern sky. It is a new day, a new week, a new month… and yes a new year. It is an awakening of sorts, where we have an opportunity to set our course on perhaps a new path. It is a perfect time to reflect on the past and take what went well and bring it with us. The negative that we experienced in the past, well, we can just leave that behind as we move forward on our journey.

While it is a new day and a new beginning, we are still who we are. We may have pretended to be someone else in the past. Perhaps the best promise, as we renew this day, is to remove the mask of our past and be just who we really are, ourselves. If we truly remove and throw away the mask, we are free… free to be who we really are without the shroud of falseness.

It's a new beginning, where we make new promises and set forth on our path. Great things lie ahead and if we go forward, renewed and refreshed with whom we are, the path opens up to the wonders of a great life. Enjoy the journey.

January 2

*D*emons and monsters lie under our bed and have been there all night, just waiting for us to get up and start our day. These demons manifest themselves as stress, anger, fear, powerlessness, low self-esteem and when we discover these monsters creeping into our day, what do we do? What do we have to battle these demons and monsters?

These demons and monsters are our character defects and play imaginary mind games with us, truly becoming the 'enemy within' our body. Not only will these demons take over our day, they will take over the lives of others we interact with, if we don't rid ourselves of these monsters.

Our weapons to combat these demons of character defects are our swords of values. The powerful and might swords of courage, faith, honesty, and love, as well as the many other values we hold dear to our heart. We have the weapons to fight those demons and defeat them.

If we live our values each day the demons and monsters of character defects will not be part of our day, but each day we awaken we need to remember they are still waiting under the bed.

January 3

I t matters what we think; or does it? Our mind is constantly processing information and our thoughts go from one idea to another to another. We begin one thought process, and another idea or situation comes to mind, and we begin thinking about it. Or conscious and subconscious mind is thousands of thoughts each day. All this activity is all contained in the mass between our ears and matters to no one, except ourselves.

It matters what we say; or does it? Sometimes, there is a connection with what we say and what we were thinking, but then again, sometimes we speak without thinking. What we say is now out there for others to hear. While what we say may have a limited audience, we are now causing others to think. Our spoken words are just the audible manifestation of our thoughts. Do our words matter? Yes, they do and will make an impact on others.

It matters what we do; yes, absolutely it does. Our actions make the biggest difference and matter the most. We can think and say all sorts of things, but when we put our thoughts into action, that is what will make a difference and will matter the most. We can think we need to forgive, but it's not until we take the action to forgive does it matter. When we move into the action of serving others with care and compassion, it then matters.

Our actions and what we do on our journey matter. What we do will not only impact those around us, but will soon be paid forward by someone else. Our actions have now doubled, tripled, and live on. What we think matters, but only to ourselves. What we say matters to those that can hear us. What we do matters; we make a difference, and the world is just a little better because our actions are more powerful than our thoughts and words.

It matters what we do. What will you do today to make a difference?

January 4

Our life is like a novel, divided into many chapters; consisting of many paragraphs and sentences. Each word of each sentence is another minute in our lives. And with each minute becomes another day, another sentence in our life's novel.

So what is our story? We are the author of our story, but there is something within us that 'writing' our story. Each day we add another page to our novel, adding it to the current chapter. Looking back we can see chapters on our school or college years. We may see chapters on family and children. And there is a common under-lying theme, though we may not see it.

'Writing' this novel of ours, we never get writer's block because every minute of every day adds another piece to our 'novel'. At some point we will finally see what has been within us, writing this novel of ours. And when we discover this force, our novel will make perfect sense.

This force that is within each of us is our personal values directing our life's purpose. The sooner we see these, the more we will enjoy 'writing' the next chapter.

January 5

A friend is someone who is #1 on your speed dial on your phone.

A friend is someone who will tell you when the jeans don't fit.

A friend is someone who will change your tire in the rain.

A friend is someone who makes you feel special all the time.

A friend is someone who can speak volumes without words, only their touch.

A friend is someone who is unselfish, caring, loving and honest.

A friend is someone who you can call at 2:30 AM and they're happy you called.

A friend is someone who knows your past and does not judge.

A friend is someone who wipes away the tears when times are tough.

A friend is someone who just shows up exactly when you need them.

A friend is someone who sees your beauty when you can't.

A friend is someone who will go through the same pain as you just to be with you.

A friend is someone who you can look into their eyes and see their love for you.

A friend is someone ...... like you?

January 6

Which way is the right way to go? What is it that I should be doing? These questions confirm that we can find ourselves in a state of confusion sometimes by all the distractions around us. We have highway signs telling us one thing, a passenger in the seat next to us telling us something different. We have ads all around us spinning the truth, trying to convince us their product or service is better. So many distractions, so many tiny tornadoes going around us, so much chaos, how do we find our way back to sanity?

The first step is to recognize these are just distractions and not necessarily our reality. We can let these tiny tornadoes just spin on by and not get us caught up in the whirlwind. We need to focus on who we are and where our path is taking us. There are attractions in our lives that keep us focused and headed in the right direction and the distractions attempt to take us away from that journey.

Find and focus on the attractions in life and if these make our heart sing, then these are the ones to follow. The chaos in distractions will be minimal if we focus on what makes our heart sing.

January 7

The road construction is getting worse by the day. There are more detours, and our commute is becoming quite frustrating. Gas prices are crazy high, going up twenty cents overnight. We get to work, and the coffee service is down and of all mornings, we sure could use a cup of coffee. We attempt to login into our computer, and a virus has taken over, and we can't start our day until we get it cleaned up. Not a good start in anyone's books.

The day doesn't seem to be on track for a good day at all. We listen to voice mails and these seem to be filled with anger. Finally, our computer is working and the flood of emails fills our inbox with urgent requests; all seemingly due within the next hour.

What has happened is that the chaos and destruction of the whirling tornado of 'things go wrong' has sucked us in, and now we're spinning with it. We are now expending so much energy within the tornado ourselves, we're adding to its power. We're complaining, slamming our fist, gritting our teeth, and perhaps saying an unkind word or two. We are now part of the problem.

Now it's time to become part of the solution. If we can step back for a moment and truly see what is going on, and not be in the center of the whirlwind, how bad is it really? Is there anything we can do to solve the problem? If so, take care of it. If not, let it go and move on. When we allow the negative aspect of our lives to consume us, it drains us. Look at all the energy and time we spend on the negative aspects of our lives, the ugly comments and thoughts, all the nasty emails, all the snickers and judging others, and all the ill-will we wish on others. If we could just take half of that time and energy and use it for the good of others in service, what a great day it would be.

Today let's focus on being part of the solution and not adding more wind to the tornado of negativity. Let's focus on helping others, living our values, and letting our sunshine light the way for others to come out of their whirlwind.

January 8

W hat leads us on our journey? We know that our feet takes us on our journey and our legs, arms and hands all play a role too, but what is leading us? Perhaps we use our mind to mentally map out a plan to where we're headed. We may be motivated by a career and that is what is leading us on our journey, but a career is merely a part of our journey, not what is leading us. Motivation is an action derived from the mind and it serves a purpose in our lives, but is it really what is driving and leading us on our journey?

The drive, the fuel, the direction that our life's journey is taking us comes from our heart. Our heart is what gives us inspiration. Our heart is what fuels our passion. Our heart is what is leading us on our journey, not our mind. When we can come to that realization and accept it, our path will explode in new colors and become so much brighter. We will be inspired! Our journey will take on a whole new meaning.

Live with passion. Live with love. Live inspired! It's our heart where all of these can be found.

January 9

I t's time to get away. It's time to stray off our path a little, venture out and have some fun. When we leave our familiar space and seek new and exciting places, we broaden our life's experiences. It's time to get away for a while and leave the routine behind. Our get-a-way's let us sleep in, or get up earlier. We get to live by another set of rules. We can have a dessert at lunch; we get to be lazy for an afternoon, just relaxing in a hammock.

Our get-a-ways are an adventure where we can just escape and have some fun, do the things we want and not the things we need to in our daily life. We may think we can't afford a get-a-way, either for the cost of travel or the cost of time. Bunk! You cannot afford not to escape, even for a day. We don't have to travel far, we just have to remove ourselves far enough from our 'normal' world and let our body and soul be renewed. Our get-a-way can be to a foreign country or all the way over to the next county to relax in a park for a day. It's as simple as that.

Returning from the get-a-way and returning home, we are re-energized, refocused and see how beautiful our life really is. It's good to be home.

January 10

The car battery and gas in the gas tank are a couple very important parts of our car. We need one to get us started and the other to keep us going. If either is drained or empty we are stranded on the side of the road until we can get recharged and refueled. And the same is true for us; if we become physically or emotionally drained we become stranded on our life's journey. But where is the refueling/recharging station for us?

Some may suggest that some time away for relaxation is a way to replenish our bodies and that is true in many cases. Others may seek meditation to find to be another way to recharge. But there are times when the battery is so low, or the gas tank so dry neither of those are effective. It is then that 'road service', in the form of a good and caring friend, is needed to get us back on our journey.

A caring friend can hold our hand just so gently and softly say the right words that our emotional tank begins to fill back up. When that tank is full, the physical one will also be replenished.

Let's not let a friend be stranded with drained batteries or empty gas tanks on their journey, let's be the 'road service' to get them back on the path.

January 11

hildren are running and laughing all around. It's a party! Colorful balloons, tied with ribbons, float through the air; swaying in the gentle breeze of the backyard. Tables are lined with birthday decorations, and all the party-goers are playing games and having fun.

A small wand is dipped into the soapy mixture, and bubbles begin to form; some big, some small. Each one floats in the wind, and we can see the multi-colored rainbows glisten on each bubble. We're mesmerized watching them float through the air. The children chase each one, trying to pop them with their fingers. The atmosphere is filled with fun and not a care in the world.

Why can't we have fun and not a care in the world? Why can't we have a day filled with balloons and bubbles? We can! It's a matter of us taking life a little less serious today. It's convincing ourselves that we deserve a little fun in our life. Whether or not we buy a small bottle of bubbles and simply sit in our chair and create the little spheres of the soapy mix, it makes no difference. We just need to imagine that bubble, or that balloon floating on a ribbon. We imagine hearing the laughter of carefree children. We need to see that our life can be fun too. We can have our own party, and not worry about any cleanup.

So break out the bubbles and balloons, throw the confetti in the air and enjoy life today like it is the first day of a very long party. Laugh and smile for no reason other than to celebrate our life's party today.

January 12

From the moment we begin our journey to the day our journey ends, each and every day should be filled with joy and happiness. But along our journey there are days of sadness and despair, but we need to find our way quickly back into the light of love and laughter.

We are not here to travel in the darkness, but in the light of what is guiding us. We shouldn't merely exist on our journey; we need to live on our journey. We need to live a life filled with happiness. We need to live a life of serving others. We need to live a life of love, not only for others, but a love of ourselves.

Travel today with a song on our lips, kindness in our touch, and love in our heart.

January 13

The sun warms the sand on the beach, while the ocean is many yards away, with its small waves lapping the shore. It's so peaceful and serene. A small mound on the beach begins to come alive and small sea turtle eggs begin to hatch. Instinctively the small creatures begin to dig their way out of the warm nest of sand that has been home and head to their destination, the ocean.

Without a compass, a mother or father to guide them, they begin their trek to the water. Motivated at this point, their tiny flippers push the sand, struggling they inch forward, one stroke at a time, closer and closer to their destination. Motivation is the drive on this part of their journey, but this part is not without the perils of the beach. Many young turtles do not make it to their ocean.

The first sea water wave washes over the small turtle and motivation has changed, it's now inspiration. Inspired by the joy of finding its new home, its new life, the turtle rejoices. Its flippers now gently propel the little turtle into the wonders of its new world, the beautiful ocean.

Have we found our inspiration like the little sea turtle? Have we found our home and see all the wonders and beauty that surrounds us?

January 14

That feeling we get when we close the lid of the paint can after painting the baby's room is that sense of accomplishment. It's the same feeling we get when we finish a big project at work, knowing we did our best, and the boss smiles as he looks it over. When we bring a task to a conclusion, and have applied all our talents to the best of our ability, it fills our heart with a sense of pride and a feeling of accomplishment.

The bands may not play or the crowds cheer when we finish our task, but we didn't do it for their praise and recognition anyway. We did it for ourselves. We did it because it was some we wanted to and that's all the reason we need. We don't need to boast about it, for that diminishes our work to an ego-filling exercise. We should be proud of our work, but not seek the praise of others.

Accomplishment of any task, big or small, fills our lives with a sense of purpose. It gives us that warm feeling that we are worthy and that we can make a difference in the world, if we just try.

January 15

I n the open field, stands a tall replica of a Native American Indian totem pole, a tribute to a culture. At the top is the head of an eagle. Its beak, bold and prominent signifies power, yet a peaceful grace envelops it. Below the eagle are other figures, representing various animals and symbols. At the bottom is a worn figure, almost unrecognizable. It has been kicked, scuffed and is covered with dirt as it is the bottom of the statuesque totem pole. It has been abused by the wrath of nature, but had little choice because of where it is on the totem pole.

So where are we on the totem pole? Are we on the bottom, taking the abuse of others? Are we putting ourselves on the bottom by our own choice? Or are we at the top, majestic and powerful? The answer lies in our mind and not where others place us. If we value ourselves and are honest, we should find ourselves somewhere in the upper half.

We may not be the eagle on the top of the totem pole, but we're certainly not the unrecognizable figure, beaten and scorned, on the bottom. It's time we put ourselves in the right place on totem pole.

January 16

Comfy and cozy, we pull the covers around us, lying in our bed. We feel warm and safe. Our sanctuary for the last few hours has given us the rest we needed. We may want just stay in this cocoon of protection, safe from the outside world, but we can't. We must break the bonds and greet the world.

Our world awaits and needs us. What will be our mission today? What will we do, consciously or unconsciously, that will make a difference? We don't know for sure, but we do know we have to venture out from the safety and security of our covers to start.

We can and will make a difference today. Our lives will also be changed when we take the step in helping and being of service to others.

The warm and cozy bed will be there later tonight, but right now we have something more important to tend to...life.

January 17

United We Stand. It's so encouraging seeing examples of ways we support causes such as Red Shirt Friday in support of our American troops, wearing a pink ribbon that is looped over itself supporting an awareness of breast cancer, or being part of another charitable event, supporting a great cause.

But what about the other, less visible, ways we stand united? Don't we stand united against the fight on terrorism? Don't we stand united in making the very best life for the children in this country? Of course we do, but don't show a visible symbol.

We are united as a small group, a larger community, and as a great nation. We should be proud to stand beside our brothers and sisters, united. United We Stand and no one can ever take that away from us; for we are one, and one that is strong in whatever cause we fight.

Be strong. Be brave. Be united and stand proud.

January 18

The good deed done today is not done because we expect something in return; it's given because we are living the values that are within us. It's the act of caring and doing something for someone, and not doing it in a selfish way. Doing a good deed is like adding to our own legacy by demonstrating that we can live in a world where not everyone is out for themselves. Random and anonymously at times, we give of ourselves, making the day just a little better than it was a few hours ago.

We're standing in the grocery line behind the single mom struggling with two children in the grocery store; counting out coupons and sees her total is more than what is in her wallet. Wondering which items she will have to put back, we step up and pay for her groceries. The single mother's eyes fill with tears, while the two children sit quietly in the shopping cart. Her eyes say thank you; her gratitude is from her heart and someday, she will do a good deed for some other stranger.

Acts of kindness are not hard and don't require a lot of money. They are for us to think of others before thinking of what's in it for us. We need to reach out our hand to help, with our palm turned down, and not turned facing up looking for some sort of payback.

A good deed will make for a good day. If we can do a good deed each day, we have made someone's journey today just a little better than it started. Give, inspire, and make a difference today for it is within each of us to do that little thing for someone else.

January 19

"Knock, knock… who's there?" We, of course, would follow this with a joke of some sort, and as corny as they are, we just begin to smile at the moment; we hear the first two words. Instead of focusing on the first two words, which brings our attention to the door, let's focus on the last two, "… who's there?" On a serious note, when we hear that knock, do we ask who is on the other side, peek through the peephole, or do we simply open the door?

So what could be possibly knocking on our door? Could it be an opportunity? Will we miss it and not open the door? The opportunity could be one of a career change, a new relationship, time to spend with family, or an opportunity to share ourselves with others, giving the gift of time. Opportunity is a gift in its self and comes in so many forms.

The knock may be faint, and we may not hear it thus missing what or who awaits us to open the door. If we never open the door after the knock, that knock may never come again and are we willing to accept that? If we are, then we may miss that turn on our path; that change in the direction on our life's journey that leads us to our life's purpose. We shouldn't ignore the knock, at least look through the peephole.

January 20

When we get the wind knocked out of us, we collapse on the ground. The moment before we were just fine and then, without warning, BAM!! It hits us like a truck, and we are flat on our back, barely able to breathe or move. What was that we ask ourselves?

There are events in our lives that come in quietly, while others hit us like a truck and knock us for a loop. We need to catch our breath and get back up. The hand of a friend can help us to our feet, but we need to brush ourselves off and face that 'truck' that just knocked the wind out of us. We cannot simply lie on the ground and accept defeat. We must get up and face the world.

When we get up and face life's challenges, we experience hope. We put our courage into action. We bring that inner strength from deep within our heart and soul, and face the challenges that are ahead of us on this journey. We do this not for others. We do it for ourselves. It is our journey.

January 21

Memories are those little pieces of history we retain in our mind in little file cabinets. These little pieces, filed away, are sometimes pleasant thoughts, while others are not so nice. We file them in the file drawers of our mind. Many times we played a role in the memory, and some memories we were just observer. It could be the memory of a freshly baked apple pie coming out of our grandmother's oven. Other memories may be times of painful relationships that turned ugly and their images are etched in our minds. Good or bad, these memories are ones that we have put away in our minds.

Each and every day, our actions may be creating another memory. Perhaps this memory is one for ourselves, or it could be from someone else. So if we're creating memories; are they ones that will be filed in the "pleasant file drawer", or the drawer we don't want to open?

We create memories and we need to remember that these are not only ones that will be filed away in our mind, but the minds of others that we touch. Each day we have a choice of the memory we're going to create. Let's create ones based on our values and not the character defects that haunt us.

January 22

Without you, the world would have one less smile to enjoy.

Without you, we would have one less person to enjoy as casual lunch.

Without you, the world would miss the gift of your time.

Without you, we would have one less shoulder to lean on when we need it.

Without you, the world would miss your kind words.

Without you, we would have one less friend that shares our joy and happiness.

Without you, the world would have one less loving soul to inspire others.

Without you, we would be a little less than what we are today.

Without you, we, and the world, would be sad.

You see, you make a difference in the lives of many. Just be yourself. We, and the world, love you for who you are.

January 23

*P*ush this button and we will go up in the elevator. Push this button and we will get the candy bar from the vending machine. Push this button and we select the gas to be pumped into the car. There is even an "Easy Button". Buttons, we use them in our daily life. There are some buttons that are unnecessary and should not be used.

It's when people start pushing our buttons that things start going wrong. Some of our buttons are so big and exposed; it is easy for others to push them and get us to react certain ways. It's easy for them to manipulate us by pushing our buttons, knowing how we will probably react. Certain people even know the secret button, so secluded and hidden from view. It's that button begins a spiral of our emotions. Buttons are manipulative.

It's time to disable our buttons as best we can and not allow others to control our lives. We, in turn, have no business pushing the buttons of others either to cause them to act a certain way. We don't need buttons. What we need is to recognize we have our values and by living them, inspire others. It's by doing this, do we lead and inspire, not by pushing their buttons.

January 24

The rose bush, stressed from draught, insects, and other cruel forms of nature is almost to the point where it will die. Sad to see this once beautiful bush, once filled with roses, is slowly slipping away. But we have the ability to bring life to what is almost lost. We begin to water it, give it the nutrients it so needs. We nurture it back to health, slowly but surely the brown leaves are replaced with new green growths. We continue to nurture it and then one morning, it rewards us with a beautiful red rose. Perfect in color and shape it is a gift from the rose brush for not giving up on it.

We also see times where we need to nurture others. We need to find ways to bring water and nutrients back into their life. We need to nurture hope for them. We need to be a friend, when others have walked out, leaving them to shrivel up. We nurture with care, compassion and empathy. We nurture with a hug, a gentle touch of the hand, and a kind word of hope and encouragement. In return, they give us the same beautiful gift the rose bush gave us, but this time it is love. And what a beautiful gift it is.

January 25

The warm water from the shower cascades over our bodies. Beating down, from head to toe, the water washes away the all that we collected since the last shower. We can feel the water cleansing our body. It feels so good. All the 'dirt' has now been washed off our body and flows down the drain.

Just as the shower washes our bodies, our personal values will wash away those defects that we gather. Courage and faith will wash away fear. Forgiveness will wash away anger and resentments. Joy will clean us from the dirt of sadness. Gratitude will wash away self-pity. Love, especially love of self, will wash away the feeling of low self-worth and low self-esteem.

Like the shower, we can use our personal values to make us 'clean' again, each day, each morning; we just have to put our personal values as a top priority in our lives. When we do, we will feel just as refreshed as coming out of the morning shower.

January 26

3-D is the new technology wave that brings three dimensional viewing to the home. It adds new life to the once black and white televisions of the past. But today, 3-D means something else to some. It can mean discouragement, disappointment, and depression. These 3-D's are not ones that add to our lives, but are ones that take away from life. We find this to be debilitating in so many aspects, it is scary.

We need to recognize when one, two or all three of the 3-D's begin to impact our life. We need to take corrective action and eliminate these from our day. It's time to look at what is good in our lives. We need to focus on what we are grateful for and not what has brought the 3-D's into our day. The more we add to our gratitude bucket, and see the wonders in our life, the less the 3-D's will play a role in our day, or our life.

Life is too short to allow the 3-D's to be part of it. We need to find a solution and be the person we want to be.

January 27

So what's the answer? We pondered this all the years in school and we looked deep within our mind to pull out the answer to the question on the paper. Is it A, B, C, or all the above? We studied long and hard for this test and our brain is just so saturated, we think it would leak out our ears. With all the knowledge we could possibly muster up, we answer the question.

So what is the answer? Not to the academic test on the paper, but the one we face each day in our lives. What is the answer to the many decisions we face? We can't really pull an 'all-nighter' in this test, because it comes to us in so many forms each day. Each question is a little different than the next. But the answers are not always in our mind, but are in our heart. The answers come to us when we look and live our personal values. Is the answer to be honest and sincere? Is the answer to be loving?

The answers are not always easy in the test of life and the good news is, we will all pass this test, if the answers come from the heart.

January 28

The mother is preparing fresh home-made cinnamon rolls for the weekend breakfast. Having a little extra dough, she prepares it with all the same special ingredients, just as the larger rolls, but this one she takes a little extra time. She takes the dough and rolls it out and shapes it as a heart and puts it in the oven. As the mother takes it out of the oven minutes later, all brown, the sweet smell fills the kitchen. Letting it cool a little, she then brings it over to us and says, "I made you a special roll this morning."

A simple act of kindness can make the difference in the world. The memory of that special, heart-shaped cinnamon roll will last forever in our heart. It wasn't a lot of extra work, it was thinking of someone else and doing something special.

A simple act of love is what lifetime memories are made of. What simple act of kindness, or simple act of love can we do today that will make a difference in the lives of those we touch?

January 29

A new day begins and we begin another part of our journey on our life's path. What is store for us as we travel? What joys or tribulations lie ahead? What beauty is just around the next turn? We don't really know until we take the next step into today and leave yesterday behind.

We should focus on the beauty of today and see all the wonders that are around us. Let's see the beauty in the friends that walk along beside us. For our friends are the angels in our lives. Let's also see the beauty that is within us. Our journey is our journey and we need walk it in the very best company we can, with our angels and ourselves.

Are you an angel to someone else, helping them on their journey? If so, what a great gift you share with each other.

January 30

*I*t is over. It is in the past and we cannot bring it back. A little dark in tone some might say, but is it? We can look at "it" as being someone that we loved; perhaps a person that is we no longer have a relationship with. This brings a sad feeling about "it" and our heart weighs heavy. Perhaps "it" is something bad that has happened in our lives and now we can move forward into the light along our path. Good or bad, "it" is over and lies behind us on our journey.

These events in our lives make up who we are and who we become. We can allow all those "its" to drag us down and bring us to a low point on our path, or we can learn from each and every "it" and become a better person. Our path then will be brighter as a result.

The only rule we really must apply to "it", is that "it" can never diminish who we are as a person. We are worthy and deserve our own love and respect. Never let "it", whatever "it" might be, ever convince you otherwise.

January 31

The little furry creature sits quietly beside our bed in the morning, waiting for us to stir. Its tail wags as the slightest movement on the bed, knowing their 'human' will soon share some attention with them. Maybe a small yelp will bring them the love and attention they so desperately seek.

We swing our legs off the bed and our little furry creature goes crazy; tail wagging faster than a hummingbird's wings, it is so excited to see us up. Its excitement may be partially to go outside, but more likely to receive a small token of love from us. Our furry creature gives us unconditional love and is always there. What do we share in return; maybe simple pats on the head or a little treat as we rush out the door? They are there to sit in the couch with us, all curled up on our lap, safe and content in its feeling of love. Our furry creature knows no boundaries in sharing its love with us and only hopes for a little in return. A simple scratch behind the ears, or a little rub under the chin, is their reward for the love they so freely share.

While many of us may not have a furry creature in our lives, do we have someone that is trying to share their unconditional love, without boundaries, with us and we not see it? Do we simply give it a passing pat on the head too? Look closely. Love is what we all seek and is within each of us to share, if we love ourselves too.

February

February 1

I t's a moonless night and we look up to the dark night sky above. The sky is filled with a blanket of stars, twinkling ever so bright. Like tiny diamonds, glistening on black velvet, we can see deep into the endless space above us. How peaceful, serene, and humbling it is to be part of this vast universe, knowing we are here. We must also believe that we are part of this whole universe for a reason.

As we continue to stare into the dark, star-filled sky, a shooting star streaks across the black velvet sky, ever so quickly. As a child we were taught to wish upon on a falling star and that is what we must do now, make a wish. What will be our wish? What will make our life in this vast universe complete? What is it that is so deep within our heart and soul that is waiting to be revealed? Is it what will lead us to our life's purpose?

As all the stars above us as our witness, make a wish, not a shallow one, but one that is real and meaningful to ourselves. With our wish in our mind, now push it to our heart, for our heart is where our values live and these will give us what we need to make our wish come true.

Make a wish and now live it.

February 2

Confused, uncertain, bewildered, we find ourselves at a point on our path where we don't know which way to turn. We know our journey is not over, but which way do we go? Left, right, or straight ahead… we stand idle, waiting for someone to whisper in our ear the answer to our conflict of what path to follow.

While we have friends that walk with us along our journey, and help us through some tough spots, it is ourselves that must answer the question of which way to proceed. Many times it is not an easy decision to make, but making no decision is not an option.

With each turn on our path there is new hope, new inspiration, new life and new love. With each turn, we use our value of courage to take that next step. If we are living our life's purpose, and living our personal values, each decision on which path to take will be the right one.

February 3

Happiness is that feeling when the burdens of the past are gone.

Happiness is that feeling where things are right in our world.

Happiness is that feeling when there is a smile in our heart.

Happiness is that feeling when we are filled with gratitude.

Happiness is that feeling of being helpful to others.

Happiness is that feeling when we can let go of things we cannot change.

Happiness is that feeling when we discover the real and authentic self.

Happiness is that feeling of finding our life's purpose.

Happiness is that feeling when someone loves us for who we are; nothing more and nothing less.

Happiness is that feeling that we can create for ourselves.

Happiness is…

February 4

To fly above the earth, like the graceful hawk, its out-stretched wings, effortlessly soars through the air. How beautiful it is to see an example of nature's wonders. We, too, want to fly, to soar through the air with the same grace and beauty, but we have no wings.

But what if we had only one wing, would that gives us what we seek? With only one wing would we struggle and only fly in circles? But what if we found a friend that had only one wing too and then holding on to each other, we could fly together. We would no longer struggle with our dream of flying and we would no longer simply fly in circles. We would fly with grace and beauty because we found a friend to help us on our quest.

Having one wing and actually flying is silly, but having a friend to help us along our journey is not. Friends lift us up when we're down and hold our hand to comfort. They encourage and push us when we need a nudge. A friend will walk along side us as we just need someone to talk with.

A friend is another example of nature's beauty. They share their one wing with us; that wing is also known as love.

February 5

There are so many things on our list today to do. We have to do this, do that, run here, and run there. We have so many things to do; a house to pick up, laundry to wash, take the kids to school and oh yea, we have a job. Yikes! How will we get it done? We know somehow all the important things will get done today, but how well is another story.

So with all that we face today, we need to try to do the best we can. Now our best may not be 100%, or it may be 110%, but all we should strive for is our very best we can. So who defines our best? We do, not someone else. We know, in our heart, when we have truly done out best. If we finish the race in third place, but know we gave it all we had, isn't that our best?

Face each event, each task, each job with the spirit of doing the very best we can and then we at the end of the day will judge whether we did our best. And if we honestly say, maybe not, then all we can do is try to do our best tomorrow.

February 6

"This line - No Waiting" is the line we are always in search of, whether the grocery store or the Department of Motor Vehicles to get our car registered. How nice it is just to walk up and do what we need to without 'wasting' our precious time in line.

How ironic it is that we create our own line and it's the one that is not moving. We're waiting in our own line for the next step on our journey. We're waiting for the next job to make us successful. We're waiting for the next relationship to go out and have fun. We're waiting for this or for that before we do anything else. We have created our own waiting line and it's not moving.

If we stay in our stagnant waiting line, the opportunities of life are passing us by. It's time to step out of this self-created line and go to the "No Waiting" line and begin to live life. It's time we stopped waiting for everything to be perfect before moving forward.

Our journey is there, we just have to get in the right line. Which line are you in?

February 7

A dark cloud creeps over us, and suddenly we feel overwhelmed with the situation surrounding us. We may have an exam that is today that we must pass. We studied all semester and now the day of the exam is here, and we feel we are not prepared; we feel we're not smart enough. Doubts float around our head, mixed with the facts that we must know about this Government 202 exam today. We soon begin to believe all the doubts, and we question whether or not even to take the exam; surely, we will fail. Well…. GET OVER IT! We need to stop doubting ourselves. We need to focus on winning, not failing.

Perhaps our situation is not in the classroom, but in the boardroom. We're interviewing for a new position. Our resume is good; we dressed professionally, and we answered all the questions as best we could. Yet as we walk out, that dark cloud of doubt looms over us. We feel we're not good enough, smart enough, or 'whatever' enough. Again, we just need to get over it. The question we should ask ourselves is… "Did I do my best?" The answer will be yes, so it is time we cast aside the cloud of doubt.

Doubts create that sense of doom, a feeling of failure. We stop believing in ourselves and think we are unworthy or not smart as the person that sits next to us in class, or not as pretty as the person that interviewed before of us. What we forget is we are smart; we are pretty and are capable of many great things in this life. We also forget we have so many friends and family that believe in us and have no doubts about our ability. We need to clear away the clouds of doubt and replace them with the sunshine of confidence. We need to believe in ourselves because so many others already do.When you believe, great doors open and life becomes filled with joy, happiness and love. Today believe in something. Today believe in yourself.

February 8

*E*nveloped in darkness we cannot see anything, total blackness surrounds us. Which way do we go? Is there something that is in our way and we may stumble?

But are we really in total darkness? The answer is no. There is a tiny flicker of light deep within our heart and soul and it's called hope. If we just recognize it and let it shine in our darkened world, we will begin to see. That tiny spark, that tiny glow will slowly turn into a small candle-like flame and it will be called faith.

If we have hope and faith in our lives we will not find ourselves lost in darkness and fearful of what may be in our way as we continue our journey. If we let the light, the spark, the tiny flame burn bright within out heart, our journey will never be filled with complete darkness.

February 9

The rain comes down, sometimes hard, while others times a light sprinkle, but it still comes. If we get caught out in it, we will become wet, chilled, uncomfortable and miserable. We know that rain is needed for nature to flourish and grow, so we welcome the rain in that respect. So before we venture out into the rain, we should take our umbrella to keep us from getting wet and miserable.

The adversity in our lives is like that rain; it makes us uncomfortable and miserable. But we need the rain, the adversity in our lives to grow too. If everything was always sunshine and soft puffy clouds, we wouldn't appreciate them as well without going through the rain. But we need to have an umbrella for this rain too. This umbrella is one called acceptance.

Acceptance, our umbrella, is that life will bring us some rain into our lives, but we don't have to become uncomfortable and miserable because of a little rain. Accept the rain, the adversity, knowing we will grow, just as nature does with its rain. We just don't have to allow ourselves to be miserable, as long as we have our umbrella, acceptance.

February 10

The sound of the ocean wave splashing on the shore, a sound hard to describe, but one that is so soothing and relaxing. Each wave, one after the other comes to end of its journey across the ocean and lands on the sand. Perhaps travelling thousands of miles before reaching the beach, the wave washes up the sand and bids farewell as it slowly slides back into the ocean, no longer a wave. Perhaps the wave has washed up a beautiful shell, or a perfect sand dollar. These are the gifts from the ocean that the wave has delivered.

The waves around the world are endless and millions splash on the sand each day, each one part of nature, each one unique in its own way. We too are like the waves; a part of nature and unique, travelling on our journey. When we reach our beach, the end of our journey, we will wash up the sand and then slowly drift back into the ocean, leaving our legacy, like the shell and sand dollar on the sand for others to see.

February 11

otivated today? If not, is that a bad thing? Motivation is that drive that has some sort of carrot dangling in front of us. It is the bonus the boss promises us if we get the project done early. It's the prize at the end that is driving us to perform and accomplish any given task. Motivation is the drive that is centered in our brain that causes us to push ourselves and to work harder, break a sweat, to get to the end, so we can be rewarded. Motivation is about ourselves and motivating others is causing them to work toward a goal and win a reward, and we in turn will be rewarded as well. Motivation is a good thing, for the right reasons.

There is another human drive that is not centered in the head, but is a little flame that lives in our soul. That drive is inspiration. The candle-like flame lives within each of us, some dimmer than others, but is still there. Inspiration is soul-driven, and we go through life living out our purpose for being on earth. We are serving others because someone else inspired us by their actions or words. Inspiring others is taking our soul candle and lighting their candle. When we are inspired, we have a glow; that glow is our soul flame. Being inspired is awesome, but inspiring others is a feeling that words cannot express. Our own soul flame is turned up when we inspire others. Inspiration is not about self; it is about serving others though our actions and words.

Do we need motivation? Yes. Motivation is that drive we need for those sprints on our journey. Inspiration is that drive that is for the marathon we must run. Make a difference today… Inspire others for their marathon.

February 12

Today is the day.

Today is the day we will begin with a smile.

Today is the day we will take a moment and see the beauty of nature.

Today is the day we will reach out to help a friend.

Today is the day we will count to ten before we lose our temper.

Today is the day we will do something for someone else.

Today is the day we will find another way to express love.

Today is the day we will be who we really are and not put on a mask.

Today is the day we will dream and believe it is possible to achieve.

Today is the day we will make a difference in our life and the lives of others.

Today is the day because tomorrow is never promised.

Today is <u>the day!</u>

February 13

*I*t's simple. It's free. It's easy to do and makes a difference. So what is it then?

It can be given to your family and friends. It can be given to the stranger in the grocery store walking up the aisle. It takes a matter of seconds to create and give away. So what is it then?

It doesn't need to be wrapped in package and tied with a bow. It is something we have day or night. But it's sometimes hard to give away. So what is it then?

So what is it then? It's a smile. One of the easiest and simple ways to express the love that is in our heart and makes a difference to everyone we share it with.

So, what are we waiting for? Share a smile today and do it often.

February 14

Today flowers will be delivered to work places and homes. The words, "I love you" will be spoken. Chocolate-covered strawberries will be placed on a white doily, and cards will be exchanged. Today young couples will become engaged to be married. And today a sweet kiss or two will be shared. Today is about love. Love is that hard to describe emotion, that wonderful connection between two people that makes our heart sing. Love is that twinkle in someone's eye and that ever so slight smile.

Today we celebrate with special dinners, roses, cards, chocolate, hugs, and kisses. It's the one day we express our love openly for another person. It is a little sad that today is the only day we show our love. What about the other days of the year? Why do we limit it to just one day on the calendar? Of course we celebrate birthdays, anniversaries, and other holidays with cards and gifts, but that still leaves many more days that are void of being that special day where love needs to be shown.

We shouldn't limit showing affection or saying, "I love you" to just one day a year. Tomorrow is never promised, so we should be sure to share these three words more often than once a year. Today is about love, but so is every other day on the calendar too.

Happy Valentine's Day my friends. May love live in your heart and in the hearts of those close to you.

February 15

The race car virtually flies around the track at speeds of 180 MPH. Lap after lap the speed seldom lets up and the race car adds another mile to the odometer every 20 seconds. But how long can the race car driver keep up this fast pace? Sooner or later the driver must come in the pit stop for fuel and tires, to replenish what has already been spent in energy.

We too cannot keep up a fast pace, going 100 MPH without our own pit stop to replenish our energy. Going faster and faster all day can wear us down and at some point we collapse in exhaustion and run out of fuel and lose the race. We need to recognize that we need to pace ourselves and that we cannot go lap after lap without stopping to refuel.

Take time to refuel; rest and enjoy the race... maybe at a little slower pace.

February 16

A friend comes into our lives and touches our heart like we've never know before. A friend walks with us as we face the storms in our lives and holds our hand, comforting and giving us guidance along the way. A friend shares our laughter and tears as we face life's challenges and milestones.

Sometimes a friend has to leave us and follow their own journey. While sadness fills our heart we need to be grateful for each moment, each kind word they shared, every touch of their hand, and every ounce of the love they gave us freely. Our friend made a difference in our lives and their love will remain in our memory, in our heart forever.

It's now our turn to return the same gift of friendship to another person as they walk their path. It is our time to be of service, to share our love and wisdom. We have learned our lessons; it is now time for us to teach.

Be a loving, kind and caring friend. Let them feel our compassion and strength. Let them know we are there for them whenever they need us. Make a difference in someone's life today by being the same kind of friend that touched our life.

February 17

I t's very early in the morning and is the darkest time of the night. The sun will not make its appearance for a while, and we look upward to the crystal clear black sky. The sky is covered with stars, like tiny diamonds on black velvet; they twinkle ever so slightly. As we stare into space, we sense the enormity of the universe, and we are humbled, with what we think is our mere existence. We focus our gaze to one area of this black velvet sky, and we see deeper and deeper into the blackness, only to discover tinier diamonds twinkling. Each twinkle of each star gives it life, and it's no longer just a tiny light in the sky; it is more, much more.

We imagine each star; each tiny twinkle is an angel looking down upon us from the heaven above. Each twinkle is telling us that an angel is looking over us, protecting us. How vast the universe and the countless stars that blanket the night's sky. We suddenly feel we're no longer alone, or insignificant; we are a part of the wonderful universe.

Each day and each night another star is born; another angel has joined the heavens above to watch over us. Suddenly, we see a shooting star streak across the black sky. It is an angel coming back to earth in the form of a friend. We look back at the tiny diamonds in the night sky and see we have many friends, many angels. Our heart is warmed with the feeling of being loved by so many angels and friends.

The black night sky gives way to the twilight of the sunrise. The tiny stars slowly disappear with the coming of the day. The sun is rising and we can no longer see the stars, but we know the angels are still there watching over us.

February 18

The oar slices through the water like a hot knife through butter. Each team member of the racing crew, in perfect unison, pulls their oars and the sleek racing water craft slides over the water. The crew listens as each oar hits the water at the exact same time, as if it were just one oar. Pulling back with each stroke, the team works together to race to the finish line.

We too are part of a team; all pulling together toward some finish line. The question is, are we in perfect unison like the racing team? Or are our oars clashing with each other and causing our boat to flounder in the water?

We need to find that timing, and work together. Our oars pulling, each of us doing our part as a member and becoming one of our racing team. We each play a part and each of us makes a difference. We will make a bigger difference when we are in unison with those on our team.

February 19

I t didn't go our way... We didn't get what we wanted… We feel like we were cheated out of something that we think we deserved… Life sometimes brings disappointments and that is just reality.

What would it be like if we got everything we wanted? Would we truly be happy? Would we appreciate the things more? We know the answers to these questions. With disappointments in life, we can celebrate the successes with greater joy. With sadness in our life, we can appreciate the happiness that comes to replace it. As we find anger and resentments, we see love and forgiveness in a different light. Each emotion has a counter-emotion that teaches us that life is what it is, filled with disappointments, sadness, and anger, but it is also filled with success, joy, happiness, love and compassion.

With each emotion and counter-emotion, we have the choice to focus on one or the other. Which one will we choose will depend on how long we want to suffer and not enjoy the life we are given.

February 20

From ghosts to goblins and from monsters to ghouls, today we dress up to hide our identity from others. We attempt to scare others, pretend to be someone we're not, entertain friends, make fun and bring smiles to most as we put on various costumes and masks. Today is a day to smile and enjoy the fun of Halloween's madness.

But what about the mask we wear all the other days of the year? Why are we wearing it? Are we pretending to be someone else? Are we trying to scare someone? Make fun of others? What are we hiding? Sadly we wear masks to hide the 'real self' from the world because we may think our 'real self' could appear to be weak and insecure. When we put away our masks, our 'real self' is visible, yes vulnerable, but it's who we are inside. We now are authentic, not only with ourselves, but with those around us. Wearing a mask is a form of lying; lying to others of who we really are, but mostly lying to ourselves.

So as the day ends, let's take our scary mask off, for Halloween is over. And let's not put another one on in the morning. Let's be our 'real self' until the next Halloween.

February 21

A warm cup of tea, wrapped in a soft wool blanket, sitting in our comfy chair, and reading a good book, brings to our mind a very warm and comfortable image. We can imagine exactly how this feels. It gives us a sense of being safe, and all is right with our world. We find peace in this warmth. We are safe.

Imagine a new-born baby, being held by its mother, wrapped in a soft cotton blanket, nursing on the mother's breast, and how safe and secure that baby must feel. That baby doesn't know the word 'love' yet, but in this moment that sense of love surrounds that child. The bond of a mother and her baby is one that cannot be explained, and the depth of that love is endless. We can only imagine in our own heart that feeling of comfort, peace, and serenity.

Why can't we find that peace and serenity? that warm comforting feeling today? We're envious of those that can find that in their lives. The good news is that we can have this peace, this serenity, this sense of being safe, and most importantly, the feeling of love. We find all these with a simple hug. Two sets of arms, wrapping around each other, embracing is a connection that is so simple, yet so powerful. Two souls connecting for just a few seconds; can bring an overwhelming sense of comfort, compassion, and love.

The human connection of a hug between two people can make all the difference in the world and yet; we are too embarrassed to do it. We're too afraid of looking weird, crossing a boundary, or any number of weak excuses; we hold back this one simple gift. If we look into the eyes of the others person, we can see it's what they need, and we can see it is okay to reach out and bring that comforting hug.

A hug brings comfort, peace, care, and love to both sharing the embrace. Reach out today and share some love.

February 22

Imagine that five years ago we were asked to write down what our life would be like today. What would we have written? Where did we imagine our professional life to be? What did we write down about our personal life; a new relationship, another family member? Would we have come close to where we are and what we have in our lives today? Would we have sold ourselves short in achieving and growing to where we are? Are we better than we imagined?

It's likely that we are in a better place today than we were five years ago and in fact, looking back, we are amazed where our path has brought us today. We sometimes don't give ourselves credit for our own abilities and the potential we each have in making our lives go beyond our expectations. We should see that we are limitless, only restrained by our own short-sightedness.

So, if asked to write down what your life looks like five years from today, what would you write? Stretch your imagination and reach for the stars, because you see, you will be among them, just wait and see.

February 23

*I*n order for us to get the most out of life, we need to take in as many experiences we can find. We need to open our mind to see all that is around us; the beauty of nature or the beauty of the human soul. If we don't open our minds to see and learn, then we will have missed out on so many wonders of the world.

It's not only our mind that we need to open; we also need to open our heart. By opening our heart we make ourselves a little vulnerable, and put ourselves at risk of being hurt. Though we may feel the hurt at times, it will make the joys that much sweeter.

But we cannot go about our life, walk our journey all tightly closed up like a turtle that has retreated into its shell. We need to open up our mind and our heart to truly see what the wonders of life await us.

Come out of your shell, the world awaits.

February 24

The coward hides in the shadows, strikes when the time is right, then quickly retreats back into the shadow. The coward is afraid of standing up for himself, because in reality, he knows his actions are unjustified and are the actions of the weak. He thinks he's being courageous as he faces his foe, but will quickly run at the slightest sense of harm or confrontation.

The brave soul, on the other hand, stands straight and tall and does not need to hide in the shadows. He finds the courage to face his foe, whoever or whatever it may be. Scared at times, he is diligent in knowing that the courage in his heart and soul can withstand and overcome the foe that is waiting.

The coward is like our character defects and the brave are our personal values. Our character defects hide and wait, striking out only to retreat again; still lurking in the shadows, waiting to come out once again. It is our personal values, our brave, that will face this coward of character defects and defeat it.

The brave and the coward, two enemies that faces each other and will come to battle, but which one will defeat the other? At times, the coward will win a fight but it will be the brave, using all the courage within them, will win the battle.

February 25

Make a difference…. tell someone how much they mean to you.

Make a difference…. hold the door for someone.

Make a difference…. share your smile with others.

Make a difference…. take off your mask and let the world see the real you.

Make a difference…. take time today to call or email a friend just to say hello.

Make a difference…. be the friend you want to have as a friend.

Make a difference…. do your very best today at the task you have in front of you.

Make a difference…. let go of any anger in your heart and replace it with forgiveness.

Make a difference…. love others, but love yourself too.

Make a difference…. it's not hard. Just be aware that every action, every word we do or say makes a difference not only in our life, but in the lives of those around us.

Make a difference…. Inspire!

February 26

The young child sits on his grandfather's lap, looking out over the pond in the park and asks, "Why are there ducks in the water?" The grandfather replies because that is where they like to play and swim. "Why do they like to swim?" the child now asks. The grandfather explains that the duck's feet are special for swimming. Sitting on the bench, the young child continues to ask the 'why' questions and the grandfather continues to answer as best he can.

The exchange of question and answer is no more than seeking the answers; seeking wisdom and answering the curiosities of our mind. Do we ever stop asking 'why'? If so, do we think we have all the answers now? When we ask questions we continue to learn, we continue to grow. We also need to listen to the answer. We should never stop asking questions because there is always more wisdom to be gained in the answers. The questions that are not asked are tiny bits of knowledge and wisdom that we will miss from learning.

So, why are there ducks in the water?

February 27

The morning light illuminates our path and it's time to begin another part of our journey. Our path has happiness, joy and love in the steps ahead, but only if we choose that path. Many times we step off that path and find ourselves on a different one, allowing resentments, anger and regrets get in the way of our journey. How did we find ourselves on this part of our journey? We can reason our way to justify how we got here, but if it is joy, happiness and love we seek, the reasons really don't matter.

Instead of continuing down this path and find our way back to the path of peace and serenity, we need to just stop where we are and search deep within ourselves for the answers. The answer may be forgiveness, not only of others, but for ourselves. The answer may be compassion and empathy. The answers are within each of us, we just need to be willing to look. But looking and seeing the answers are one thing, we need to live the answers in order to wipe away that what blocks the heart from the sunlight of love.

February 28

An indulgence is something that is extra special and something we normally don't get in our normal everyday life. The indulgence could be a wonderful ice cream sundae in the middle of the afternoon. It could be a special pair of shoes that we have seen in the mall and finally decided to buy them. The indulgence could be that special piece of electronics that has more bells and whistles than the one we already own.

An indulgence once in a while is not bad. We need to spoil ourselves just a little and have some fun. But we need to be careful the indulgence doesn't turn into an everyday event, otherwise the indulgence turns against us, causing us physical, financial or emotional discomfort. The old adage, "Too much of a good thing…" certainly applies to how an indulgence can turn into something detrimental.

Indulge once in a while and savor every minute, because it is special. Don't let the indulgence become the new everyday lifestyle, for then it is no longer an indulgence.

February 29 (Leap Year)

Our journey, our path is our life and we should not be in any rush to reach the final destination. We have so much to do on our journey and we need to live it to the fullest, experiencing all the wonders our path has to offer. But we're just not on the ride, we have a role in this our life, a huge role and we cannot just meander along without contributing to it.

We have the opportunity to make this, our life, so very special and make a difference in the lives of others too. Being of service to others on our journey not only helps them on their journey, but adds so much to our own. When we serve others, we add love to our journey, for serving others is an act of love. How else can we make our journey more meaningful? Simple, random acts of kindness will brighten someone else's path. Perhaps we need to lighten the load of a friend and help carry their burden by giving them a little of our time and a little piece of our heart by listening.

It's when we get out of ourselves and just not focused on our path, but look to find ways to help others on their journey, that we will make our journey, our life one that we can be proud of when we do reach our final destination.

March

March 1

What happens when we don't get our way? We throw a tantrum, of course. We get upset that things are not happening according to the way we think they should. We, of course, know what's best and it just needs to be that way and there isn't any other way, period! Right? It's our way and there is no more discussion.

Sound familiar? Well, we all know that this isn't reality. We don't always get our way. There are times in our life that we a forced into doing it another way, someone else's way. Now we can stew, remain upset and pout, or we can accept it and give it a chance. Perhaps it might even be better and that we will now adopt it as our new way of doing something. This is learning.

We need to open our mind and sometimes our heart to learn new ways and new things. If we remain so steadfast in our own ways, our learning is restricted to learning and expanding our mind. We almost become stagnant in growing our knowledge.

Let's open our mind to new ways of doing things and learn from others. In doing so, great events will suddenly appear to us.

March 2

The morning's light is barely visible as we sit on the dock overlooking the lake. The water is smooth as glass and acts as a mirror, reflecting the scenery all around. The morning light now gradually reveals more and more of itself and the blues and pink colors are reflected on the lake's surface. It's quiet. It's serene. It's a time to reflect and look to our new day.

Just as the lake reflected the beauty of nature and the morning sunrise, we reflect onto others what is within us. Be aware of the beauty, or not so beautiful image we reflect as we go about our day. Cast away the reflections of evil characteristics and replace them with the reflection of our values by living them each day, each moment. See the beauty within and then let others see it too.

March 3

O ur path today is not open and easy to travel. The vines, thorns, and mud cover our path, and we are bogged down; each step harder and harder to take as we work our way on this given journey. The path has not been cleared by others in the past, and we are slowly doing our best to take one step at a time. Each cut of a thorny branch, each step into the mud and mire, we find ourselves in a survival environment. We're simply trying to hold on and not sink into the mud or be wrapped up in the vines and thorny bushes. We don't see the light of our previous path, and today we struggle.

Life's journey is not always clear sailing or a path that is open and free from worries. And when we find ourselves with these challenges in life, the thorns and mud, we cannot allow ourselves to fall into the simple, raw, basic lifestyle of survival. We have worked too hard, traveled too far, and made great progress in living our life's purpose to allow a little set back, a little difficult path on our journey to take away our passion for life.

An attitude of merely surviving the day and what lies ahead is a sad existence. In fact, that is all it is, an existence. We're just breathing in and out and barely nourishing our body. We need to find a way out of that horrible path and get back onto a path where we can thrive, not just survive. We need to work hard to get through the tough times in our lives and see the sunshine and clear journey. Sometimes it will be hard, but just surviving is not living. Our journey is too short not to live it to its fullest.

Thrive to live, not survive to exist.

March 4

Sometimes the day just doesn't start out on the right foot and we get off track. And sometimes we stay off track the whole day, but in some cases we find ourselves back where we wanted to be in the first place.

What throws off track? It could be a cross word with our child as they get ready for school because they are wearing shorts and t-shirt when it's 40 degrees outside. Or perhaps it was a flat tire on the way to work causing us to be late for work on the busiest day of the week. Regardless, this event has done a job on us. Now it's up to us to find a way back to the norm.

We can continue to focus on what has ruined the start of our day, or we can just let it go and move on. Letting it go can sometimes be hard, and if we drag it around with us the whole day will continue to be bad. Letting it go allows us to start our day over, regardless what the clock says the time is.

Just remember, we have a choice to start our day over any time we need to.

March 5

*F*amilies come in all shapes and sizes; functional and dysfunctional, loving and not so loving, involved and estranged. In any case we have a family in which we are a part of and play a role in that human unit called a family. Like many other things in life we have choices and we can be the loving element or the not so loving one. We can engage and be an active participant, or we can ignore all the others and isolate. It's a choice.

There is another choice we can make as it relates to families. We can be part of another family, just as if we were born into that family. We can develop a love and deep feelings for this small group of people that we're not related to, but share many ideals, if not more, than our biological family. We find a sense of acceptance and love that is unexplainable.

It's all about family, biological or not. It's about being a loving, caring and compassionate member of a family that adds joy to our lives and to the lives of our 'family'. We are not here on earth to be alone, we are here to fulfill a purpose and be part of a family. Let's share our love with our family.

March 6

"An attitude of gratitude" is a phrase we hear often, and it's true that we need to develop an attitude and be grateful for what we have in this life, but perhaps it's only one part of the greater whole. Yes, we are grateful for family, friends, employment, and the gratitude list goes on. Our heart is warm and full of love as we bring this gratitude attitude to life, but again we need to take our gratitude to the next level.

We feel blessed for all that we have in our life and we realize how good our life is and say a blessing at the Thanksgiving table for all the good in our lives. Consider this... take it another step, be of service to someone else. Demonstrate your attitude of gratitude by being a living example of how to help another person. Instead of walking away from the dinner table and sitting on the couch, help clear the table, do the dishes, or take out the trash. As you see a stranger struggling to open the door because their arms and hands are full, smile and say, "Let me get that for you."

We have it so good and while others struggle. We can help; we can make a difference in the lives of others by living and acting our attitude of gratitude. Let's be of service and make a difference in the lives that we touch today and tomorrow.

March 7

When an act of kindness is shown to us, we feel good. We feel a little special that someone took the time, maybe went out of their way to do something for us. Even the smallest act of kindness can be so special when it's given with a little love. Our thanks to this person could be a simple 'thank you' and a smile. But the greatest way to show our appreciation is to pay it forward and show someone else a small act of kindness.

We get so wrapped up in our own little world we forget. If we simply open our eyes and look around there are so many ways we can repay whoever gave to us, by showing a little kindness to another person. They in turn may follow our example and touch someone else's life with a little of their love too.

A simple act of kindness shown and then paid forward makes a difference. We have made a difference when we get out of ourselves and demonstrate a little act of kindness. The world is just a little better for it.

March 8

*W*hat is the measure of success in life? Is it the amount of money in our bank account, or what kind of fancy car we drive, or perhaps it's the designer clothes we wear? Not only do we measure ourselves by these material benchmarks, but we measure others by the same. These measurements are just temporary and can be wiped out in a short amount of time. And if there are gone, are we then failures?

The true measure of success is not of material, sometimes short-lived objects, but is of how we live our life. If on our journey we can touch the life of someone else and make a difference, even in the smallest way, we add to our success in life. If on our journey we discover our life's purpose and find the means to fulfill it, we add to our success in life. We find success by living our values the best we can each day.

We measure success not in money or things, but the amount of love we share with others and making a difference in their lives. The more we give of ourselves to others, the greater our success will be. While others may not see our success as we do, it really doesn't matter. It's what we know in our heart to be true of our measurement of success.

March 9

We have a companion, a friend that walks with us on our journey. Our paths are adjacent and we can walk together as we travel along the way. We find a place to sit and share this special time. We talk about all sorts of things. We smile, we laugh and we may even shed a tear. Our friend has touched our heart in such a special way and we have touched theirs too.

As we prepare to continue on our journey, our traveling companion says, "This is my destination and I will not be continuing with you. But you need to continue on your path toward your destination. Thank you for being part of my journey." A sudden sense of loneliness overwhelms us as our friend disappears and we stand alone on our path. We look around and they are gone. We look back on our path we can see how our companion was there for so many steps along our journey.

While our friend reached their destination and is no longer there to hold our hand, guide us, or wipe away a tear; they are still in our heart and will always be part of our journey. We need to take their love that is still within us and move forward. We have our own journey and it begins with our next step. We carry the memory and love of our travelling companion with us in our heart.

March 10

FREE RENT!! We see this sign and the skeptic within each of us says, what's the catch? And we will soon see there is a catch.

The actions and words of others are seldom within our ability to control them and yet, we allow them to crawl under our skin and find their way to our head. We continually allow their actions and words run around in our head, over and over and over; replaying the same irritating scenario in our mind. It bothered us the first time and with each time we replay it, it only gets worse and festers. We are allowing them, their actions, their words to live 'rent free' in our mind. They have moved on with their life and probably don't even recall the event, yet we play it over and over, as it continually eats away our peace of mind.

It's time we took the "FREE RENT" sign down and give an eviction notice to all that is still playing the bothersome game in our mind. It's time to let it go and move on with OUR life and stop letting THEIR life live rent free in OUR mind.

We need to remember, we are the landlord of our mind and we can control who gets to move in and who gets evicted. It's time we learn this hard lesson and lock the door when the irritating words and actions of others come knocking. It is time to bring in peace and serenity back into our life once again.

March 11

We are only one among many, but we are a part of the whole.

We are unique, but are no different than others.

We are loved, but only if we give our love away.

We are making a difference, but only if we get out of self.

We are real, but only if we take off our mask.

We are human, but only if we seek humility.

We are courageous, but only if we have removed fear with faith.

We are forgiving, but only when our heart is filled with love.

We are at peace, but only by acceptance and loving ourselves.

We are who we are and no one can change that, except ourselves.

Who are you today?

March 12

As we go about our day, making decision after decision; turn here, go there, do this, do that. Many of these decisions and actions are just unconscious ones and we barely even think, but once in a while we come to a decision and in the back of our mind or in the pit of our gut, it just doesn't seem right. This is a "Red Flag" warning. It's time to stop and think. Why are we doing this? If it doesn't feel right, why are we doing it?

These little twinges of questioning are our intuition, our 'values coach'. Our 'values coach' is reminding us of our personal values and making sure we are think through what we are about to do making sure they are in alignment with our values. If our 'values coach' has sent up the red flag, it's for a good reason.

We live our lives making decision after decision and our personal values are the principles that guide us in each one. Our 'values coach' is there to subtly remind us that we cannot allow character defects to take over and make our decisions today.

Intuition, 'values coach', red flag in the back of mind, or the twinge of pain in our gut, it makes no difference what we call it, we just need to give it some credence before we make a quick decision. Think before we act.

March 13

We hear the sounds of the cars whizzing by, or the sounds of the police sirens in the distance. We hear the night owl hoot as it patiently waits for its prey. We hear the rain drops' pitter-patter on the roof and the distant thunder of a storm approaching. We hear the words of our friend as we talk about all sorts of things concerning life. We hear with our two ears and process the noise in our brain. We hear the noise and quickly move on to process new noises or process new thoughts that are running in our mind.

Instead of hearing noises, perhaps we should listen for a change. Listen to the night owl hoot and picture its beauty perched on the branch of the tree. Its eyes wide open and its beautiful feathers fluff in the night air. Listen to the drops of rain and appreciate each sound of each drop as they surround us and provide the beauty of nature. Carefully listen to the words of our friend and by listening we touch their life a little deeper.

We hear with our brain, but we listen with our heart.

March 14

The tear… a clear liquid that that flows from a tear duct that is located in the corner of the eye. The tear itself washes the eye and removes irritants and protects the eyes from infection.

Enough of the biological explanation of tears; tears are liquid emotion. Humans are the only animal that generates tears because of emotional situations. Tears well up when we're happy or sad and tears come when we hear a song, or see a movie. Yet, when tears come we're embarrassed, ashamed, and don't want others to see us with tears. Is it because we don't want to appear to be weak? Probably, but it means we are human. Tears are generated from the heart and we should never be embarrassed to shed them. It tells others that we feel, that we care, that we have a heart and are willing to allow our emotions to manifest themselves in the form of a tear. We are human.

There are days we just want to cry and allow that liquid emotion just to flow for no reason… so go ahead… it will help… we may not know why but it just will.

March 15

Living life... we live this life we created each and every day. Each moment of each day is living the life we have and it's just for today. During our early years under the protective care of our parents, our life was being formed by their influence and the influence of others such as grandparents, teachers, clergy and friends. Gradually we break away and begin to create our own life and live it as it unfolds, but it is now our creation. We are now responsible for the outcome. We are responsible for our life.

It's our life now and we create it every day we get out of bed. We cannot blame anyone else for its outcome, for it is our responsibility to make it what it is. It is our life and we can make it miserable or one filled with love and joy. We have the choice to form our life in any shape, size, or fashion. Certainly outside influences will be part of our life, but it's our choice how we allow them to change our life. If we make some bad decisions in our life, well, that was our choice and hopefully we learned something and now can move on in creating and living the life we want for ourselves.

It's OUR life and we need to live it to the fullest. We need to live our life today the way we want, for tomorrow is never promised. Our life, our path, our journey... it is up to us to make it what it will be for the rest of today.

March 16

Two tin cans and a piece of string make a great communication device when we were kids. And when the string broke we either got another string or moved on and played with something else. It wasn't the end of the world. Today, we have phones/smartphones or small electronic devices that now carry with us all the time and it has all our information; personal contacts, addresses, phone numbers, email, an 'app' for this or that and so much other information. We become so dependent on them and when the 'string' breaks we go into a tailspin. We are lost, frustrated and feel like we have lost an arm.

STOP!! WAKE UP!! It's NOT the end of the world. We still have family and friends, they didn't go anywhere. We still have our health (though we may be a little sick to our stomach now). We still have a place to sleep and food to eat. Come on!! It's not the end of the world! It's time we look around and see what we should be grateful for and not focus on one small facet, one small thing of our life. So the 'string' broke, big deal, go get another 'string', or move on with your life.

If we created all those things on our electronic 'appendage' before, we can recreate it. Yes it may take a little time, but really… is it all that bad? Is it really the end of the world?

March 17

How far is our dream away from reality? What if we quit just before the miracle happens? How sad it would be that all the work and effort we expended in working toward our dream that we give up just before it reveals itself to us and become real. We don't know when we will turn that corner and find all that we have done has paid off and we see and live the dream, our miracle of living life's purpose.

We all have dreams and many of us are working toward some of them very hard and yet we get discouraged along the way. We become overwhelmed and sometimes tired. We can't see the finish line, or the dream seems too distant and we have stopped believing in miracles will ever happen to us. This is when we must absolutely kick in the turbo of life. We need to dig deep within and find that extra boost, that turbo power in our heart and soul and push ahead. We can't use a 100 percent; we need 150 percent or more. We need that turbo of life, that turbo of confidence and faith in ourselves, that turbo power of willingness to push ahead and not quit.

That turbo of life is ready to each of us to use. We have that turbo fuel, we just need to ignite it and great things will happen… our dreams and the miracles of our life.

March 18

A hand reaches out to help us and we turn away, thinking we can do this all by ourselves. Are we that smug and conceited to think we are so much better than they are that we don't need their help? How foolish it is to turn down the offer of someone else's help. Whoever was reaching out was merely trying to help, to be of service and we have now cast their helping hand to the side.

Now how do we feel when someone pushes our helping hand away when we reach out to help? Discouraged? Feel slighted? If we find ourselves in such a predicament, it should not let it stop us from reaching out again and again. Helping others and being of service is what we should try to do each and every day. Just because someone turns away from our helping hand, doesn't mean that the next person we reach out to will truly need it. What happens to the person that truly needs it and we don't offer? What then?

We can make a difference in the world, one helping hand at a time. Reach out today and offer your hand and accept the hand that reaches out to you.

March 19

et's pretend we can be someone else, past or present. Who would we want to be? Perhaps we would want to be a great leader in the past, Abraham Lincoln or General Dwight D Eisenhower. Perhaps we would want to be a spiritual leader like Gandhi, the Dalai Lama or Mother Teresa. Maybe we would want to be a famous scientist that discovered something that changed the world as we know it. Still perhaps we would want to be a notable philosopher like Ralph Waldo Emerson or an author like Stephen King. Who do we want to be?

We can wish were someone else and if we could make that come true, then the world would be without one special person, you. You are you and not someone else. We can strive to be like someone else, but only in the fact of how they made a difference in the world and how they made a difference in our life and in the lives of others. We can do this by being ourselves and finding ways to make a positive difference in the lives of others.

You are special and never let anyone ever tell you otherwise. You make a difference and will continue to make a difference in everyone you touch today and tomorrow. Be yourself and the world is better as a result.

March 20

The minutes of the light of day and the minutes of darkness of night are equal today; it is the equinox. It is the first day of spring. While many still see snow on the ground, there is a sense of beauty, knowing that old man winter will be leaving and the snow on the ground will give life to the seeds of blooms that will waken from their long sleep. It is a rejuvenation of life. Flowers will soon fill the gardens; the wild flowers will cover the landscape with vivid color. The warmth of spring is nature's way of showing us its love.

Just as there is a balance of the minutes of night and day today, we can find a balance in our lives too. We can put away the heavy garments of what has weighed us down over the last few months, and bring out the airy, light, and beautiful clothes that make us smile. It's time to let go of the winter burdens of isolation and fear, and replace it with new friends and hope. Today is a new day; a new season, and the beginning of a new life.

Just as the winter snow moistened the seeds of the spring flowers, let the emotions of anger, resentments, and hurt, give life to forgiveness and love. Today is the first day of spring. Today is the first day of the rest of your journey. It's time we allow the spring flowers align our path.

March 21

"Quit complaining!" Wow... how many times have we heard that? And yet, we still do it and it's usually about things or situations that we have no control. We complain about the weather, of which we have zero influence over. We complain about the traffic because of highway construction, and of course we have zero control of highway development. The list will go on about things we complain about and we will voice our complaints to anyone that will listen. We rant and rave and rant some more, filling our mind and the minds of other people around us with negativity.

So here's an idea... if we find ourselves getting ready to complain about something, let's ask ourselves, can I do anything about it? If the answer is no, then quit complaining. If the answer is yes, then take the action necessary and quit complaining. Complaining is spreading negativity and is certainly not very appealing to anyone on the receiving end, because they can't do anything about it either. So why vent on them and add negativity to their day.

Instead of complaining, spreading negativity, wouldn't it be awesome if we spread positivity? Let's share the blessings in our lives and how grateful we are for what we have and make a positive difference instead of a negative one. People want to feel good and spreading positive thoughts and words will make a difference in their lives. So quit complaining.

March 22

Things go wrong in our lives and we are quick to look how we can shift the blame to someone or something else. It's their fault the project wasn't completed on time. It's their fault that we're late for the party. It's the other driver's fault that we had a fender bender. It's their fault for whatever goes wrong today… it just is.

Let's take a step back and give an honest look at what happened. Did we have any part in the event? Could we have changed the outcome if we took some action? Don't blame others without honestly looking at our role and in many cases, we will see that we are just as much to blame. Our hand should never point fingers at others and blame them, without pointing the same fingers back at ourselves first. We should look to see how we could have changed the outcome and learn from the lesson.

It's too easy to blame someone else for what has gone wrong today. It's time we step up and take some of the responsibility. Remember, we are quick to take the credit when things go well, it's time we take the same approach when they don't.

March 23

Our path is not always flat and easy to travel. There are times where we will find ourselves either knee deep in mud, or trying to climb over a huge obstacle that stands in our way. While we enjoy the easy and carefree parts of the journey, we must also take a positive approach on the not so easy times too. These difficult challenges make us stronger. Each one we overcome, we gain not only strength, but wisdom. When we overcome whatever faces us and reach the other side, we can look back and see how our courage and confidence in ourselves gave us the strength to conquer what was put before us.

The strength and willing determination is within us and we need these life's challenges to be placed before us so we can grow and become stronger. Each day, each step is another opportunity to become a better, wiser person. As we grow stronger on our journey, we can then help others that struggle and help them overcome their obstacles so that they can grow stronger too.

Never doubt the strength, courage and determination that is within each of us and with this belief in ourselves, no obstacle will be too big or too difficult to overcome.

March 24

*I*t's the time of year when gifts are exchanged and many times in the back of our mind we have set an expectation of gift giving. At times it is just the mere fact that a gift will be given to us, or it may be that we're expecting a certain gift from a person. When we set these expectations there are several possible outcomes. The first is that we get the gift we expected... and now we're only mildly happy because we expected it. Next might be that we don't get what we expected but still got a gift and we feel it is less than what our expectation was... and now we have to put on a smiley face and pretend to be grateful. The last is that we don't get a gift at all... and now we feel hurt and resentful.

How ugly the scenario can be when we set expectations to feed our ego. Setting greedy expectations can only be the first step toward disappointments, leading to full blown resentment and beyond. Is that what we really want? It is when we give and truly expect nothing in return do we get to feel that joy in our heart. It's that joy and love in our heart that we look for, yet we set ourselves up for just the opposite when we set expectations.

When we give, and truly expect nothing in return is when we truly discover that we were given a gift... and that gift is the joy and love in our heart; that we have touched another person's heart. There is no better gift than that.

March 25

We awaken to the smell of freshly brewed coffee and our senses begin to come alive. We walk outside in the cold winter morning and smell the soothing scent of a fire in a fireplace. We walk in to the bakery and smell the fresh cinnamon rolls just as they come out of the oven.

When we become more aware of all our senses, we begin to realize how wonderful our life truly is. We touch the soft skin of a baby and our heart is warmed. We hear soft mellow voice of a stranger say 'good morning'. We taste the creamy chocolate morsel and a sense of pleasure washes over us. We see a stranger hold the door open as we walk out, our hands filled with packages and we feel gratitude.

Awaken our senses and life takes on a new meaning. We can stop the hustle and bustle of life and simply enjoy the moment when we become aware of our senses. For this moment will not come again as it is right now and if we don't stop and 'smell the roses' they will be withered and gone.

Enjoy life today and allow your senses to bring new joy.

March 26

The packages were all carefully place around the Christmas tree. Each one wrapped in beautiful colored paper, each crease perfect and the corners were precisely folded. The ribbon, so colored coordinated with the paper, was perfectly tied as a beautiful intricate bow. Perfect in every sense, we don't want to destroy all that work by ripping it open. We just want to admire it. We suspect it was wrapped by a professional.

We notice another gift that is set aside in the corner. The paper is wrinkled and the corners can hardly be called corners. The paper is torn in one place and a piece of tape covers the tear. The ribbon is loose and the bow contrasts sharply with the paper. But we see it as being perfect too, not wanting to destroy all that work either. We look at it, hold it and a tear forms in the corner of our eye. We know this gift was wrapped by a child. The child's wrapped gift is not just wrapped in wrinkled paper and ribbon, it is wrapped in love, and that is far more valuable.

The wrappings of love are the true gift.

March 27

The eighteen wire-ties securely hold the toy car in the box and we didn't notice that the required tools on the outside of the box included wire cutters. Nor could we find the tiny Phillips head screwdriver that was need to open the battery compartment to get the batteries in place, while the little one anxiously is waiting to play with the new toy. The plastic box, so tightly packaged we a special tool to open it. Little did we know we also needed an electrical engineering degree to set up the new surround sound system and magnifying eye glasses to read the small print in the instruction book. Have we over complicated our lives and made it more difficult?

We may have lost the concept of simplicity. The homemade gift; a scarf, a home-canned jar of relish, or a simple collage of special photos are just as special as any of the others. The common thread between the high-tech and homemade is that bother were given with love and that is what counts.

We don't need to drain the bank account when we give gifts, we just need to tap into our heart and give our love. Love is a gift that required no batteries, no engineering degree; it just requires a willingness to share from our heart. Love is the priceless gift that can be given each and every day.

March 28

There comes times when we think we really don't matter and that we make little difference in the world. We think that our lives are without purpose and we are just here to occupying space, that our existence is just that, existing. When we find ourselves in is mind-set, we are walking down the steps to the pit of low self-worth. This pit is dark and lonely. But it's of our own doing that we're taking these steps.

As soon as we see these steps in front of us we need to stop and just look around and ask ourselves some questions. Did we make someone smile this week? Did we share some of our time with others? Did we reach out to someone in need? Now looking at the answers to these questions... Did we answer 'yes' to <u>any</u> of these questions? If so, we made a positive difference in someone's life and without us, their life would not be the same.

We should never doubt that we make a difference in the world. We make a difference in the lives of others when we just get out of ourselves just a little and share a little piece of our heart. We make a difference, even though we sometimes don't see it. We should never doubt that we make a difference in the lives of others when we have love in our heart. With that love in our heart the world is just a little better, because we share a little of ourselves and our love with others.

March 29

Gloating, bragging, showing-off are various forms of our ego running wild and completely out of control. When allow our ego to take over like this, we lose the respect of others. As we accomplish things in our life, mark milestones, we should not flash them in the faces of our friends. By doing so we may cause them to feel a little less than and we in turn become a braggart.

Winning is not such a good thing when we walk away gloating causing someone else to feel like a loser. If we win or receive something special, accept it with grace and humility. It will be a rare situation that someone else wasn't a part of that milestone and made it possible. If we allow our ego to take over, we are virtually saying that those that helped us are not important. We do not live in a bubble, void of the influence of others and we in turn influence them.

Bragging and gloating are born in the mind and are fed by our ego; casting a negative influence on others. Grace and humility are values that clearly come from the heart and are admired by others that witness such beauty.

March 30

There are times when we are asked to do things we don't want to do. These tasks are ones that seem to consume our precious minutes in the day and we just don't want to spend our time doing them. It could be cleaning out a closet at home that has piled up until the door doesn't close. Perhaps it's work related; a set number of hours of continuing education requirement, or any number of other things.

Now we can stew over each of them and procrastinate until we no longer have a choice but to begin to work on them. So we do a little here and a little there and very little is really accomplished until we finally make our minds and face the task and do it. Low and behold we make progress and something special is revealed. As we clean our closet we find an old black and white photo of our grandmother and grandfather when they were young, and we smile. As we work through our continuing education we learn something that we use the next day when asked a question, and we knew the answer.

The daunting and perceived unpleasant tasks we face are not always as bad as they appear to be in the beginning; sometimes we find treasures. So let's face the task at hand as an adventure, as an opportunity to grow, learn, and discover new insights into the world. We never know what we will discover until we begin the adventure.

March 31

Ninety-six percent of the people we will encounter today are focused on themselves, their lives and how they can get this or get that. Their world is self-centered and strictly revolves around them; spinning in only one direction, theirs. The ninety-six are living a life that has suppressed their personal values and not allowed them to become part of their life anymore and in fact are allowing their defects of character rule their life.

On the other hand we have the four percent place their values ahead of their character defects and live a life that is centered on being of service to others and loving them. This minority shares a smile with a stranger in the store or holds the door open for them to enter first. The four percent is finding ways to make a difference in the lives of others, and in turn will make a huge difference in their own.

So each day as we get up and get on with our day we have a choice to be a ninety-six, or a four. Who will we be today? It's time we decide to make a difference in the world.

April

April 1

Today is the day of the year when we play jokes on our family and friends. It is the one day many will forget that it's April Fools' Day, and they will be caught off guard by our antics and jokes. Some will be spontaneous, while others have been planned out for several days. However, there should be rules with the jokes we may play today.

No joke should be played with the intent to harm someone or be disrespectful. Jokes should be funny and light; showing that we care enough about them to play a light-hearted prank. We need to remember that today is not a blank check to do whatever we want, thinking it's funny to us; it must be funny to them too.

Our actions are measured by the way we treat people. If we treat others with respect and honor them as a person, we in turn will be respected by others. If we care about someone, and love them; we will find the same love within ourselves.

It's April Fools' Day. Have some fun, just not at the expense of someone else.

April 2

We get giddy when we are given an opportunity to meet, or even come close to a celebrity. How exciting it is to see this person, face to face, whether they are an actress, actor, author, famous speaker, singer or anyone else, we get excited about this opportunity. Oh my gosh... what if we got an autograph??? Why do we get so excited, along with hundreds just like us? We see these people as famous, influential, powerful people in the world, using their talents to entertain or influence others. Yes, they are worthy of some adoration.

These celebrities are just people like us. Their basic physical make up is just like ours; they don't have an extra arm, or leg. They have just found ways to use what they have to become who they are. We too have many of the same abilities and we use them to influence and make a difference in the lives of others too. We may not be on television or perform on a stage, but we do make a difference when we use our talents to help our fellows. We are celebrities too, just without the camera flashes and mobs of people around us.

Let's be the celebrity today that uses our talents, gifts and values to reach out and make a difference. While we may not make the cover of a magazine, we will make the cover of someone's heart.

April 3

Many times we think we can do this by ourselves and don't need the help of others. We take the approach we can 'go solo' on our journey and that we have the will and determination to just do it ourselves. Well, that many be true in some situations, but not all. There are times when we need help, and yet we are so stubborn sometimes we don't reach out and ask.

Our stubbornness has now become one of those unforeseen obstacles on our path. We created this barrier that we must now face and perhaps our travel is more difficult as a result of this ego-driven decision not to ask for help. There are times when we must learn this lesson the hard way and it also shows us that we have the ability to do things on our own. So when do we ask for help and when do it face our journey alone?

The answer is not easy and is different for each situation and for each individual. We shouldn't throw up a wall along our path because of our ego, but have the humility to know our own limits and ask for help when we need it.

April 4

 ho's counting on us today? Who is relying on us to be there for them and to do certain things? Some may say no one, while others will say their family. Others may even broaden the group to those with whom they work are relying on us, but that will probably be the extent. Is that all? Really? That few? We're just ordinary people, right?

If we believe we have such a limited influence and see ourselves as ordinary, run of the mill, just generic brand type people we really need to take a second look. We touch the lives of so many each and every day. If we weren't who we are and did the things we do, then their lives would be different. So our sphere of influence has now grown to the grocery clerk, to the waitress where we had lunch, to the other parent at daycare, to the friend that needed a comforting touch.

With this reawakened realization, we need to step it up a bit. We need to be amazing today, not run of the mill. We need to be extraordinary, not just ordinary. We need to be name brand, not generic. People are counting on us to be all those things; special, amazing and extraordinary. It's up to us now to be those. People are counting on us.

April 5

The super powers will we all possess lie dormant, locked away within us but there is a key that will unlock that box, we just have to find it. There are many times we don't even realize there is a box and that we have these powers, but we do.

The power of a gentle touch can move mountains. The power of a kind and caring word can speak volumes, louder than any other sound. The power of a smile radiates with the brightness of the sun. And the power of a listening ear dispels all chaos and calamity. So with all these powers right at our fingertips, what is the key that will open this box and release all these powers? They key is love.

Open our box of powers with that key of love and discover all the miracles each one possesses. Great things will happen all around us and lives will be changed. The world will be changed… and…we will be changed.

April 6

With a batting average is .425; we step up to the plate, with bat in hand. We look out into the field of players and see each one very attentive as we take our stance over the plate. The catcher crouches down and umpire leans forward, each of us waiting for the pitcher to throw the ball. There's the wind up, and 'SWISSSHHH', 'SMACK' into the catcher's glove goes the ball. The umpire shouts, "STRIKE ONE." We step away from the plate and gather our thoughts; we barely saw that one coming.

We step back up to the plate, and we're set for the next pitch, just as all the other players. The ball leaves the pitcher's hand, 93 miles per hour, rocketing towards us. We have a microsecond to make a decision, swing, or let it go by. 'SWISSSHH' … 'SMACK' into the catcher's glove again. "STRIKE TWO." We hesitated and now we are one pitch away from going back to the dugout, unable to advance our team, and feeling we have let them and ourselves down. We're left with one ball, one microsecond to make a decision to swing at the next ball or just let it go by. There's the pitch...

Our batting average in life does not mean anything. What is important is that we take a chance and swing our bat at the balls that are thrown our way. It takes courage to step up to the plate, and it takes a willingness to take a chance at life to swing our bat. We will miss one-hundred percent of the balls we never swing our bat to hit. Sometimes we hit a foul ball, and sometimes we hit a double… and occasionally we hit a home run… because we swung our bat instead of letting life just 'SWISSSHH' on by us.

"BATTER UP"…

April 7

Megabyte, gigabyte, terabyte are a measures of memory that a small chip can contain. Thousands and thousands little pieces of information that can be recalled in a matter of seconds. When we go to extract that piece of data from the memory, it's just that, a small piece of data with nothing else attached.

Our mind is another place that stores pieces of information and we recall pieces of data from it too. When we go to our own internal memory bank sometimes we get more than just that piece of information. Sometimes what we pull from our memory brings along with it an emotion as an extra bonus.

Memories, bad ones, sad ones or happy ones each bring with them an emotion that is much greater than the memory itself. Can we recall a memory of when we were playing in the snow, making a snowman and the snowball fight that followed? There is a small smile that spreads across our face as we recall that memory. Other memories that we recall bring other emotions that are not so pleasant, and we can become overwhelmed with anger or sadness. The sadness in our heart is heavy and consuming as this memory is brought up. If we can look to see if there is some happy times associated with this memory also and then focus on those memories too. As we concentrate on the good times, and not the sad times, the sad emotion our memory becomes less overwhelming.

Memories... cherish the good and happy ones, letting the others simply fade away into the memory bank, locked away for good.

April 8

It is our time just to be…

… be caring ~ there is someone that needs us.

… be willing ~ it's time we step out and try something new.

… be passionate ~ there is a fire burning within us. It's time we add more fuel.

… be serving ~ reach out and help others with their challenges in life.

… be honest ~ while not easy at times, it is the best way to live life.

… be respectful ~ if we want others to respect us, we must practice the same.

… be hopeful ~ that tiny glimmer of hope may be the only thing we can hold on to.

… be humble ~ be our right size and don't let our ego become inflated

… be loving ~ the value of our love is immense, share it.

… be yourself ~ for there is no one better to be you… than you.

April 9

What's fair in life? And who are we to judge what's fair and what's not? Our idea of fairness is based on our values and those that we hold true to our heart. With our values as our core belief and the way we live life, we weigh circumstances and judge their fairness. However, life is imperfect and we make mistakes. Others make mistakes too and we need just to understand that we all are just human.

When we think the scale of fairness has tipped in the unfair direction we need to dig a little deeper into our personal values and find the courage to face the day. We need to search deep within our heart and soul and find love that will light our path and allow us to continue on our journey. Hold true the value of integrity, doing the right thing, when our path becomes difficult to travel.

Things are sometimes not fair, but if we rely on our personal values, we can face the day, find goodness in our life, and place yet another step forward on our journey. Our values must never waiver, for they are the fuel that keeps us going.

April 10

*L*aughter is such a great reliever of stress, anger, and just all around gloom. It takes us from the cloudy gray side of life to the lightness of our day. Who cannot smile when we see a baby giggle, or see someone that is laughing uncontrollably? Laughing takes us away from the drudgery when find ourselves in sometimes and adds a little joy to our day.

So what do we have to laugh about? We can find laughter in comical everyday situations. We can find laughter in some of our daily blunders we commit. But there is caution ahead. Never laugh at someone else and their life, because if you do, you laugh alone. Laughter is to be shared with others so we can add a little joy to their day.

It's time we find took a little bit of our day and find some laughter. It will lighten our heart, rejuvenate our spirit with joy, and make the day just a little better.

April 11

*P*lans get changed. Priorities are shifted. Our day is unfolding differently than we anticipated. So do we get angry, upset, or throw a tantrum? Of course not, we adjust. We don't dwell on circumstances that are out of our control and we move forward, maybe in a slightly different direction, but still forward.

Life's journey has turns in it, some expected and some not, coming to us as a surprise. Our day's journey depends on how we react to the changes to our schedule and the action of others around us. If we react negatively, then we are certain to influence others with our foul mood. However, if we take these changes in stride, our outlook on the day remains positive and we can continue to make a difference in the lives of others in a positive light.

These changes… this shift in priority… how big of a deal was it anyway? If we are honest with ourselves we see it's not that big of a deal. If we can check our ego, we will see we were making it all about us and not thinking of others. So before we 'pop a cork', throw a fit, or lash out because things are not going our way… take a peek inside and be honest. Is it really a big deal?

April 12

So when we receive a compliment or someone helps us with a task, do we think in the back of our mind... why are they doing this? Are we suspicious of their actions and wonder if there is some motive? In some cases their motive is less than admirable and in fact quite the opposite. What about the person that talks behind our back or does things that may bring us pain or harm? Do we wonder why are they doing these things?

In both cases we can see that their motive, their motivation, to act this way is driven by their ego that has run amuck. "What can I do for you that you in turn will repay me?" Or, "What's in it for me?" And last, perhaps the saddest, "I need to destroy this person so I can look better." Looking carefully, we see that ego, selfishness, and greed are the character defects that cause people to act this way.

We shouldn't be suspicious of everyone's willingness to help us, or that they made a positive comment about us. But if we discover there is a hidden agenda and their motive was ego driven, we simply need to find it within ourselves to forgive and move on. Yes, that is not easy, but the burden we carry weighs us down, not them. So release it with forgiveness. Maybe the best we can do today is the willingness to find forgiveness in our heart.

April 13

We seek to find the answers to questions that have no real answer. The answer could be this or it could be that, but which one is the right answer? Perhaps there isn't a wrong one or a right one. Our mind races weighing all the facts as we know them and figuring out which is the right answer. What is the solution to the situation or question we are facing?

The more our mind races from one solution to the next, it becomes more complicated and we become more frustrated in seeking the answer. Maybe we can find the solution if we just slow our mind down. Calm the chaos of our racing mind by taking a deep breath and close our eyes. Take another deep breath and focus strictly on our breathing. Like the rushing stream filled with the heavy rain water, we cannot see the river rocks that lie below, but we know they are there. Once the stream slows down and the water becomes calm, we can now clearly see the rocks below. Just like the stream, once our mind calms the chaos, we can clearly see the rocks, our answers that are right there.

A brief recess from the rushing mind reveals so much to us. We perhaps will find the answers to our questions. As a bonus to this new found serenity, we can see the beauty that is all around us and more importantly, the beauty within.

April 14

There are givers and takers in this world. In some cases there is a combination of the two, called the giver/taker. The takers of the world are only taking away from others, just for themselves. They take time from others. They take knowledge from others and soak it up. They are like a sponge that has unlimited capacity of taking and taking without limits. The true taker seldom gives, unless it's to take more. These individuals are focused on themselves and allow greed and selfishness to control their lives.

On the other hand, there are the givers. These people constantly give and give and give more, expecting nothing in return. They volunteer, they find ways to help others, and they share everything they have, accepting nothing in return. They simply love giving freely to others. In some cases there is a risk for the giver in that they will drain themselves and never replenish their own body and mind.

The giver/taker is one that gives freely and accepts what others have to offer too. It is an exchange of sorts. We give away our time and energy, but we also accept what others are offering to us too. It's a win-win scenario. We give away and we allow others to give away too, thus replenishing our body and soul. We need to find humility in our giving and be thankful in our taking. We need to give with love and take with gratitude.

Be a loving and caring giver, but also be a thankful and grateful taker.

April 15

As we turn the corner on our morning walk we see a pair of shoes on the edge of the sidewalk. The brown leather shoes are old and worn. One shoe, lying on its side and the other, toes facing the sidewalk. Some mud covers the toe of the shoe and the finish of the leather is worn down to the rough leather. The shoe laces are old and knotted, broken several times and tied together again and again. We can clearly see a hole worn in the sole of the shoe. We wonder who was so thoughtless that they would throw away these old shoes and clutter the sidewalk. How inconsiderate they must be.

If the shoes could tell us of their journey, we would learn this about them. The brand new shoes, nicely polished, walked with a young family to church each Sunday. Then one day, these shoes found themselves standing in the rain as they lowered the shoes-owner's only daughter to her final resting place after a drunk driver took her life. The journey of the shoes continued, but lost their shine and found their way through many dark and tough places. With each step, the shoes helped the shoe-owner travel his journey until the journey ended for him. Now discarded, the shoes just lie there with no place to go any more.

Let's not judge the shoes or the shoe-owner by their outward appearance, for we see, we have not walked in these shoes and we do not know of their journey.

April 16

*I*ntimidation is a self-imposed fear of feeling 'less than' when around others. Being around doctors, lawyers, famous authors, great speakers, or our boss we may feel inadequate and intimidated, though they are probably not intentionally doing so. We climb into our shell, like a turtle when we find ourselves in situations when we are expected to interact, in some capacity, with these people whom we hold in high regard. "What will I say?", "Will I look stupid?" are the questions we have rolling around our mind as we listen to them. "Oh, please don't ask me a question..." is that thought that plagues our mind.

We may not have their level of education or social position in life. We may not have the fancy car or the big house on the hill, but we have something that is just as important, if not more. We have our personal values. We have a set of values that are deep within our heart and soul. We can hold our head up and not look down or away. We should be proud of whom we are and not let anyone ever cloud our pride with intimidation.

We make a difference in this world just as those that intimidate us. We need not retreat into our shell when placed in situations with others because we have something to offer too, our belief and passion of our personal values. These values are just as important as any college degree, position in the business world, or anything else.

April 17

We may have heard a phrase that a stranger is a friend we haven't met yet. And if we look closely at that, it's true. The friends we have in our life today were once strangers at one point. How did this relationship grow from stranger one day to friend today? It probably took giving of ourselves to another person. That giving of ourselves just may start with a smile in passing or just a 'good morning' with a smile. In any case, it could be the start of a friendship that could last a lifetime.

We are the 'stranger' too, and don't we feel a little better when someone else initiates a smile and a greeting? Or do we just grunt something, look away and continue on with our day? If we look directly into the eyes of a stranger we can connect at a slightly deeper level, even for just a fleeting moment, if we simply smile. Eye to eye contact is just another way one heart smiles to another.

Reach out to a stranger, share a smile and look them in the eye, for they may be your new best friend. We just may need this friend someday.

April 18

The night air is cool, but not cold. The night's sky is cloudless and stars are like twinkling little diamonds in the sky. So peaceful… so relaxing we sit and enjoy the peace and solitude of our late night rendezvous with nature. The silence of the darkness is deafening as we allow our mind to reflect on who we are, how we got to where we are today and contemplate where our journey is taking us.

As if in a hypnotic state, we stare at the stars above us. How humbled we feel as we continue to gaze deep into space, the universe, the dark blanket of night. Suddenly a shooting star streaks across the midnight sky. Its speed is fast and the shooting star's tail creates an arch as it rockets through the sky. The arch is like the arch of a rainbow after a spring rain.

The midnight's rainbow is gone in a fleeting second, but its image remains in our memory. We make a wish on that star. What is our wish? Is it to follow our dreams? Just as the spring time rainbow promises a pot of gold, our dream is that pot of gold. The shooting star, the midnight's rainbow, is what reminds us that we need to follow our dreams, follow our passion, and make a difference in the world.

Midnight rainbows are special and rarely seen. We need to follow them to where they are leading us, to our pot of gold, to our life's purpose, to our dreams and beyond.

April 19

We stand on the sidelines and the game continues to be played on the field. We watch as others play some winning events while others lose some. It all plays out in front of us, but we just stand idly by on the sidelines. We're tempted to get out there and play too, but we're too afraid of losing, or making a fool of ourselves so we just remain in place.

What will it take for us to get into the game? What needs to happen for us to step out onto that field and be part of the game? Sometimes it is a simple, light push from a friend or that we simply decide to take control of our life and take a chance on the field. That game, that field... is the game of life and we need to get into that game and begin to participate in it instead of allowing life's game to be played out without us. We forget we have a team in this game and that team is our friends. That team is there to protect us, push us, lead us and be part of our life, but we cannot experience it, but standing idly by on the sidelines.

We need to get in the game; get involved, take a chance and be part of the winning team. We are a team in this game called life, so we need to help our teammates as they have helped us so we all can win. Make a difference, be part of the winning team.

April 20

The early, early morning's darkness is eerie and foreboding. The silence of this time of day is the most quiet, for nature has not awakened from its deep sleep. We look at this time as maybe the darkest of times, not only for today, but perhaps we see it as the darkest time of our lives. As we focus on our darkness, our self-imposed despair, we look up and now there is a glimmer of light in the eastern sky, the day is beginning to makes its presence. Slowly the sky begins to fill with the soft pastels of a beautiful palette of colors.

That morning palette of color, that little glimmer of light on the horizon is a reminder to us that if we simply look up and see the light, we see it is our hope. It is our hope that will take us from the deep darkness of the early morning and bring light into our life. Having hope is that little glimmer of a flame, deep within our soul that can pull us from the depths of our darkness.

The morning's twilight begins to envelope the darkness of the early morning and it is hope we see in this twilight, that comes to us each morning, and we finally figure out it is the hope in our heart that will take away the darkness we feel inside ourselves.

April 21

W hat brings us here? Why are we where we are and doing what we're doing? It's easy to ask these questions, for no one can tell us we're wrong in the answer we come up with. We may find the answers in prayer and meditation, or perhaps we will find the answers in personal journaling. Whatever the method, no one can argue with us that it is wrong.

Deep within our soul is a compass and it gives us the direction we need to travel along the pathway before us. The direction our compass points may not always be clear and our compass may sway from side to side because of interference of outside influences, but once the interference subsides, our compass points us in the right direction again. We are on our journey, following our path with a purpose in life. At times we will face challenges along the way, or may make a wrong turn, but we will find our way back to the path that leads us on the purpose-filled journey with our compass.

It's time we trust our internal compass and follow its direction, not questioning its guidance. Nor should we question why we are where we are in life, or why we are doing what we're doing, simply begin to trust our compass. We need to stop questioning and begin living; begin living with a values based purpose and follow the direction of our compass. Enjoy the journey.

April 22

There are days when we just don't want to do certain things. We may not want to get out of that warm cozy bed or take the dog for their walk on a cold morning. We may not want to exercise today or have that healthy salad for lunch. We may not want to go to work or do our homework for the college course we're taking. We just don't want to…

But we do… We do get out of bed, we take the dog for its walk and we get on the elliptical for 30 minutes. We make our way to work and eat the salad we made for ourselves and not the big fat cheeseburger we dreamed about. We do these things because we have discipline in our lives. We fight through the all the "I don't wanna's", with that internal drive of discipline and determination.

Discipline is work, and may be the only thing that will get us through the excuses we find sneaking in, preventing us from doing what we know to be the right action. The discipline we demonstrate in our daily lives inspires others and what better gift can we give to them than to inspire some discipline into their life.

April 23

The fireworks rocket streaks upward in the night sky and suddenly explodes in a beautiful array of colors, sprinkling the sky like sparkles of colorful glitter. The resounding boom follows like distant thunder and we watch, mesmerized, anticipating the next rocket; each one different from the last, each one we oooooo and ahhhhhh over. It's a celebration as the sprinkles of fireworks light up the night sky.

Celebrating brings happiness and joy into our lives. Whether it's the night sprinkles of fireworks, or it's the balloons and confetti of a party, it's fun to celebrate. We smile, laugh and have joy in our heart. Our eyes twinkle with happiness. Sadly we spend more time not celebrating than we could. One might say, we don't have anything to celebrate, and therein lies the problem, we do, and we just don't see it.

Today is a day of celebration because today is a gift and gifts come with parties and celebration. We are part of that gift. We are here to celebrate ourselves and our lives. We touch the lives of so many and what better way to touch someone's life than with a celebration of who we are. Be joyful and happy as we celebrate today; celebrate our life and those to whom we will make a difference.

April 24

It was Friday night, and this was the family eat-out night at a local restaurant. The Dad of the household had to work, but Mom didn't want to disappoint the kids, so they all loaded up in the van to go out to dinner. This was an extra-special night, but little did they know, how special it would be. Arriving at the restaurant, they were seated and menus passed out to the Mom and oldest son, Nico. The other two were too young, so they just colored on the kid's placemats.

No sooner as eleven year-old, Nico picked up his menu, he noticed an elderly lady coming through the door, walking with a cane; she was seated a few tables away. Nico noticed that no one was with her, and she sat alone. He couldn't focus on the menu, even when his Mom asked what looked good to eat; his attention was solely on the elderly lady, very concerned she was all alone, and perhaps his Mom would let him sit with her during dinner, so she wouldn't have to eat alone. Nico's Mom could see a little tear in his eye, and she asked him what was wrong. "That lady is all alone, and I want to sit with her and eat dinner." said Nico. The mother explained that was not a good idea. So he asked, "Could we at least buy her dinner?" The Mom agreed and Nico wanted to tell the elderly lady, and his Mom said okay. He walked over to her and said, "Hello. My name is Nico and my family, and I want to pay for your dinner." The old lady was very touched and thanked the young man. They chatted for a few minutes, and Nico gave her a hug before returning to his table.

Nico now satisfied, he devoured his dinner. As they left the restaurant, the old lady was still enjoying her dinner, and she thanked Nico again. She looked into the mother's eyes and said, "You have a fine son. Thank you for my dinner." What the family didn't know was this lady had just lost her husband this past week and Friday was the night they went to eat out too, and that is why she was alone in the restaurant that night.

On the drive home Nico's Mom called her husband to tell him what had happened at the restaurant. The next morning at breakfast, the Dad told Nico how proud he was of him in helping the elderly lady in the restaurant. Nico simply said, "What? No a big deal Dad. It's just what you do." Nico has taught us kindness, care and compassion. He teaches us respect and doing the right thing. This is all wrapped up with a huge example of true humility. Random acts of kindness are not hard, but touch the lives of so many.[1]

---

[1] This Thought of the Day is based on a true story and has now reached hundreds of people, maybe thousands… and has made a difference. This story was told with permission of Kimberly M. of Pennsylvania and her son, Nico. Thank you for allowing me the honor to tell your story. You both inspire me.

April 25

"Would I rather be kind or right?" is the question we seldom ask ourselves as we go about our day, facing one situation after another. We have this drive in our mind that we have to win, we have to be right. It's our ego filling our head with this drive to be better than those around us. It can be a very small issue and we know we're right, but is it that important that we win? Will the argument have a better outcome if we insist on having it our way? Or will the overall situation have a better outcome if we're kind and let the other person 'win'?

Forcing the issue to be right, at the cost of someone else's situation, usually has a counter effect on the issue in the first place. Yes, we are right and we win the conflict, but we lose maybe something even greater than the win, we lose respect. Not only do we lose respect from those involved in the situation, but we lose self-respect. We bullied ourselves into being right and having the outcome feed our ego, but we diminished ourselves as a result.

We need to stand up for what is right and do what we can to make a difference in the world. It's just sometimes we make a bigger difference in the world when we decide to be kind instead of being right all the time.

April 26

*L*ove is noun and a verb. ~ **Love** is too big to be just one four-letter word, it needs more letters. ~ **Love** is one of those emotions that can invoke feelings from one end of the spectrum to the other. It can bring comfort with the tender touch of our hand and a kind work spoken from our heart. ~ **Love** can bring pain and hurt like no other emotion can. ~ **Love** is being there for someone that is walking in a tough part of their life's path and their journey is difficult. ~ **Love** is shared with friends, family, a spouse, a partner, coworkers, pets, and yes, even a stranger. ~ **Love** is having a smile on our face, but more importantly, a smile in our heart. ~ **Love** makes each moment seem like an eternity. ~ **Love** makes the world go around, yet stops it at the same time.

Love is so special and such a beautiful gift we can give each other, yet we hold so close to our heart we don't want to express it, or share it, we just want it for ourselves. ~ **Love** when given away or shared with others comes back to us a hundred times more powerful. ~ **Love** is what we all need and most desire.

So it's time for action. It's time we share our **Love** for each other. Find a way to share it from our heart, and make a difference in the lives we touch each day.

April 27

The physical pain of a sore muscle or joint is an indicator that we have stretched or extended our body beyond what it is accustomed in doing. Sometimes the pain is intense, while other times it's merely a subtle reminder to take care of our body. We seek relief from this pain through medication, physical therapy, physicians or other medical professionals. And sometimes the greatest healer is just time.

There may be times in our lives when we also face emotional pain. This pain is just as real and just as intense at the physical pain of injuring our body. This pain is isolated to one part of our body, our heart. All sorts of events in our lives will cause this emotional pain to erupt. It could be the loss of our long time family pet that is truly a family member or perhaps the loss of a dear relative. The pain can come from an argument with a loved one, or any number of other reasons. This pain is real and we need to find relief from it. Some may find temporary relief from medication, advice from medical professionals, but there are two things that will bring the greatest relief, the love of a friend and time.

The love of a friend, holding our hand, listening to each word as we allow the pain to pour out from our heart, brings comfort and relief. The pain may not be totally gone, only time will take it away completely. So... can we be part of the healing today? Can we be the one that listens and comforts, removing the emotional pain our friend feels? We can. It just takes love.

April 28

Accepting responsibility for our actions or the actions of others representing us is sometimes hard. We should remember that we are responsible for what transpires in our lives, both personally and professionally. If we're wrong, then we need to step up and accept the consequences of our actions. We lessen our credibility when we try to blame others for mistakes we make. The same holds true for the errors that others make, if they are acting on our behalf.

We're not perfect and we make mistakes and we will probably make some in the future. And making mistakes is okay as long as we accept them as ours and we learn from them. We only compound the problem when we shift the blame, when it is truly ours to accept. The lesson of accepting responsibility is a hard one, but in reality we are a better person as a result and will be forgiven quicker.

Respect, integrity and truthfulness are the values that shine when we accept responsibility for our actions and make right any wrongs. In our heart we know what we need to do and that feeling in our gut are our values reminding us of the right action we need to take. We should learn to trust our values for they are our legacy.

April 29

The sun begins to settle in the western sky as our day comes to a close as we walk up our path. The sunny day is replaced with the soft color palette of dusk and it's time we take a rest from our journey. It's like closing a chapter of a book, our book, of our day. We lean against the tall oak tree that soars above us and we look back on our journey today and ask ourselves some questions. "Did I touch a life today?", "Did I live my life today based on the values that are in my soul?", "Did I make a difference in the life of someone else today?", and "Were my words and actions filled with love?"

The answers to these questions may not be the answers we had hoped for, but we realize we may have another opportunity to change those answers when we awaken to a new day, and start on our journey once again. The final page turns over in this chapter of our life as we drift off into a comfortable sleep, knowing the answers to our questions and realizing we do have a purpose in this life.

We can make a difference in the lives we touch and the morning will bring us new opportunities and new people to meet and make a difference. We just need to look for ways to make a positive difference in their day and in their life. Our path is merely the road we travel fulfilling our life's purpose.

April 30

People are counting on us each day. A part of their lives is sometimes dependent on us doing certain things. Our lives are intertwined with so many others; we can hardly claim that we are so isolated that we don't touch someone else's life each day. If we're a parent, then our children are dependent on us each day to nurture and help them grow. Our friends count on us to be there when they truly need us. Our employer depends on us to do our part in making the company profitable.

Our day and what we do with it touches someone else. It is then our action that is carried through from one person to the next and then another. We should never feel that our actions really don't matter because they truly do. Our actions are seen by people outside of immediate sphere of influence, and we made a difference to them too; we just don't see it.

The one person that is counting on us to do the right thing every day, to live a life with integrity, respect, courage and love, is… ourselves. If we don't live a life that reflects our personal values, we are selling ourselves short of the best life possible.

May

May 1

The morning fog is very thick as we awaken and step onto our path to begin our journey again. We can barely see more than fifty feet, and we can't see where our path is taking us today, but we move forward. Early on today's journey we come to a split on our path; a path to the left and one to the right. The fog obscures our visibility, so we can't see what may be ahead on either path, so we must choose.

We can stand there trying to analyze which direction to follow, or we can dig deep within ourselves and find that courage, that faith to step out in whichever direction. Was it the right choice? We may never know that answer, but what we do know; our courage and faith can walk us through whatever may lie ahead.

There may be some point along our journey when we think we did make a bad choice, and we become angry with ourselves in not choosing the other path. We can beat ourselves up and miss the point of what can we learn from our choice. If we have faith, then the choice was the right one for we have now learned a lesson and have become just a little wiser.

Have the faith and courage to step out into the fog and follow your path without fear.

May 2

We are constantly in search of something. We're thirsting for knowledge, so we go to school, letting the educators of the world teach us. We're looking for a companion, someone to walk with us on our journey through life, so we interact with friends in a social aspect of our life to help us find that one and only person. We seek wisdom, so we read great books, filled with words that will enlighten us and bring clarity. We're in search of the meaning of life, while some may climb the highest mountain, looking for the Tibetan Monk, seeking the answers from him, many will seek spiritual guidance from clergy.

Unaware that we are really looking for all of these, we go about our day, doing the best we can with what we have. In the quiet of a day, we may ask ourselves, why we are here on earth and what is our purpose in life, or do we even have one. We can go to the educators, our friends, clergy or the great authors to find the answer, but the answer is closer than we think. The answer is within us and us alone.

We must start with revitalizing our personal values, and if we look closely at them, then take the next step and look a little deeper within ourselves, do we discover a passion. Finding that passion is the first step in answering the ultimate question, what is our purpose in life? Reawakening of our values will lead us to our life's purpose. Look honestly within and the answers will be revealed.

May 3

We hear of the lives of law enforcement officers being saved by a body protective vest. The vest is made up of complex material, specifically designed to protect the person wearing it. If they are struck by a life-ending bullet, and their vest protects them from the potential damage that this bullet could impose. Without question, the officer is knocked down, bruised, and is hurt, but not dead. Their life was saved by their protective vest.

We also wear a protective vest that shields us from what many might call life-ending incidences. Yes, these 'bullets' that strike us may knock us off our feet, bruise us and even bring tears to our eyes with pain, but… we're still alive. Our protective vest is not complex; it is actually quite simple, but it is not without some flaws. Our protective vest is made up of our personal values, and these flaws are our character defects, which weaken our vest. Character defects such as greed, selfishness, ego, hatred and many more may cause our values vest to be weak and not protect us as well from the bullets of life.

We put on our protective vest each morning and each day. We make it impervious to the bullets of life by making sure are values are what the vest is made up of, and not allowing the cracks and flaws of character defects weaken it. We should wear our values vest with pride, knowing it will protect us. Yes, we may still get hurt, and we may still shed tears, but we're still here to live another day.

May 4

*W*hen injustice strikes us, we cannot just lie down and accept it. We cannot allow injustice just to run over us without a fight. We must take a stand and face that demon square in the eye and bring courage, honesty, and integrity as our weapons to defeat it. Our battle we face may be fierce, but if we stand up for our rights and stand up for true justice, we should never feel ashamed for our actions.

But what about the injustice, we see that has happened to others? Do we just let them be trampled down by their unjust demon? What if they are no longer capable of fighting their battle, do we just stand on the sidelines and feel sorry for them? The answer is no, if we have an ounce of compassion, an ounce of fairness, we will fight their battle with every ounce of energy and just as strongly as we fight our own.

Will injustice win? Maybe... but if we know in our heart, we fought our battle and the battle for those unable to fight, with all the weapons at our disposal, with all the passion that burns within us; we should never look down in defeat. We should feel proud that we took a stand and used our personal values as the weapons to defeat the demon of injustice. We should never bow our head in shame when we take a stand for ourselves, and those that we love.

If we defeat the demon, we should not gloat or sing our praises to all around, but simply feel the warmth in our heart, we did the right thing, and we defeated the enemy. Stand proud, head held high, for we today made a difference.[2]

---

[2] Today's thought of the day is based on a true event, happening today. It is inspired by a young lady who has traveled a long distance to stand up for her brutally murdered sister at a clemency hearing for the convicted murderer. Her courage, her desire to make sure justice prevails should be an inspiration to all of us. I won't use her name, but if you believe in the power of prayer, please consider taking a moment and saying a prayer for a very strong and very brave young lady, facing the demons of memory of this horrible event.

May 5

We made the team. Now we have to win the game. We can win the game as long as every team member does their part, and maybe just a little more. If we don't pull our own weight and work together as a team, there is little chance we will win. Each of us has the ability, and each of us brings to the team special talents. It's up to the collective us to pull together, and make this team the best it can be and bring in a winning season.

The game has started, and we're off to a pretty good start. Gradually, we seem to fall behind a little. We look around to see if we can figure out why. We look at other team members, and we think they're not playing to capacity. We see others that seem not to be pulling their weight too, while we are doing our very best. We will surely lose if they don't do their part too. Soon, we seem to be one of a few that are playing to win. We think, well, if they are not going to give their best, neither will we. This way of thinking will now take our team to defeat with certainty.

We are a part of a team, and we are responsible to do our very best. Once we allow the thought of doing less than our full capacity, we weaken the team. We can encourage others to do their best, but in the long run, we can only control how we work on the team. We shouldn't judge others about how they are playing on the team, because we may not have all the facts. Our part of this team is to do our very best, and if we lose the game, we can hold our head high, knowing we did our best.

When we begin to accept the actions of others as the new standard, when that is less than what we are capable of performing, we have added another weak link to the chain. We shouldn't judge others on their performance based on what we think they should be doing. We need to focus our energy on something we can control, ourselves. Today, let's play our very best to win.

May 6

E yes bleary from the night's sleep, we begin our day with our routine. At some point in that routine, we look into a mirror and see a reflection of ourselves. What do we see in that mirror? Do we see a person that doesn't like themselves, or see a person we think is unattractive? Do we start our day, looking in our mirror, setting the stage for our whole day with thoughts, which bring us down and make the day miserable before it's even started?

It is time we break that mirror, and if you think that will bring seven years of bad luck, well so be it. It's time to get a new mirror that will reflect back our true self. We need to look into our new mirror and see a different person than before. We will see the true reflection of ourselves. Looking into our new mirror, we see a person that helped a friend yesterday. We see a person that smiled at the baby in the grocery store and made them smile back. We can see our reflection is one that has goodness and compassion in their soul. We now see a person that has love and joy in their heart, and we smile. We finally see a person that has values in their life, and that they make a difference every day.

The ugly duckling of the old mirror is replaced by the beautiful swan in the new mirror. We are that attractive and graceful swan. As we look into our brand-new mirror and see ourselves as a beautiful swan, we have now set the stage to make a bigger difference in the lives we will touch today. Maybe our purpose today is to help someone else find a new mirror.

May 7

Patience is the ability to remain quiet when things around us are chaotic and not going at the pace, we want them to progress. Patience is restraint of pen and tongue when there are words boiling inside us that we think we need to say because of someone's action. Patience is not easy; it takes work. It takes being diligent and strong in allowing whatever is impacting our life to play out and wait for the right time for us to take action. Patience is the willingness to bring calmness to what would other be chaos.

Being impatient usually ends up with words that cannot be unsaid, or an email that cannot be unsent. Impatience is more likely to cause further chaos than solve the situation and could cause it to escalate even more. Rash, quick, over-reactions, because we just can't wait for the situation to play out, will only add to the problem.

What is the cost of impatience? Depending on the situation, it could be minimal or none at all, but it could also be very devastating. What is the cost of patience? It can bring serenity to calamity.

Patience is remaining in the calm harbor as the stormy sea churns; waiting patiently, allowing the storm to subside before we set sail.

May 8

The horizon on the eastern sky becomes brighter as a new day begins and the sun makes its appearance, bringing new light and new hope to our day. So once again we begin our journey, another day and another set of challenges and rewards. Our path is set before us, taking us through our life, challenging us with obstacles placed on our path. Each obstacle, once overcome, brings the reward of accomplishment and growth. Each one makes us stronger and wiser, so we can face the next one.

There will be times when the challenges seem insurmountable, and we see no way over or around them. We try every conceivable approach to overcome, and we become exhausted, mentally and physically. We think our journey came to an end, and we begin to consider giving up. The solution to our dilemma is only an arm's length away, our hand. Exhausted from our efforts, we lie on our path, but if we simply reach up with our hand and ask, 'Can you help me?' The hand of a friend is there, grasping our hand, pulling us up to our feet. Our friend's hand is strong and together helps us overcome the obstacle that seemed to defeat us.

We have friends in our lives that will help us overcome any obstacle that is set before us, but we cannot always take; we must also give. We must extend our hand to help someone else that is facing their challenges. We will discover by helping others with our hand of strength and hope; we become stronger too. A day should not go by when we don't offer our hand in service to others. By giving of ourselves, we grow and our path, our journey becomes brighter.

May 9

A tiny green shoot begins to make its appearance through the winter's soil. The winter brown earth is hard and void of life, but the tiny green shoot finds the strength to break through. Slowly, but surely it finds its way through the hardened soil and begins to reach upward, climbing to the light of the sun. It's new life, a new beginning for our tiny part of nature. The mystery remains, what beauty will our new green shoot bring as it continues to grow?

Like the tiny green shoot bringing new life to the season, we bring new life to the day as we break through the night's solitude. We awaken and find the strength to start a new day and bring our lives in tune with nature. But just as the tiny green shoot needs the will power to break through the winter's soil and bring beauty, we also need to set our will and determination to bring our beauty to the day as well. We need to recognize we have a beautiful gift to give to the world today. We begin our day by letting our beautiful flower bloom with the rest of nature. Our beautiful flower is living our life's values.

As the tiny green shoot will bring a beautiful flower to the world to enjoy, what will we bring to the world? What beauty will we add to the day and make a difference in the lives of others. It's time to blossom.

May 10

W e look and see the stage is dark. We can barely see the scenery on the stage, but it is all in place and we know the show will begin soon. Faint music begins to play, and the lighting behind the backdrop begins to illuminate the set. It's almost time for us to make our entrance. It's almost time for our play to begin.

The music begins to get a little louder, and the lights begin to get brighter. The whole stage is now filled with lights and music, and we step out of the wings and move to our mark and to begin. We are joined by others, many others, moving to their marks, then the curtain rises and the play has begun. We say our lines as best we can, sometimes not as perfectly as we wished, but hopefully well enough not close the curtain. Our dialogue serves to lead to someone else's script and one after another, we play out act one.

We should remember as we move about the stage and reciting our lines, we are merely a player in this play. We're not the lead and needn't have the spotlight on us, but our role is important, as the actor beside us is depending on us to deliver our line, so they may play out their part. As long as we play our part and not try to direct all the others on the stage on how they need to play theirs, we will find act one will go well.

With each act, scenery is changed; other actors have come onto the stage, while others have left our stage, and we continue to play our role. We play our role on stage until the music fades; the lighting dims and darkness engulfs the stage, and the curtain comes down. Our play is over for today.

We don't need to wait for the reviews for in our heart we know whether or not we did well in our play today. We don't need to listen to praise or criticism. It is what is in our heart that counts. If our play today touched the life of someone else and made their day a little better, we were a success. And we may never know whose life we touched, but tomorrow will bring another play and other actors. Our role in the next play is to do the very best we can. This play is called, "Our Life."

May 11

The gavel strikes the wooden base, and the judge makes a decision of what has been brought before him. All the evidence and all the arguments are done, and a judgment is made. Weighing each proposed fact, the scales of justice are tipped in one direction or another, without regard of personal opinions or prejudice; the judge does his sworn duty and passes judgment. This is his job, and he has done it with all the experience and education that has brought him to where he is.

There are days when we judge others and in fact, act as the jury too. We judge based on our personal feelings, not necessarily based on the facts, but only as we perceive the situation. We don't call witnesses, listen to both sides of the story, or allow for detailed examination; we simply strike the wooden base with our gavel. We condemn that person without just cause, simply because we think we have the right to pass judgment on someone else.

The most difficult case that may be brought before us is the case where we pass judgment on ourselves. This case is very difficult to defend, because we have already made our decision; guilty is too often the verdict and the punishment is a constant mental beating of ourselves.

Judging others and judging ourselves doesn't leave very much room for compassion and love. So before we slam the gavel on our wooden base, think, are we choosing to condemn rather than show care, compassion and love? And who are we to judge anyway?

May 12

*O*ur day starts, not necessarily when the sun breaks the horizon, but as we begin to awaken from our night's rest. Our mind begins a conversation with us. It may start with events of yesterday, or the possible events of today. In any case, our mind starts our day and sets the stage for where our path may lead us. If this inner conversation with our mind focuses on the ills of yesterday, our journey has begun down the dark and gray path, and it may be difficult to find our way back to a more pleasant journey. However, if our mind's conversation is of happy thoughts and the positive potential of today, then our path is filled with soft warm breezes and sunshine.

If we can begin our mind's conversation with listing of what we are grateful for, we can be sure our journey will be one filled with joy. We look into the morning mirror and smile at ourselves. Being grateful for what we have in our life and feeling rich with the treasures that have been so generously given, our heart glows. The gifts of friends and family, the gifts of love and happiness, the gifts of self-respect and other personal values are what we should see as we look into the mirror. Our conversation with our mind continues, and now it is filled with affirmations and a full sense of gratitude.

Our day has begun; our feet are set on our path, and we begin our day. Our mind's conversation does not stop throughout the day and if can keep the conversation focused on the gifts in our life; we will find our journey is filled with the sweet smell of spring and the warmth of a sun. Let's focus on the gifts in our life, give thanks and be of service to others. Make a difference today by simply adding our smile.

May 13

 ith little energy, we move along on our journey,
taking one step at a time and are really not very
focused as one foot goes in front of the other.
We look ahead, and we can see something lying across our
path. As we come up on it, we see it's a rope, stretched
across the path and our mind thinks back to a day, long ago,
when we played jump rope with our friends. Suddenly, the
rope is spinning in front of us and two of our childhood
friends are on each side of our path, twirling the rope and
shouting to us to play. So we watch carefully and jump in,
timing each hop as the rope strikes the ground. After a few
moments, we jump out the other side, smiling at the fun,
and as we turn to see our friends, they are gone as is the
rope. A little sad we couldn't play longer we turn back to
our path and continue.

A few steps later we come across squares drawn with
chalk, with numbers in the middle, and we hear the voices
of our childhood friends again, encouraging is to play hop-
scotch to the end of the squares. We hop on one foot to the
end, leaning down to pick up the rock we tossed, and finally
hop out. Joyfully we turn to see our friends, and they are
gone. Again, we turn back to our path and start again on
our journey. Soon we come across a large round circle
drawn in the dirt and glass marbles, in various sizes are in
the circle, and we hear our childhood friends shouting to us,
it was our turn and we take the steel round ball and shoot it
into the middle, knocking out the cat-eye and the big red
marble. We smile at our accomplishment and just as the

other events today; the marbles are gone, and our friends have gone too.

So what is the meaning of this little story? We need to remember that no matter how long we walk on our journey; we find our friends have never really left us. We can still play games, laugh, smile, and fill our heart with joy of the memories of yesterday. We should never lose sight that this journey we're on is a journey to be enjoyed and not dreaded. Now imagine, at the top of the hill on our path, we see a sled; the down slope of the hill is covered in snow… now go have some fun… we hear our friends calling our name to hurry up.

Mother's Day

Sweet, gentle, kind, beautiful, and loving are words that come to mind when we think of our mothers on this Mother's Day. We recall the times when she doctored our boo-boo from the playground. We remember the times when she made her special chocolate-chip cookies for our class party. Her words of wisdom are etched in our hearts as she guides us through our teenage years. She's there to give us a smile filled with love as we hold our first child. Mothers are so special, there are not enough words or ways we can express the way we feel.

Some of us have our mothers still here with us today, and we will call them, or visit them, bringing flowers, a sentimental card, trying to express our gratitude. While some, our mothers have passed and are not here for us to call or visit, and we are very sad today. We're sad because we can't talk with them and hear their voice. We can't hug them and give them a kiss on their cheek. A tear forms in the corner of our eye because we're sad, and we just can't help it. Our mother is now a memory in our heart, and her presence is always there; we simply need to look inside our heart, and we will find her.

To all the mothers who may read this message, we love you. We may not always tell you that every day, or express it in the best of ways, but we do. The bond we have is special and one that cannot be explained. You are in our hearts, and we are glad you are there. You are there to whisper the words we need to hear and the hug we need to feel. You are there to give is us your love, and we love you.

Happy Mother's Day. We love you mom.

May 14

hat does it mean to give 110 percent? How is that possible? How can we do more than 100 percent? If we did what it took to accomplish the task and meet the requirements and nothing more, then that is giving it 100 percent. But what if we went just a little beyond the standard, is that 110 percent? Sure it is, and if we step it up even more we can continue to exceed it too.

Why is it important to measure the percentage anyway? There isn't any good reason. What we should strive for is doing the very best job we can, or being the very best person we can be, or giving ourselves to the service of others as best as we possibly can, holding nothing back. If do this every day, we can look back on the day, exhausted, depleted of every ounce of energy, and be proud of ourselves. We gave it our very best today and left it all out there on the playing field of life. The true measure of our accomplishments is not in percentages, but how we feel at the end of the day.

Each day we need to strive to do our very best in whatever is placed before us. In doing so, we will make a difference in the world. And the percentages never really matter for we know in our heart the true measure of our work.

May 15

*A*lone in the corner the child sits on a small wooden chair, facing to the wall. Tears slowly trickle down their face. Very sad and hurt from the scolding and subsequent punishment of sitting in the corner, their play time is taken away. All the shouting and scolding are over, and the child sits in isolation. The child thinks not only of the accident of knocking over the special cookie jar, breaking it into many pieces on the kitchen floor, but are also thinking of how telling the truth may not have been a good idea.

We are taught that telling the truth is something we should try to live by and practice in our life. We don't have to remember the truth, but we do have to remember every single lie and to whom we told it. A world of people not telling the truth leads to the lack of trust, suspicion, anger and deceit. Telling the truth, while difficult at times is the best decision we may make today. Accepting the outcome of our actions is part of learning.

Shouldn't we thank the person for telling us the truth? When someone tells us the truth, we shouldn't punish them, because if we do they may never tell us the truth again. Instead step back, survey the issue and find a solution with the truth-teller to correct whatever has happened.

We should teach our children that telling the truth, no matter how egregious the situation is the best choice. We do this with love, and not anger.

May 16

The wooden slats, cracked and worn span the deep gorge. The green jungle and raging river are below our trembling feet. Each slat is attached with frayed rope. We step cautiously from one to another, stepping lightly to see whether the splintered slat will hold our weight. The knuckles on our hands are white as we clinch the rope with each step. Each step is a step of faith. Each step is a step of courage. Each step brings us closer to the other side, so we can continue our journey.

Courage and faith are the two personal values that can get us through some of the most difficult times we will ever face. Courage doesn't eliminate fear; it gives us the strength to face it. We can face fear squarely in the eye and not back down when we have the courage to stand up to it. Courage supports our other values that are within us. We cannot love without having courage. We cannot be honest without courage giving us the understanding, we can accept the consequences. Courage is the base which supports many of our values.

Faith is that invisible belief that we are making the right choices. Faith is a belief that we can do what seems to be impossible. This inner drive is given a turbo boost when we find the power of faith. Faith is believing in ourselves.

We can cross that rickety rope bridge and get to the other side when we have faith in ourselves and the courage to place our foot on the first splintered wooden slat.

May 17

*T*here may come a day in our lives when we contemplate whether our life truly matters. Perhaps we ponder how we can do something that will matter, and we begin to feel we have no purpose in life and that we are just here and nothing we do really matters. And feelings like this can bring us down into the pit of self-pity so quickly. The good news is that we have no reason to feel this way at all, because if we just look around we can see we do matter.

> ➤ If you served in the military, protecting this country and maintaining our freedom, you matter.
> ➤ If you're fighting for justice for a sibling who was tragically taken away from this world, you matter.
> ➤ If you stopped to help an elderly lady out of her car after a car accident you witnessed, you matter.
> ➤ If you raised your children to be polite and have manners, you matter.
> ➤ If you simply wiped away the tears of a friend and listened with care and compassion, you matter.

We should never doubt for one moment that as we travel our journey in life, that we matter. We matter because we care, because we have dreams for ourselves and for others. We matter because we love others, and we love ourselves. We matter and we make a difference in this world, one day, one life at a time. Never doubt, whether or not you matter, because you do. The world would be less than without you and that matters to the rest of us.

May 18

*E*ach morning we start to formulate our day. We think about what has to be done today; grocery shopping, meetings at work, taking children to school or the pile of laundry that is piled high. We tend to get our minds all spun up and lose sight of one very important aspect of our life, and it begins with the letter, "G."

Grace – that calm sense of serenity that speaks of love.
Respect – that which to honor another or honor ourselves.
Authenticity – that we remove our mask and be who we really are.
Truthful – that where we tell the truth with courage.
Integrity – that where we do the right thing though no one notices.
Trustworthy – that sense where others can be assured of our word.
Unity – that where we stand together with our friends and family.
Dutiful – that where we feel a sense of duty to serve others.
Empathy – that where our heart touches another's with care and compassion.

G.R.A.T.I.T.U.D.E. is more than attitude it is a way of life. It is a way of seeing our values and how our lives are changed and how by acknowledging and living our values we can make a positive difference in the lives we touch each day. Are there other values that belong to us, of course, and we should be grateful for those too.

So as we formulate the start of our day, begin it with G.R.A.T.I.T.U.D.E and our day will be filled with a sense of joy and happiness, and it will pour over into the lives of others.

May 19

We need to be strong today. We need to find the strength, not in our muscles, but in our conviction to stand up for ourselves and be proud of whom we are. We need to be strong and reach down and help a friend who is struggling. We need to be strong and not afraid to remove our mask to live an authentic life. Being strong is not always easy, it takes courage. It takes pushing fear out of our lives and replacing it with that inner strength to live a life filled with values.

A life filled with fear and intimidation or filled with solitude and loneliness causes us to quiver. All balled up in a fetal position, we shake at the slightest sound, fearing the worse is about to happen. Our fears are our perception of what may happen in the future and looking back we see our previous fears were baseless. So now it is time we stood up, find that inner strength and be strong. We need to be strong for our friends and family that depend on us, but just as important; we need to be strong for ourselves.

That invisible muscle that gives us strength and courage are centered in our chest. It is as strong as any muscle in the rest of our body, but like those, we must exercise it. Today is a great day to give the soul muscle a workout. We only have to be strong today, so give it a workout. Be strong!

May 20

There are many things about our life that are nice-to-haves, and that we could live without. We can live without television, laptops and smart phones. We can live without expensive clothes, fancy cars, and a big house on the hill. These are the easy ones that we can live without, but the list can be a little harder.

We must have food and water to live. We also need some sort of shelter to survive. There are some things we just cannot live without. We can't live without love, for love is that one hunger shared by everyone. It is a hunger that is not met with food, but is nourished by the soul. It is the one single emotion that each, and every one of us seeks to have in our lives. Some may say we can live without love, but then we're not living; we merely exist and just existing is hardly a life.

We need to help nourish the souls of our family, our friends and even the stranger we meet in passing. We need to nourish them with sharing our love, even in the simplest way with a smile, or caring word. When we seek to nourish the souls of others with the love, we find our heart is filled and overflowing.

So we need to look at what we have in our lives and what we are not living without and be grateful. We need to cherish every minute.

May 21

We never know what we will do in our day that will make a difference. We might stumble on a huge breakthrough on a project and save a bunch of time and money. This may lead to special recognition and rewards or bonuses. Today we may find a wallet on the ground and call the owner, who was panicked at the thought of cancelling all the credit card, getting new driver's license and losing the picture of his pretty blonde granddaughter. We arrange to give it back to him, and he is immensely grateful. His precious smile as he opens the wallet to show us the picture.

We do things all the time, and we never know when those little things will make a difference in someone's life. We may talk to a friend over the phone, completely unaware they needed a friendly voice, just at that moment. Our friend doesn't say anything, afraid that it may seem silly or embarrassing. Perhaps today we sent an email to an old classmate we came across on a social media web site, just to say hello. Their life was touched by your simple email just to say hello.

We never know when we make a difference in someone's life. If we're waiting for praise and recognition in what we're doing each day, then our ego is driving our actions. Our ego is robbing us from doing a random act of kindness, expecting nothing in return, other than knowing we may have helped make someone's day a little better. Ego-driven acts are selfish and lack the love of a random act of kindness.

Be wary of our motives and don't let the selfishness of our ego rob others of our love and compassion in serving them. We make a difference each day, make it positive.

May 22

The worn wooden door is massive compared to the small child who stands before it. He doesn't see the huge door as blocking him from the other side; in fact, he doesn't see it as an obstacle at all. The young man is determined to see what is beyond the door and without fear the child reaches up, turns the handle on the door and pushes it open. The door handle represents faith and as the door handle of faith turns, no fear is present. The heavy door swings open and the innocent child without hesitation walks through the doorway and into the next room to see what lies before him here.

We come to these doors too, but we see these massive doors as obstacles, and we fear what may be on the other side. The doors we face are the doors of change. We look at the door, but don't see a door handle for our fear is blinding us, and we cannot see the door handle of faith. We fear what may be on the other side of this door of change. We are afraid. What will happen if the door opens, and we walk in? We imagine darkness will be on the other side and not great opportunities. It's when we replace our fear with faith, will we see the door handle and have the courage to open it. Just as the innocent child, we walk into a new room, a new chapter in our lives, with great opportunities, which are abundant. It's not darkness that greets us as we walk through the doorway of change, but a new path that is bright.

We cannot fear the doors of change; otherwise we will always be in the room we're in today. It's when we have faith and courage that we open these doors with determination to see what great dreams are waiting for us on the other side.

May 23

The white water of the river relentlessly splashes over the rocks, each wave crashing from one rock to the next. Turbulent water speeding through each path the rocks dictate, but never stopping. The power of the water never lets up as the river works its way to its destination.

A lone kayaker paddles against the current, each stroke of the paddle sliding into the water. Each stroke pushes the kayak and its lone human engine a little further upriver, but every muscle of the kayaker is working very hard to move merely one short distance. The current is strong and never needs to rest and yet our kayaker tries to fight the river with every ounce of energy. His muscles tremble with every stroke until the force of the river cannot be defeated, and the lone kayaker turns his small boat around. Now flowing with the current, he uses the force of the water to give him speed, while using his paddles to steer his path through the rocks.

We find ourselves in similar circumstances where we are fighting a powerful river, getting nowhere. Expending all our energy we may be washed away in defeat. However, if we can find ways to use the energy of what we're fighting and use its power, we then take our paddles and focus on steering through the rocks ahead. When we use all the available tools, we have, flow with the energy and steer our own path with our paddles, the journey is still ours. We need to stop fighting the raging river and start steering our path within it.

May 24

The morning sun begins to make its appearance on the eastern horizon. The light of a fresh day pushes the darkness of the night away, and the sky begins to fill with the beautiful pastel colors of dawn. It's a brand new day, a fresh start and an opportunity to make our lives and the lives of others better.

However, the morning's light is blocked by our blinds that cover our window. There isn't even a faint glimmer of light peering through. We have shut out the light of day, and we remain in our own darkness. Just inches away are the beauty of a new day, yet it remains blocked with the blinds we have pulled closed on our window. When we shut our blinds we miss the faint orange on the horizon turn into yellow and then the blue sky is unveiled. We miss the early chirps of the birds, singing their sweet song of joy. We miss all the wonders of nature when the window to a beautiful world is shut out by the blinds we pulled.

There is another set of blinds that we pull close too. These are the blinds that cover our heart, our mind and our soul. With our blinds pulled we shut out people, our friends, our family and the rest of the world. Isolated in darkness, with our blinds pulled, we are void of light; we are void of joy, love and happiness. It's when we open our blinds that cover our heart, soul and mind do we allow the sunlight of love, joy and happiness come into our window and into our life. We need to open our blinds and by doing so we allow the love within us shine for others to see and feel.

Let's open our blinds that shut us away in darkness and allow the beauty of the world, all the people around us, our friends and family, and just as important, allow ourselves to shine in. It is truly beautiful with our blinds open.

May 25

The large mound of rocks, grass and mud could hardly be called a mountain, but that was our challenge. Our challenge was to climb that "mountain" and declare ourselves as king/queen of the mountain. Wet from last night's rain, the slope is slippery and the traction of our feet is poor. Grabbing at every handhold we can find and putting our feet in just the right places, we make our way up the 'mountain'. Almost reaching the top, reaching our goal, our foot slips, our wet fingers lose their grip, and we slide down the slippery slope, scraping our chins, knees and elbows. We are not defeated by our slip in trying to get to our goal; we have learned from it. We now know where not to put our foot or which rock not to grab, so we go back to our climb.

As we look at the goals in our lives, these are small mounds filled with obstacles, which make our climb challenging at times. We take each step toward accomplishing our goals with determination and perseverance. If we take a wrong step and slide backwards, we have two choices; we can sit on the hill, looking at our bloody knees and elbows and not get up sitting in defeat and weep, or we simply need to get back up, brush ourselves off and start again.

Our slip on the hill probably won't take us back to the bottom, so our work so far has been good. We need to learn what caused us to slip and not follow that same path. We need to set our sights to reach the top and imagine achieving our goal. It's then we place our foot and hand back onto the 'mountain' and continue our journey. Giving up on our goal is never a good option. It is ours to dream, and it is ours to achieve.

May 26

The wild surf beats against the sea wall. The waves crashing against the concrete, sending water high into the sky and then is blown over the land with great force. The flag on its pole flaps violently as the wind of a hurricane begins to rip them to shreds. Standing tall on the shoreline is a granite monument with a weathered sea captain standing on top, facing the violent ocean. Leaning slightly forward, the sea captain's one hand is covering his brow, as if he is looking out in the distance. The fierce hurricane winds and rain are a force that lasts for hours, yet our sea captain remains steadfast, facing the storm that beats against him.

We too will face storms in our lives that are relentless and seem to last for hours, days, and even weeks. The wind and rain of our storm try to knock us down, or make us concede to it and seek shelter. Like the sea captain facing his hurricane, we must face our own and be just as diligent in standing up to the ferocious force that is beating against our shore. With courage, strength and diligence, we endure the roar of the storm's wind, the crashing of the ocean waves all around us and lean into our storm with defiance.

Still standing, still facing the direction from which the storm came, we feel the wind subside, the beating rain and crashing waves at our feet slowly diminish. Our eyes looking in the distance, we can see the light of the sun; the storm is over. We stood against a mighty force, and we were stronger. We did not waiver. We stood our ground.

We have the inner strength and courage to face the 'hurricanes' that blow into our lives. We have our values that will withstand any force of nature, and we will be standing tall when the sunlight once again shines on us.

May 27

We wear our ball cap with the "Mr. Fix-It" proudly displayed on it. That's a title many of us carry around with us, though we may not even be aware of it. We like 'fixing' things, or 'fixing' people and their problems. We think we have all the right tools in our tool belt and with these 'tools, we think we can fix whatever we may perceive to be 'broken', not in our life, but in the lives of others.

We feel this need to fix things because we care. We care enough, and maybe too much, that we want to fix their problems, so we try to fix them. While we think we have the right tools, we may not. We may be using a Phillips-head screwdriver on a flat-head screw and in some cases actually make the situation worse. We don't do this intentionally; we just want to help.

By 'fixing' their issues, we rob them of learning how to fix things in their own life, and we rob them of that experience. Sometimes it's better to hand them the tool and let them fix it. It's called, learning. While we may remain close by to help, if asked, we need to let them gather their own tools and learn how to fix things in their own lives. They need to learn because we may not always be close by with our tool belt.

To the Mr. Fix-It's of the world, thank you. Thank you for teaching us how to solve our own issues. Our thanks to them are learning how to fix ourselves so that we may teach others later in life.

May 28

O n our path, we will find joy and happiness along the way. Many times it is of our own making, while other times it is because of the action of others, and we get to share in their joy and happiness. There is a spring and lightness in our steps. However, there are days when joy and happiness are replaced with disappointment and hurt. These feelings cast a shadow over our journey, and we walk with less of a spring in our step. It seems we are weighted down, and our feet feel like they are cast in cement. These are not the good days of our journey.

When it is others that have disappointed and caused us this pain, what was it that made us feel this way? Did we set the standards too high or place them on a pedestal, and they fell off? Do we feel they betrayed us in some manner with half-truths or other actions? It is us that carry this burden, and it is us that can release it too. The hurt and disappointment can be wiped away when we accept others as being human and imperfect. When we accept and forgive, the burden of the rocks of disappointment and hurt are taken away.

There comes a bigger challenge when we are the reason for the disappointment and hurt in our lives. We look at ourselves and make judgments. Did we expect too much of ourselves or think we are super-human? This pain we carry may be one of the harder ones to find relief. We can beat ourselves up over the smallest of things and hold on to that disappointment and hurt for a long time. It's when we see the solution for releasing it because of others is the same solution for releasing it because of ourselves. We must accept we are human and make mistakes. We must find it in our own heart to forgive ourselves and when we do, our rocks of burden will be taken away.

Our journey is too short to allow it to be cast in shadows of disappointment and hurt. We need to seek the light of joy and happiness with acceptance and forgiveness.

May 29

The little ticket dispenser is teasing us with a little yellow tag with a printed number. The sign says, "Take a Ticket to Be Served." We look up and see the electronic number counter mounted on the wall displaying the last one served. Above the red electronic display is a single word, "Serving." So we can take a number from the ticket dispenser and wait to be served, or we can be the electronic counter and serve.

So how can we be of service to others today? We understand that serving others gets us out of self and causes us to make a difference. So how can we be of service? Let's count the ways…

- We can wash the dishes after the big family Sunday dinner.
- We can take the shopping cart back to the rack from the lady who just loaded her groceries into her car.
- We can make the coffee for the office staff, even though we may not drink coffee.
- We can volunteer our time for a charity on our free time.
- We can hold the door open for a stranger who is walking in, as we're walking out.
- We can pick up a friend who has to drop off their car at the auto repair shop.
- We can leave a little sticky note on a coworker's desk with a simple smiley face.
- We can … serve others.

Being of service is not hard. It is a thoughtful action where we put our life on hold for just a few minutes and help someone else. It's caring enough about our friends, family, and even strangers whom we reach out to help. Even the smallest act of service is appreciated. It is truly a loving action where two hearts are touched. When we serve others, we don't focus on ourselves, but concentrate on the needs of others. The reward is phenomenal. Our serving others have made our world just a little better. We made a difference. We can make a difference in serving others.

May 30

We climb into our small sailboat and push off the dock. The spring breeze is gentle as it fills our sail, and we begin to venture out into the ocean. The cloudless sky is brilliant blue, and the sun feels good as we slip slowly through the clear blue water. The sound of the waves lapping against the hull is soothing as we continue to sail out from the shore. Lost in time, we sit back and relax as our small sailboat makes it way out to sea. Solitude is what we sought, and solitude is what we found. The slight rustle of the wind in our sails, the water splashing against the sides of our sailing vessel and an occasional squawk of a sea gull are the only sounds we hear.

We take this time to reflect on our life. We look forward to seeing where we are on our journey and are sad for a moment and happy the next. We wonder if our life has been worth all the effort and wonder where our journey is taking us. We lose track of time with our inner reflection and look around, and we can see no land in sight. Have we become lost at sea? We feel so alone now and lost. Which way should we steer our sailboat? Which direction is the way back to the safe harbor?

Suddenly, a porpoise surfaces right beside our small boat, blowing air from its small blow hole in the top its forehead. Startled, our attention is not on our new traveling companion as it stays close to the side of the boat. Gracefully, it swims alongside our boat as the gentle wind continues to push us through the water. We look into the porpoise's eye, and we see another living being. We don't feel alone any longer. The gray porpoise turns ever so slightly and we turn too to stay with it. Our friend looks at us as we look back at it and there is silent communication between us. No longer alone, we follow our friend. Our new sea friend dives below the surface and disappears. Seconds later it shoots out of the water, flying high into the air just forward of the bow of our boat. As we watch it jump in front of us, we now see a familiar landmark in the distance, we are no longer lost.

Our sea friend swims alongside once again, making eye contact, as if to say good bye. The porpoise swims away, and we know that this creature has brought us back to the safety of the harbor. Our friend has come into our lives with a purpose. Our sailing venture has renewed our faith in ourselves and faith in those around us. We are not alone in this world. We have many traveling companions to help us and we in turn can help others that seem to be lost in their sea.

We each have our own journey to travel. Look for guidance of companions, friends and family to help guide our boat back into the safe harbor, so we can continue to sail once again.

May 31

We work hard. Whether we're employed outside the home or are responsible for inner workings of our home, we work hard. We spend many of our waking hours doing jobs and tasks to make a living. What is making a living mean? Perhaps it is working for a paycheck to buy food and necessities, put a roof over our head, put gas in the vehicle, and whatever is left, we may buy an occasional "thing" that makes us feel good. Each day we spend working hard at whatever job we have, we are focused on how to spend the paycheck.

With little warning, and absolutely and totally out of our control, a force of nature takes away all that we have in mere seconds. The roof over our head is now a football field away. The food and necessities are scattered all about. The vehicle we put gas in is now flipped over and is in our neighbor's living room. Devastated, destroyed, all our hard work, all the 'things' we provided for our family are lost and given to Mother Nature. How selfish of her to take away all the things we worked so hard for; it's not fair.

We are sad when we see this happen, but in reality, we also should be thankful. We are still alive, maybe scratched and bruised, but alive. Though the family albums are lost to the devastating force of nature, we still have our memories. We still have our values of faith, integrity, honesty, respect, courage and love. Things are just things. What we stand for and the values we live by are what are important, and no force of nature can take those from us.

We work hard. We're making a living, and perhaps making a living has a whole new meaning. Perhaps we can see that making a living means living our values every day; being of service to others, sharing our time, and never letting a moment go by without making sure someone knows we love them. We work hard, so let's work hard on what makes a difference; our personal values make a difference, and we can change the world by living them each day.

Memorial Day

*I*t's very early in the morning; the sun has not come up, but the faint light of dawn fills the sky. There is a light morning fog laying low over the ground. An old man sits on a bench looking over a green grassy field filled with white marble monuments, each one with a name and two dates. Through the fog, the old man can see an American soldier in uniform, his backpack filled with American flags, placing a flag at each tombstone. With each flag he puts in the ground, he steps back, stands at attention and salutes. The light of day becomes brighter and through the fog, the old man can now see the soldier has placed many flags already, but sadly has many, many more to go. However, each one deserves no less attention that the first one he placed at 0300 this morning, for today is Memorial Day, a day to honor those that paid the ultimate sacrifice.

The old man stands as the soldier comes near and walks over to him. He simply raises his right hand to his brow and gives the best salute he can possibly render. The soldier turns to old man and returns his salute. After the salutes are given, the soldier simply says to the old man, "Thank you for your service." As tears slowly roll off the old man's cheeks, and he says, "I am honored to have served this great country." The soldier turns away and continues his daunting and respectful task to honor the fallen heroes.

Now A Personal Story...

As many of you know I usually don't write in the first person. I don't want to make my Thoughts of the Day about me; I want them to be about us; that is why I write in the third person. Today I am making an exception, and you will see why in a minute.

I served twenty years in the United States Army as an aviator. I went to Vietnam and flew medical evacuation helicopters called "Dustoff", where I took injured soldiers out of rice paddys, or lifted them out of the jungle, to medical facilities for treatment. Sadly, not all the ones I picked up survived, and they paid, serving this country, with their lives. I say to each one of them, I'm sorry I couldn't have done more for them. I tried my best. However, I am grateful and honored to think there may be some Vietnam veterans who are alive today because I could help them, and for that I am truly grateful. I witnessed first-hand the pain in the faces our young Americans from wounds they received; many visuals too graphic to write. Just know that it's not all movies and television, it was real, very real, too real.

Today, I want to remember two of my friends; two of my flight school classmates that did not come home from Vietnam the same way I did. Their names are on the wall that is shown in the picture at the top of this Thought of the Day.

Edgar Franklin (Frank) Crouse, Jr.; Warrant Officer. Born - August 19, 1949. Killed in Action - July 20, 1970 while flying a low-altitude helicopter, engaging the enemy, was shot down and the helicopter exploded and burned, killing Frank and the other pilot, Mark Webb.

Paul Robert Brass; Warrant Officer. Born - January 25, 1949. Killed in Action - December 14, 1970 while flying a medical evacuation mission, crashed into the side of a mountain during extremely bad weather conditions at night. Paul and his crew were not letting poor weather or night keep them from trying to save another soldier's life.

To Frank and Paul, my dear brothers, I salute you. It was a true honor to know you and call you my friend.

I write this, not to seek praise, but just to tell another personal story from one soldier that served this country with pride and honor. I salute all that served, and I am honored to serve beside you to protect the freedom of this country. Salute!

So today, or any other day you see someone in a military uniform, man or woman, have the courage to walk up to them and say, thank you. Better yet, buy them a cup of coffee or pay for their lunch. I mean, it's the least we can do for all they lay on the line for us, right? Right!

June

June 1

How can we be kind instead of being right today? How can we not judge too quickly without all the facts? How can we give the benefit of the doubt? These are some challenging questions and answers that are tough and not easy to live by.

When we feel the need to be right all the time, it's our ego poisoning our relationships with others. We go around with big-shot-ism and we give the appearance that we are right and everyone else is wrong. With that attitude, we actually diminish ourselves with those around us. It's time to let some kindness into our heart, kindness in our action and words. We don't always need to be right. When we act with kindness, our ego is put in check, and we will find some serenity and love.

Our scales of justice are not always so blind. We are quick to judge and many times unwarranted. We think we know the facts and won't seek the truth from whom we're judging. Why is that? Don't we want the truth? It comes back to ego, where we think we have the 'power' to be judge and in some cases be the jury. We have no such 'power' or right to think this way. When we allow the benefit of doubt to enter into our heart, the real answer in judging others will come. The key word is 'benefit' and the real answer is not to judge others, but treat them with kindness and love.

Life is too short to go around allowing ego to control our day and our actions. Ego will take us down paths on our journey that will not be pleasant. Ego feeds on selfishness, greed, and resentments. If we can find a way to take away its food, we can be a better person. It may not be easy, but the rewards are immeasurable. We can be kind instead of right. We can give the benefit of doubt and not judge. We can love others, just as we want them to love us.

June 2

A large hour glass sits on the table. Pure white sand fills the top vessel and slowly a single grain of white sand falls from the top and into the lower globe. It is time in motion. Each tiny speckle of sand represents a moment in time, a moment in our life. The tiny granules cannot be stopped, nor can they go back into the upper vessel. Time never stops; it comes down one grain, one second, one minute, one hour, and one day at a time. Each tiny sand crystal is an individual speck; each one is an opportunity for us to do something with them.

We all have this hour glass in our lives, and we never will know when that last tiny grain of sand will fall from the upper vessel leaving it empty. What we need to do is to make the best of the moments we have. With the small crystals of sand, let's build sand castles; the spires reaching tall on the castle's walls. Let's play and make every crystal of sand play a part of our journey. Let take the sand at our feet and build a path, lining it with gratitude, respect, integrity, honesty, authenticity, and most importantly line our path with love.

Another small grain of sand falls, and it is another gift from the Vessel above. Each moment is a gift, and it is our responsibility to make the most of each one. We shouldn't scorn the sand, but be joyful another grain was given. We should treasure every crystal of sand as if it were a precious gem, for, in reality, it is. Use the gems of time wisely and with the crystals of time we are given, will be the legacy we leave behind when the last grain of pure white sand falls from the upper vessel.

June 3

Most of us would agree we hate standing in lines. It takes away our precious time, and we cannot get anything accomplished, other than posting our frustration on a social media site. And, if that line is the line to the complaint department, it's even worse. Whether we in a physical line of people, or simply on hold on the telephone, when we're in this line, the frustration, anger, and impatience build to a boil. In fact, in some cases the waiting on hold or in line increases our blood pressure greater than the original complaint. So what are we to do?

We can complain to our friends about the problem, and they may agree there is an issue and be on our side. So now that we have some moral support, we complain to yet another and so on. Now we have an army of supporters, but unless we're willing to take some action, complaining does nothing to resolve the problem.

Before we get in that line or get on the phone, let's examine our issue. Can we fix the problem? Yes- then do it and stop complaining. If the answer is No, then who can? No one? – then stop complaining. If there are some who can help, seek their assistance and stop complaining.

We don't have to get in that long line in the complaint department. Complaining and not doing anything about it is a waste of our time. Complaining not only brings ourselves down, it brings those around us down too. Life is too short to complain about things we cannot resolve or drag ourselves and others into that pit of self-pity.

In the corporate world, companies reorganize for efficiency. In our world, let's reorganize and dissolve the complaint department. We don't need it. We take on the action necessary, and we don't need a complaint department in our lives to run to when things need to be resolved. We do it and not complain about it.

June 4

Our journey has been long, and we are tired. We still have a little way to go before we can rest. We come to a turn on our path, and we look to the left, down the path and see that there is a small bridge that crosses a small stream and green grassy banks filled with beautiful Texas Blue Bonnets. Those same grassy banks and Blue Bonnets are in front of us too, and we can see the path just on the other side. On the edge of our path is a sign, "Do Not Walk on Grass." So we look around, no one is near. We can ignore the sign, walk across the grass, jump the small stream and be on our path much quicker than walking to the left to the bridge that is a half-mile out of our way. We can find rest the sooner we get to the path on the other side and finish today's journey. No one will see us if we cross the grass. No one will know.

The decision is easy when we are aware of our traveling companions; our values. We walk to the left, following our path to the bridge, crossing the stream and green grassy banks filled with the beautiful Blue Bonnets. We walk onto the bridge and stop for a moment, looking at the clear water running underneath. We see our reflection in the water, and we see integrity. We did the right thing though no one was there to witness it. We made the right decision, though no one will ever know. We walk the rest of the way of the bridge and onto our path and continue our journey. Another traveling companion now makes its appearance, self-respect.

Integrity and self-respect walk together with us on our journey. They are but just a couple of the companions that are with us always, though, at times; we may forget they are there. Values are within our heart and soul. When we let our companions be part of our journey, our journey is one we cannot regret.

June 5

reams are not just given to us; we must work for them. In doing so, when the dream becomes reality, it is much more meaningful, knowing we worked toward the accomplishment of this dream. We dream of new homes, fancy cars, exotic vacations and even new careers. We should not expect these will be handed to us just because we dream them. We need to have these dreams for they stretch us to learn more, do more, and be more. We work, focused on the sweetness of how wonderful that dream will be when we move into that new home, or we bask in the sun on an island paradise. Dreams are so important for they give us drive and purpose.

With dreams comes discouragement at times. We dream lofty goals, and we work hard toward them. We expend many resources to get there, and we just don't see progress. We consider changing our dreams to a smaller house, a weekend vacation instead of the island paradise, or sticking with the current job and let the passion of a new profession simply fade away. STOP!!! We cannot allow small setbacks to extinguish big dreams. We need to stay focused on the journey and not the short part of the path we're on today. We need a pep talk once in a while and since many of these dreams, and the feelings of discouragement are not known by others, we need to be our own pep squad. So LETs DO IT!!! Refocus on the goal; picture it in our mind again. Do it now! And do it often.

Great dreams are fulfilled by perseverance and determination and do not come true by giving up. Don't quit before the miracle of the dream. Don't quit, keep living a life that will bring these dreams to reality.

June 6

hat kinds of friends do we have? We have social media friends, and that count is in the hundreds. We have friends whom we see casually and that number will vary. Then there are dear friends and that number is less than the others. And finally, we have one or maybe two or three that we call true friends whom we can trust with our lives. These friends are rare in our life. This friendship takes time to cultivate and nourish. It takes commitment, honesty, trust and love to have such a rare friend in our lives. If we are so blessed to have this kind of friend in our lives, we are very rich.

There are a couple of things we need to make sure we are aware of in these friendships. First, we must be the same kind of friend to them in return. We must be caring and loving to them, just as they are to us. We have to live up to our part of the relationship; otherwise a good friend will be lost. We also need to recognize that if we use and abuse a friend for our own selfish needs, we will soon lose that friend; use, abuse, and lose.

Good and true friends are a treasure, and we are rich when we have one and richer beyond that is if we have two. Good and true friends are hard to find, but the start of this kind of relationship is we need to be a good friend first. Love is the key, and it is what makes the connection so strong. Are we a true and good friend to someone else?

June 7

I need you… to help me when my hands are full.

I need you… to encourage me when I'm feeling discouraged.

I need you… to hold me accountable for my actions.

I need you… to be a compassionate friend when times get tough.

I need you… to listen, not with your ears, but your heart.

I need you… to be by my side as I walk this journey.

I need you… to wipe away the tear on my cheek when sadness comes.

I need you… to love me when I can't love myself.

I need you…, and that's all there is to it!

Are you the 'you' someone needs? If so… they need you… to step up and be that person; to be that one-of-a-kind friend, that soul mate, that special one. That one is YOU. Are YOU ready to make a difference in someone's life? Make a difference in the world? Well… are you?

You are and the world is a better place because you are who you are. Don't pretend to be someone you're not, because you are just the one, we're looking for, just as you are, by being yourself. Thank you for being there for us that needs you.

June 8

The potential problem begins with a misunderstanding. Whether it's a statement, verbal agreement, email, whatever, if one person perceives it differently than the intent of the first person, there are two versions of the 'truth', and problems can happen. Both parties believe in their own interpretation of the stated issue. While in many cases this is easily resolved or may not even be that big of a deal, but misunderstandings can end friendships, business agreements and relationships. The person's 'truth' is what they believe to be fact and act accordingly, while the other believes in a slightly different version of the 'truth'.

For instance, if we give permission for our son or daughter to go to the movie with their friend, we may mean this one time, but don't articulate that succinctly. The son or daughter interprets it as they can go to the movie with this friend anytime that want. This misunderstanding turns into an argument and may escalate into angry words.

We need to be aware that we may not always clearly convey our message and that our 'truth' may be different from the 'truth' of the other person. When discovered, the truth needs to be clarified before it turns into angry words and hurt feelings. We need to be clear in our words and intent as much as we can. Seek to have one version of the 'truth' and misunderstandings will be few.

June 9

We practice and practice. We want our game to be perfect. We want to win. So we make sacrifices in other aspects of our lives, and we push ourselves to be the very best. We look for our weaknesses and make them stronger. We find our strengths, and we sharpen them to a razor's edge. We are ready, ready to take on this critical match and show others our skills that we have worked so diligently to perfect. It's game time.

We're in the game, nervous and our adrenaline is pumping. We're focused and a small blunder, right at the beginning gets the game we practiced so hard for, gets our game off to a bad start. We know we have to let it go and get back into the game, and we do. We make some headway and our confidence returns. Our opponent is sharp and keen, but we remain focused on our game, and we are in the zone. The final minutes are coming to the end, and we stumble slightly, but enough for our game lose its momentum. Did we win or lose? The judge will make his ruling in moments, so we wait; time seems to have stopped as we wait to hear the winner's name. Will it be ours?

Winning is not everything, doing our best is. We can be critical of ourselves at the end of our game and get angry at a blunder here or there, but in reality, we tried. We prepared; we practiced, and we delivered the best game we could. Was it perfect? Probably not, but that's okay. What counts is that we did our best. In our heart, we know all the hard work in preparation brought us to this event, and we delivered our best. We should feel good and proud of ourselves for whom we are. We are someone who takes pride in their efforts and will do it again when the next game comes.

June 10

We pull the tattered cardboard box off the top shelf of our closet. We lift the top off and there, in white tissue is our Christening gown we wore as a baby. The little lace bonnet is folded neatly beside the gown. What a great legacy that has been passed down. Now we prepare to put it on our newborn child for their Christening, with the hope that it will continue to be worn one generation after another.

Now the scratched and dented tin box, that holds all our 'treasure' from our childhood is taken out of our top dresser drawer. The painted images on the lid are barely recognizable, but we can still make out the Model-T car and a young boy running with his dog. We open the lid and see the Indian arrowhead our grandfather gave us. In the tin box is a marble, a steelie that we used when we played marbles with our friends. We see a shark's tooth our dad found on the beach one day as we walked together.

The physical treasures represent wonderful memories from our past. But there is only one gown, one marble, one shark's tooth to pass down to our children, and if you have many children who get to share in this legacy, how is it given out? Is our legacy things, money, or an estate? Or is there a legacy we can leave behind that can be shared by all our family, and we needn't worry about how our worldly possessions will be divided?

A legacy of being known as a person of integrity or a person that was honest and fair is a legacy worth more than any bank account. Being a person that is known to live their personal values of integrity, truthfulness, respect, compassion, authenticity, and love is a legacy that doesn't need to be kept in a cardboard box on the top shelf of the closet or in our top drawer in a tin box. The values we live by are the legacy that lives on in others and is kept in their heart.

We need to safeguard our values and let nothing take them away, but let's not hide them from others either. Let's live them and our legacy will be worth more than we could ever imagine.

June 11

With our pen ready, we take the form and begin. The first blank is today's date, and we write, 04/19/2012. We progress through the next few blocks, and we come to a blank for our birthday. We write, 04/06/1958. We pause for a moment and look back at today's date. Wow! It's almost the end of the month and nearly a third of the way through the year. Where has time gone? In this moment, we look at the year, and we think… 2012… really? 2012??? We quickly skip thinking about the year and jump into thoughts of decades. Where has the decade gone? We reflect on the time that has passed, and then we wonder about the decades ahead and what lies in store for us.

We forget one very important aspect of time as we jump from year to year and decade to decade. That one aspect is in a simple number of today's date. Which number is it? The number is "2." Our minds can scan the calendars of past and the ones of the future, but what we need to focus on is 2-day. The dates of yesterday are gone and the dates of tomorrow are beyond our reach for now. We need to recognize we have today, 2-day, and with this special day we need to make the best of it. We need to do our very best to live today with all our heart and be the very best person we can be 2-day.

The number '2' in the date field in a form or in the note we write is a reminder that we're living in 2-day, not yesterday and not tomorrow, but 2-day. What can we do to make 2-day one for the memory books? What can we do 2-day to make someone else's 2-day better? Make a difference in 2-day by being a friend, sharing a smile with a stranger, and shaking the hand of a new friend. 2-day is special; don't let it slip by like the decades have in the past.

June 12

We confine ourselves to our little bubble, and we go about our day, same routine, for the most part, and we're content. And for many, this is a perfectly fine life, and no one should judge them otherwise.

However, there are a few that want more from life and in order to break that bubble of existence and move into a world of truly living, we must be willing to step up and reach out. We need to find the courage that we can leave the comfort of our bubble of existence and find a life that is exciting and purposeful. We need to see the faith within ourselves that we believe in ourselves, and that we can reach out and touch the stars. Scared? Sure. Capable? Absolutely!

If we're happy in the bubble, we're living, great. But if we see a mountain we'd like to climb, an ocean we want to sail, or a star we want to touch, we must leave that bubble and reach out. Our companions of courage and faith will guide us on our journey, but we have to climb out of our bubble and take that first step. The first step is the hardest, but the journey we are beginning will bring all fresh meaning to our lives. It's time… step up… reach out… our journey is about to begin, and the great wonders of a brand new existence will be unveiled.

June 13

Each of us has chores in our daily life. We wash clothes, load and unload the dishwasher, fix a meal, make the bed, run the vacuum, and feed the pet, or pets in some homes. We all share in the responsibilities of living in the world we do. Whose job is it to take out the trash? That nasty and smelly task of bundling up the garbage and trash and removing it from the house is no one's favorite job. Look at the bright side, once that garbage is out; the house is cleaner and looks a lot better. It's once again fresh and renewed.

Taking out the garbage is a chore we all must do in our life. It's not the physical trash, but the trash we build up inside ourselves that we need to get rid of. We need to get rid of the trash of anger and resentments. We need to remove the garbage of greed and guilt. The trash of untruths and deceit needs to be bundled up with all the other garbage that builds up in our lives, tied in a sack and removed. When we remove the trash of character defects, our inner home, our inner-self is once again, clean and fresh. We look better inside when our clean inner-self can let our personal values shine and not be cluttered and smothered with the trash that builds up in our lives.

It's time to take out the trash, a chore we must do ourselves. All the other chores can wait; this is one we must do each day. Every day is 'trash' day, so get busy.

June 14

eel the soft spring breeze wash across our face. Smell the sweet bouquet of the fresh blooms of all the flowers that surround us as we sit for a moment on a bench along our path. The sunlight feels good on our skin, and we think we're sitting in paradise. The sounds of nature, the chirping birds, the babbling brook behind our bench, even the silence itself creates a sense of well-being. We are at peace; we have found serenity.

As we sit comfortably on our bench, taking a short rest on our journey, and we look down at our feet, and they are covered in mud, almost to our knees. We understand why this mud and dirt are there; it comes from where we have been and is our past that has clung to our feet. If we allow the dirt of our past to continue to build up on our legs and feet, our journey will be difficult to walk. We can allow the mud to become hard and build upon itself, or we can wash it away. The decision to remove the dirt may seem simple, but taking the action is another story. We must decide to continue to carry the muck of our past with us, or start the rest of our journey clean and lighter.

Our decision is made, and we move to the stream that is behind our bench and wash away the hardened dirt until our legs and feet are once again clean and free from the mud of our past. We are ready to continue; free from the weight of the mud, our steps are lighter, and we can travel further. With this renewed energy and sense of lightness, we know the next time the mud of the past begins to build up, we should wash it away before it weighs us down again.

It's time to continue our journey with joy, hope, happiness and a sense of renewed life. We are once again free.

June 15

There is this inner power within us that can move mountains. This self-will, this willpower can make dreams come true, but we have to be committed to focusing on positive actions with this powerful energy. If we can harness this power and focus in one direction, we can be unstoppable in whatever we're focusing on. In order to turn this power on, we need to find the 'willpower' dial and turn it on. If we're determined, seriously set on a dream or goal, we need to turn that dial to MAXIMUM and get ready for a ride. If we're not truly set on achieving a goal, we turn our dial to MEDIUM, and we will find excuses to wander off and our dream will be that, just a dream; fading as the dusk brings the night.

Willpower is that inner force that walks away from the candy bowl that tempts us, or avoids the quick drive-through at the fast-food joint. This willpower sees the end of the goal and puts blinders on, getting tunnel vision, focusing on the joy that awaits and avoids the temptations that will take us off the path to the dreams we dream.

This inner power can be used for many purposes. Perhaps we need to lose 10 pounds, take a final exam, or focus on the completion of a big project, whatever it is, if it is truly important, turn the willpower dial to MAXIMUM. No more excuses, no more rationalizing (which is rational lying), and we need to get focused on what the goal is and get our inner power headed in the direction to make it happen. Turn it up!! MAXIMUM POWER!!!

June 16

*L*et's think back to our recent past when we were introduced someone we didn't know, and they shook our hand with a firm grip, made eye to eye contact, smiled and said, "Nice to meet you, <insert your name>." Think about that for a moment. How did that make you feel? If you're like most, it made you feel welcomed, significant, and respected for who you are. That stranger just made a difference in your life, maybe not a huge difference, but enough a difference that you remember that feeling today.

That person made a difference because they were living their values openly. Their values of respect, care, openness, and love are clearly evident by their genuine greeting. For those simple few moments, we got to feel good about ourselves and have faith in others.

Today it's our turn. It's our turn to live our values openly and not hold back. When we suppress our values, we have little opportunity to make a positive and lasting difference in the lives we come in contact. So today, let's shake someone's hand; look them in the eye and smile. In your greeting, use their name; that makes a huge difference. Perhaps we can go one step further with those we know and substitute the handshake with a hug and tell them we love them. It's not hard and it will make a difference, not only to them, but to you too.

June 17

The dark-gray skies cover the sky. A light rain continues to fall as we walk our path. Wet from the rain, our feet muddy, we trudge on, one step at a time. Our spirits are down and damp like our whole body. The rain drips off our forehead; our eyes are cast downward, as one step follows another. With little enthusiasm, we know we must press on, and we do.

Paying little attention to the path before us, other than what is immediately at our feet, we come to a turn on our path. As we make this turn, and soon realize the rain has stopped. The rain water no longer cascades down our body, soaking our clothes. Instead, we feel a little warmth from a sliver of a sunbeam, and it feels so good. We bring our eyes up from the path at our feet, and we see the clouds are breaking and sunbeams are shining through. We have come out of the gloom of our journey and are now stepping into the sunlight. Our spirit is lifted. A smile comes to our face as we see the beautiful rainbow, arching across the sky. The colors are vibrant and we see the full arch, from one point to the other. We want to reach out and touch it. We stop for a moment and admire nature's beauty.

Rain will once again fall on our journey at some point, but if we can simply remember the feeling of the warmth of the sunlight and the beauty of the rainbow, we need not let the rain dampen our spirits. Another rainbow is just around the corner, and its beauty will be better than the last. Be part of the joy and beauty of nature by being the rainbow in someone's life. Let our spirit shine the warmth and comfort on those that are traveling through their rainy days. It's time for us to shine today and make a difference in the lives of others.

June 18

Wrapped in beautiful paper and a ribbon tied so perfectly, the gift sits on the table for the recipient. The box is not big, but it looks so expensive, with its beautiful wrappings. What could it be? Who gave this special gift to this person? Whoever it is must think the recipient is quite exceptional.

We watch as the gift is carefully unwrapped, careful not to tear the beautiful wrapping paper or wrinkle the satin ribbon. The box is opened. What's in it? We try to look but can't see. The recipient smiles, a tear forms in the corner of their eye as they hold this special present. Still we want to see what it is, what could it be to be so unique?

Slowly, the special gift is lifted from the box, and it is a picture in a beautiful frame. The picture is one of the recipient and a friend. The card reads, "Remember this day in the picture and remember this special day today. Each of these days is as special as the day we became friends. I love you."

The gift of friendship is a gift we give each day to someone else. It's not wrapped in pretty paper or tied with satin ribbons, but it is wrapped in compassion, care, joy, sadness, but most importantly; it's wrapped in love. It's time we shared our gift of friendship with someone special in our lives.

June 19

*I*t's this very moment that counts the most in our lives. Right now, not ten minutes ago and not later day, right now is what is important. We expand that span of time to go further into our past or look into the future, and we can become overwhelmed with regrets of the past and the fear of the future. We agree we cannot go back to change the past, and the future is just that, the future which we cannot leap forward into. We must take that journey one step at a time.

So where does that leave us? It leaves us right where we are this very minute. It's this very second we're reading these words are where we are. Stop reading for a moment and let's raise our hands to the front of our face. It's our "NOW". We have control of what is in front of us, our hands, our thinking, and our actions. It's our "NOW" and we are making decisions with it with every second of it as it passes.

What will we do differently with our "NOW"? If we use our "NOW" to get into action to serve someone else's needs, it is a good use of our "NOW". It's this very minute we can make a difference, either in our own life or the life of someone else, but it's our "NOW" and we have to take action and make the very best of it.

So as we go about our day, stop for a brief moment and think about this message and evaluate your "NOW". Need to make an adjustment? Look at your hands; where are they? They are in your "NOW". Now, do something with this minute that will make a difference. Live your "NOW".

June 20

A word: a series of letters or characters forming a meaningful representation, verbal or written, of something or someone. Words are essential to our daily life, and we string them along into sentences, paragraphs, thoughts of the day, books, novels, and we fill libraries with these collections of words, too numerous to estimate.

So we use words to describe things and what if we could use only one word to describe someone else? What word would we use? What word would we use to describe ourselves? Now think of someone, anyone and now think of only one word that best describes that person. Is that word, greedy, liar, thief, ugly, fake, hateful, or other similar words? Or is that single word describing this person, fair, honest, integrity, humble, authentic, or loving?

That person that we used in our exercise is someone who made a difference to us. Which set of words did that person fall into? The negative, character defects list, or were the words we picked from the second set of personal values? People come into our lives and make a difference, and not always in a good way. Which way will we make a difference in the lives we touch today? What word will that person use to describe us if asked they were asked the same question?

When we live our values and are not afraid to express them, we make a positive difference. What word will we live by today? Choose it, and then live it. "A word please."

June 21

Our journey is not one of isolation. There are times when we are walking our path alone, but those times are rare. We see people walking their own path, and they cross ours from time to time and in fact, maybe a hundred times or more each day. Some are walking their path, head down, staring at the ground, while others are looking up and seeing all that surround them.

So as we walk along and our path crosses another person's path, what do we do? Do we simply look down at our feet? Do we just look ahead and intentionally not make eye contact? If yes, we are missing an opportunity that may never pass by us again. That opportunity is to look into someone's eyes and get a glimpse of their soul. It's eye contact that, for a fleeting second, connects two people's souls together.

This takes a little courage to practice this openness and to let others peek into our heart too. What will they see? Will they see the emotional pain that is tearing us apart? Will their eyes show compassion in return? Or will they see the joy and love that are beaming from our heart and soul? In either case, we open ourselves up, just as the other person did to us. It is a gift we give each other by looking into their eyes, seeing their heart and also allowing them to look into ours.

Eye-to-eye contact is revealing, comforting, reassuring, and loving. So as we walk on our journey today, make an effort to look into the heart and soul of someone else and allow them to look at ours and in doing so, we have made a difference in their life, just as they have ours.

June 22

F ear is the uncertainty of the unknown, though we trick ourselves into thinking, we do know that whatever the situation it is not going to have the outcome we want. We project our imagination into overdrive, and we add to the demon of fear. It can be the fear of losing a job and thus the fear of financial security. It could be the fear of a medical issue, and our mind takes over and runs with it until we are completely consumed by the demon of fear. While there may be little moments when fear is not on our mind, it is lurking in the shadows and will jump out to scare us in a matter of minutes. Thus, we create the fear of fear.

It's our mind that feeds this demon of fear, and it is our heart that can overcome this demon. It is our heart where we find courage to face the evil and courage to stand up to it. Courage has a companion to help with this battle, and it is faith. Faith is strong, and these two personal values can defeat any fear that may come our way. It is a belief in ourselves, and in a Higher Power that we can overcome the demon of fear. Self-doubt merely feeds the demon, and we remove doubt with courage, faith and the other values that live within us.

The evil demon of fear brings darkness to our lives and can take over, feeding on itself. Life is too short to live in this darkness. We must stand up to face our fears and overcome them so that we can live in the beautiful light that shines on our day. Find the courage and faith within and fear will have no place to hide.

June 25

*A*re we the king of the land, or the pauper who works the streets? Are we the one that puts themselves on a pedestal that looks down on all others or are we the one that feels worthless, sitting in the corner? The fact of the matter is that we are none of these. The pendulum of self-appraisal swings from side to side, and we need to realize that at the bottom of the swing is where we are. The pendulum swings from extreme ego and greatness to the other side of self-pity and exaggerated low self-esteem. It is that point in the middle of the swing where we find our true self. At that point of the swing of our pendulum is where we find humility.

Humility is being the right size for who we are on our journey. We can remove our mask we hide behind and be real. Acceptance for who we really are and the role we play in this world, walking our path on our journey, is the key in finding humility. When we remove our mask, accepting who we are in the swing of the pendulum of self-appraisal, it makes us vulnerable to the rest of the world. It takes courage to accept this fact, and it takes being honest with ourselves in order to find this sweet spot of the self-appraisal pendulum swing called humility.

Now we can't get up in the morning and say to ourselves, "I'm going to be humble today." It doesn't work that way. If we get up and say to ourselves, "I'm going to accept who I am and be of service to others, the very best way I can.", then we have set ourselves on the right path to be humble.

Courage, authenticity, acceptance, and honesty are the stepping stones we need to follow on our journey today. Be strong. Be real. Be yourself. Be loved.

June 26

S ometimes we make mistakes, but with each one we learn from them, and we grow. Some mistakes are big and some are hardly enough to acknowledge, but still we learn. We try to hide our mistakes because we're embarrassed, or we may have harmed something or someone. A mistake is an event that was unintentional, but happened. If we make a mistake, we need to take ownership and not cast the blame on someone else or some inanimate object. We made it, so we should stop trying to cover it up with excuses.

We hide the mistakes we make because we're trying to protect our ego. But the truth is we're human and not perfect. Think of someone that made a mistake and took steps to hide it or shift the blame, how did we judge them? Now think for a moment, how did we judge someone who admitted they made a mistake and took steps to correct it? Without question, we hold the person that admits their mistake in higher regard.

When, not if, we make a mistake, we need to take steps to correct it if possible. Next is to accept it as ours and not hide it. We take these steps, even though no one may ever know of the mistake we made, but we do it anyway because it is the right thing to do and helps us grow. We do it because of our value called integrity.

June 27

We walk by a small group having a conversation, and we overhear part of the discussion. It appears one person is being a little gullible and the person doing the talking then ends with, "If you believe that, I have some oceanfront property in Kansas, I'd like to sell you." What kind of 'word game' do people play on others just to get a laugh? What is it about that kind of behavior that we feel good about ourselves? Do we really? Are we just feeding our evil ego?

Insulting and belittling others have no good purpose in our lives. When we insult someone else, we are really questioning our own character. When we feel the need to make someone feel less than, are we doing this just to make us look good? Belittling another person is really 'being little' ourselves. How sad it is we feel so poorly of ourselves that we have to insult, belittle and gossip about others.

When we insult another person, we push aside our values of care and compassion. When we belittle someone, we smother our ability to reach out and be of service. Insults and belittling behavior are not who we are or how we want to be treated. Our focuses are on compassion, courage, and most importantly, love. We need to stop being little and be strong by being loving.

June 28

There is a fine line of 'needs' and 'wants', and it is hard to distinguish in our mind. We want a new car, but what we need is a form of transportation. We want a new home, but what we need is a shelter over our head. We want the thick steak dinner with all the trimmings, but what we need is nourishment for our body. We get these two, 'wants' and 'needs' confused and when we do, we soon forget to be grateful for what we have.

When we begin to add to our 'want' list, think for a moment. Do we have what we need today, not what we want, but what we need? And as soon as we begin this thought process we come out with, "yea, but…" There is no but's about it. Most of us have what we need and many of us are very grateful for what we have to meet our needs. We still have 'wants', and that's okay as long as they don't over-shadow our gratitude for what we have. Our needs are met and for that we should have a grateful heart.

If we help others fulfill their needs, instead of their wants, we are helping them see the difference and with that they begin to see the value of a grateful heart. So as we ask ourselves this question, "Do I have what I need today?" Now smile because the answer is yes and for that we are grateful.

June 29

*I*t is 6:50:45 in the morning as these words are written. The watch is set to the atomic clock hidden in some mountain and is accurate to $1/100^{th}$ of a second. The measurement of time is important in many cases. We set our alarm to wake up in the morning to go to work. We set the alarm on our smart phone to take our medicine on time. The clock on the wall tells us when it's time to do this or do that. We live by the clock and allow ourselves to be controlled by the sweeping hands of a mechanical instrument of time.

Clocks and alarms have good use too, but sometimes we just allow ourselves to be overly consumed by the passing of each minute, each hour that we forget to enjoy life. We watch the clock, wishing it would go faster one moment, and then we think it is going too fast the next. We're just too focused on each passing second.

Imagine a day when we didn't look at the clock or a day when we didn't wear a watch, what freedom we feel. We don't look at the calendar either; it is another measure of time without the two hands on a clock. How carefree we are not caring what time it is or what day, we are simply enjoying the moment. This moment has no measure of time; it is simply bringing our attention to where we are right now, this moment.

This moment is life and removing the pressures of time; we can take this moment and truly enjoy it for what it offers. This moment won't be around long, so enjoy it while you can, before time takes it away.

June 30

"Can I play? Can I play?" shouts the young child to a group of other children playing ball on the playground. "No! We already have enough." replies one of the older children. Rejected, sad, and hurt the young child turns away to play alone on the swing. Each of us has had this happen to us, maybe not on the playground as a child, but later in life when we were excluded from a group where we wanted to be a part. That feeling of rejection; the feeling of being less than takes its toll on the human spirit, and it weighs heavy on our heart. We're hurt, and the pain can be one that lasts a long time. A quick flashback moment can bring back that memory of rejection, and the pain is back again.

We have this basic need of belonging, to be part of, to be accepted, to be loved. And when that basic human emotion is disrupted, we feel less than everyone else. The good news is that we are not less than those that may cast us aside and make us feel inferior. In fact, we are actually better than them because we don't act the same way with others. We have compassion and practice acceptance of others for who they are and not discriminate.

When others reject us, it's not our loss, it's theirs. We have such great gifts to share, and we just get to share them with someone else that will appreciate, and respect us for who we are. We need to feel good about ourselves and what we have to offer the world. We have beautiful gifts to share, and the most special gift is love. If we love others as we wish to be loved, and the world will be just a little better. We can make a difference by accepting and loving, not only others that walk with us on our journey, but accepting and loving ourselves for who we are. We are one of a kind, and no one can take that away.

July

July 1

*E*ach minute detail is examined. Each word is checked for spelling and proper usage. We go over it and over it and have the entire report almost memorized we have read it so many times. We have worked on this project for weeks and now the deadline is approaching. We feel the pressure; is it good enough? Is it accurate? Is it right? All these questions spin in our mind as we sign the report and submit it to the managers above us. Anxiously, we wait.

Let's just take a step back for a moment. Did we do the best job we are capable of doing? Yes. Did you follow the guidelines set and make it the best we could? Yes. Then stop worrying. We did our best, and we need to realize we're not perfect and can make a mistake. We're not perfect, so get over it!

We're not perfect? Wow! What a great relief! We take ourselves so seriously and allow our perfectionism to bring out the whips and chains to beat ourselves up when we make a mistake. When we stop punishing ourselves for being human, life is just a little better. Acceptance is the answer. If we make a mistake, own up to it. Correct it if we can, learn from it, and now move on. We don't need to kick ourselves over and over. We made a mistake, now get over it and move on with life. Once we realize we're not perfect, and then we can accept others as not being perfect too.

July 2

We should have dreams of wonderful things in our lives for the future. Dreams are what we look toward to help us, inspire us to follow our path. We dream of loving families, children, and grandchildren. We dream of great successes in our lives where we will have great wealth. We dream of creating something that will make us famous and make lives better. We dream, but unless we believe in our dreams, followed by taking action, dreams will always float in the puffy cloud, in the distance.

We absolutely must believe in our dreams. Believe they are real, and if they are important, find a path on our journey that will make them come true. It's never too late to dream; from eight to eighty, we can dream. A dream is that perfect wave for a surfer. That dream wave is out there, waiting for us and it is ours, but we have to paddle out to get to it. We may have to swim in many oceans, ride some imperfect waves, but as long as we keep believing and keep paddling; we will ride that wave one day.

Never stop dreaming, for when we do, our journey becomes dull and meaningless. Dreams give us energy and inspiration. Dreams will soon be our reality, our perfect wave, as long as we are willing to drink a little sea water, paddle a little harder and swim in many oceans.

Enjoy the wave, live your dream.

July 3

What others think of us is none of our business. This concept is very hard for many because we are people pleasers, and we seek acceptance and understanding. Nevertheless, in reality, if we do the very best we can with our lives, not the lives of others; we have no reason to concern ourselves with what others may think of us. We are who we are, doing the best we can, with what we have and no one can ask for more. However, we still get all wrapped up with others think of us. Today, we need to let that go and be happy with ourselves.

There are also days where we wish we were someone else, because we're measuring our insides with someone's outsides. When we do this, the comparison is hardly ever accurate. We sometimes want to be better than someone else, again a skewed perception of someone's outside. Instead, we should focus on the one individual we do have control over, ourselves. Today we should try to be a better version of who we were yesterday.

Stop comparing, judging and trying to be someone we're not. We just need to be the very best version of our self and what others think or measure us by is only their business not ours. Smile and be happy with our 'insides' for that is where our values live.

July 4

*M*ajestic, the large bald eagle is perched on a limb high above the rest of the land. Its keen eyes survey the land below, making sure the land below is safe. Extending its wings, he launches off the limb and begins to soar with grace and beauty. Effortlessly, with a huge wingspan, it flies through the air, watching over all that is below. Powerful with its mere presence and backed up with sharp talons and beak, it is a force to be admired and respected. The American Bald Eagle, our symbol for who we are and for those that came before us.

Our flag, 13 stripes and 50 stars, red, white and blue, stand tall and the gentle breeze adds to its beauty. Think for a moment of all this flag has seen through this transformation and how far this symbol of freedom has come; from 13 stars to the 50 we display so proudly today.

The evening's fireworks are a reminder of all the battles this powerful country has endured and triumphed. Each star burst, each loud explosion of the rockets is a symbol of the real and deadly explosions that our service men and women went through in protecting our freedom.

Each one of us should take just a moment between all the hot dogs, watermelon, and fireworks, all the fun with family and friends and recall the words our patriotic songs, America the Beautiful or God Bless America. Remember today's celebration was not free; it cost us with the lives of many brave men and women.

God Bless America. God Bless our men and women who served and are serving today to give us this day of celebration.

July 5

The music from the pipes of the calliope plays an upbeat tune as the merry-go-round continues to go around and round. At some point, when the platform slows down enough, we jump on. This is our first time, and we find a comfortable seat in a pony drawn carriage. The merry-go-round speeds up and the music from the pipes goes faster too. We are in for the ride of our life. Soon we get brave and leave the safety of the carriage and climb onto the back of a small white pony; someone helps us up, and we continue our ride. Never stopping the amusement ride continues to spin, and the music continues to play. We outgrow the pony and move the shiny black stallion and someone lifts us up high to get on its back. We hold on tight; our knuckles are white with anticipation. It goes up and down, as if galloping in a circle. This ride is much more exciting. The merry-go-round slows down; the calliope music slows its rhythm as well. We climb off our black stallion and now ride the gray mare for the rest of our time on the merry-go-round.

Our life is like the merry-go-round. It never stops. We go around and round, the music plays. We go from carriage to stallion, to mare; each one a stage in our lives. Each one is an important part of our lives. Sometime our ride slows down, while other times it's fast and furious, like the black stallion. If we look around our merry-go-round we see we're not alone. We see family, friends and strangers on their horses, ponies, and carriages. We see that we're in this world, not as one, but as one of many. We're on this ride called Life, and we're here to enjoy the ride. Regardless on which pony we're riding on the merry-go-round, we have a responsibility to help others transition from one pony to the next, just as we were helped on our ride. One person helping another in life's merry-go-round is what it's all about.

Today, look around. Is there someone whom we can help on their merry-go-round? We don't want them to fall, so let's be of service to those that are on the same merry-go-round we're riding. Life never stops, nor should our service to others ever stop either.

July 6

We each start our day differently. No one of us prepare for the day exactly the same way each day. Some may start their day with thanking a Higher Power, of their choosing, for another day. Others may simply get out of bed and begin the same routine, brushing our teeth, shower, and so forth. Each of us has our own pattern. Do we consider asking the question, "How can I make a difference today?" as we get up? The answer is probably not for many, and that's okay. But there is one question we should consider asking ourselves in the morning, "How can I live my personal values more effectively today?"

When we review our values in the morning, we set the stage for a fulfilling day. We think of Courage, Respect, Integrity, Service, Truthfulness, Authenticity, and Love and how these personal values are important to us. We then make a decision to go out into the world and live these values the best we can. When we are living our values, we are leading by example, and we will make a difference today. We may never know whose life we will touch today, but in all likelihood, we will touch someone's.

So as we begin our day, consider our values, CRISTAL, and if we focus on living these, we will make a difference in someone's life. Then that person will see the value of that difference we made in their lives and follow our example, making a difference in others. As the day ends, we may never know if we succeeded today in making a difference, but we certainly made a difference in our own by living our values today.

July 7

$\mathcal{D}$ ay in and day out, we find ourselves on this path and where it ends, we have no clue. We're on this path, and it is our journey. We get so focused on little parts of our journey; we forget it's about the journey and not the destination. Our journey has many aspects, and we become rigid and stiff because we allowed stress, anger, and other evils to rob us from what our journey should be all about, and that is happiness and joy. So when we find ourselves in this gray period of our journey, we need to break through and find the fun in life. Our path is too short not to have fun along the way.

So here is our challenge for today, and it comes in the form of a dare. As we walk by a mirror, look into it and make a goofy face, a really goofy face. No one sees us, except ourselves and the reflection in the mirror. Did we smile? Now for the double-dare... after we have done the mirror dare, go about the workplace or home and make the same face to someone close by. We don't need to explain ourselves, just do it for two seconds. Two seconds of being silly and making a funny face can make a difference to not only to us, but to those that see us being silly. It made us smile again and made the others smile too.

The journey is too short to take ourselves so seriously. We need to have fun, and many times we have to make it ourselves and by doing the silly face exercise we smiled and the evils of our journey were removed, and happiness and joy took their place. When we have the courage to be silly and laugh at ourselves, we add a little more joy and happiness to the world.

Now, it time for the dare...

July 8

An inventory is a list. It can be a mental inventory or one that we write out. It is simply accounting for various things. It could be an inventory of our personal belongings in our home or a mental inventory of what is in the refrigerator or pantry. And we have many other examples in our daily lives and in certain cases, lists can be very useful.

However, there are some other types of inventories that are not so useful. An example of one of these types is when we make a mental inventory of someone's faults or shortcomings. When we take this inventory, we are judging others based on what we think is right or wrong. Our list can be long, and it can be vicious, especially if we act on it in any form or fashion. Sharing with others the inventory we have taken on someone else is totally inappropriate and cruel at the least, if not slanderous. When we find ourselves beginning to take someone's inventory, stop for a moment and examine two things; first, look at our own faults and shortcomings and then look at our motive for judging in the first place. We're not perfect, and we should not expect others to be either.

There is another inventory that we may find ourselves taking once in a while too. If we do something for someone else, being of service to our fellow man or woman, do we subconsciously add to an inventory called, 'they owe us'? If we're being of service and expecting something in return, then it's not authentic service; it is a simple bartering game, where the other person does not know they are a participant. Genuine service is doing for others expecting nothing in return.

Inventories have a purpose, and we can benefit from them. It's when we use the wrong type of inventory in our lives when they become detrimental and useless.

July 9

The soft and formidable clay rests in our hands, and we begin to make different shapes. A ball is easy to form and of course, the old standard, the log. We play with the clay shaping different shapes, and our creative mind begins to see one thing after another as we take the clay and create our masterpiece. We imagine a great sculpture that will be displayed in a museum, admired by crowds of people. At the end, we have a beautiful piece of art, a candy dish.

We do create and mold masterpieces. We do this in raising our children. We mold them, primarily by good parenting skills and the influence of our personal values. The mold we create may not be perfect, but it is still a masterpiece in our eyes. As our children grow older into adulthood, their 'clay' is harder to shape, and we need to allow themselves to continue shaping his or her life and who they are. We have done our best, and now it is time for them to mold and shape their own clay.

Many of us enjoy shaping and molding lives because we think we always know what is best for everyone else. So we take on the task, without being asked, to shape and mold the lives of others as we see fit. Obviously, this is will be futile. The lesson here is to accept others for who they are and not how we want them to be. By accepting others as they are and not forcing our mold onto them, we create and mold a better self.

July 10

*I*t's early morning, and the sun has just crested the eastern horizon. The tall trees block its arrival from our view, but we can see the sun rays' filter through the trees. A light fog slowly floats just over the ground, wrapping itself around the trees. The sunlight reflects off the fog like spotlights on a stage, nature's stage. It's peaceful and serene.

The shadows from the tall trees surround us, but nature's spotlight casts a beam a few yards away. Its light seems to focus on a single flower growing from the forest floor. Like a spotlight at an art museum shining on a beautiful painting, the sunbeam shines on this little flower reaching up to the sky. Its beauty is striking in its contrast with the wooded ground. The pedals face the sun's beams welcoming the warmth it brings from the night.

Today we welcome a new day. The night is replaced by the warming sun, and it shines on us, just as it shines on the single flower in the forest. We should welcome the day with a smile and a promise to ourselves that we will take today as a gift from nature and be the very best we can be. Today is a gift, wrapped in the morning's sunbeams. Unwrap it carefully and enjoy the gift of another day.

July 11

*I*t is a date on the calendar. The date may reoccur each year, such as a birthday or an anniversary. It could be a date that is just special; our high school or college graduation. On these special days, we should celebrate and give thanks for another opportunity to reflect on this date and bring back wonderful memories.

Some dates on the calendar are sad dates and weigh heavy on our hearts. They weigh heavy because we may have lost a loved one on this date, and we still carry our grief. But it's this same day that we should celebrate the life of our loved one and grieve no more. This is not easy, but as long as we carry our beautiful memories in our heart, we have reasons to celebrate because this loved one touched our lives and made a difference.

Sad dates and happy dates remind us that life is to be lived with joy in our hearts. Each day in our life should be lived with love for others and love for ourselves. While sadness is a part of life, so is joy and happiness, and we get to choose how we will live our day today. Some may think today is just another day, but how sad to think today is just another bland day. Today is a day that can be the best day of our lives and we can make it so by being present in today and being aware of all the goodness that surrounds our life. We make this day special with love within our heart and being of service to others.

On a personal note, today is one of those special dates on the calendar for me. It's not my anniversary, or a birthday of any of my family members, but is a date where I changed my life for the good. It is a celebration of a "new

Doug" and a new life. Today, my heart is filled with gratitude and a belief that a Higher Power has led me to this new path on my life's journey. Today, I am blessed with another day, and I am grateful.

July 12

We have so many advances in our world today. We have small electronic devices that communicate all over the world in mere seconds. We have environmental breakthroughs that keep our earth clean. We have new medical advances that save lives each day, but there has always been one aspect of our lives that hasn't changed over history and has made such a huge difference in the world. It is the intricate, delicate human hand.

Four fingers, the thumb, and palm, the hand is such a wonderful instrument of love. Our hand can wipe away a friend's tear when the pain in their heart seems to tear them apart inside. Our hand comforts another with a light touch on the shoulder, letting them know we're here, and they have a friend. Our hand is a medical miracle in reducing the pain of emotional anguish.

Our hand welcomes a stranger in a greeting and may soon be a new friend. A simple handshake lets the other person connect with whom we are as a person. Our hand can share love by the inter-twining of fingers of someone else's hand. It is that connection of two hands; fingers wrapped around each other, that we become one with another's soul.

Our hand is the instrument of care, compassion and love. Let's look at our hand differently today and see how we can use it to touch another's life. Reach out your hand and make a difference today.

July 13

We look at our journey for today, and we see ahead on our path is a turn, but we're not sure what is beyond it. We cannot see what lies ahead so our stride slows, and we approach the turn with some fear and angst. It is the fear of the unknown that lurks on our path, causing us to wonder if we should proceed. Somehow we must find the courage to go around the corner and face whatever is there. Slowly, with caution, we proceed.

We soon realize the greatness of our day is just beyond the curve because we turned up our flame of courage. We figured out that bringing courage into every fear; fear is overcome. Facing that unknown with courage gives us self-confidence and self-assurance. With our next step, the great wonders of our life are closer, and we will soon be able to look back and see that we had nothing to fear in the first place.

Around that corner in our life is just another chapter. Do not fear taking the next step, otherwise you may miss the wonders of your life. Find the courage to step around the corner and face the unknown. Have courage and faith that whatever is on your path will be the best part of your journey so far.

July 14

The trip around the world, solo, in a small sailboat was cut short as a huge storm blew up, sinking his sailboat. Grabbing what he could, he launched his life raft and jumped in as he watched his dream sink into the turbulent ocean. With few things in the raft, he rode out the storm and as morning came, the storm had passed and the sea was calm and tranquil. Days passed, and he had eaten the last morsel of emergency food stowed in the raft; now it was time to try fishing. Hours and hours passed, and nothing seemed to work. With each attempt, he became more frustrated, but tried again and again. Slowly, but surely, a sense of futility crept in. Once that sense of uselessness came into his mind, it opened the door to accept defeat and failure. Fishing was not working and he felt like giving up, knowing death from starvation would be the result. The door to failure was opened with a sense of futility.

We find ourselves in a similar situation from time to time, certainly not to the extreme in the story, but we allow a sense of futility to creep into our lives. We try and try, but are not getting the results we want, and so we become discouraged to the point that a sense of futility has opened the door to failure. Futility is the first stage of giving up; giving up on ourselves. Who are we? We are not quitters! If something is not working out to the way we want, we need to do it a different way. Failure is not measured by the number of setbacks; it is measured by the moment we quit and accept defeat.

Futility is the beginning of not throwing the fishing line one more time into the water to catch a fish. Futility is a warning sign that needs to tell us, get off our pity pot and try again. And that is what our solo sailor did; he cast his fishing line one last time and caught a small fish which he ate and used as bait for the bigger fish until a passing ship rescued him.

Cast your line one more time, your big fish is there, don't let futility lead you to defeat and failure.

July 15

The team rushes off the field. High-fives' all around as the team runs over to the coach. The team then lines up and the opposing team does the same, and they walk toward each other, holding their hands out repeating, "Good game." Praise for a excellent job is taught at a young age, not only receiving it, but giving it too.

Most of us like being recognized for our work, maybe not always in front of a large group, but a simple acknowledgment of a job well done is appreciated. Expressions of appreciation, big or small, for doing a good job make a huge impression and build self-esteem. We never know how much a simple 'thank you' or 'great job' will turn a regular day for someone into a great day, because someone noticed and took the time to say something.

Recognizing someone, even for the smallest accomplishment, takes just a few minutes of our day, but will make the world of difference in theirs. We should not seek praise for ourselves, but give it away as an act respect and to honor others. A simple pat on the back for a job well done makes the day just a little better. It's the right thing to do.

July 16

A soft blanket… a warm cup of tea… watching a beautiful sunrise from the sand dunes of a pristine white-sand beach… all, and many more, bring comfort and serenity to our lives. Our lives slow down and we are at peace with the world, and the world is at peace with us. This inner peace allows us to open the door to deep self-reflection, and we can begin to see our path, our journey more clearly. This peace and serenity allow our mind to look back at our past and learn from it. Our mind is open, and we discover wisdom in the words of others.

This calmness allows us to see the little things in our lives and how truly wonderful they are. We see we are blessed with a life that is filled with good and marvelous people. These special moments of serenity allow us to escape the emotional steps that take us to the pit of self-pity and see that the answers in our life are on the steps of gratitude.

So where do we find this serenity? Where can we escape to experience this inner peace? The answer is simple; if we want to find this, we will find the place and time. Simply escaping from television, phones and other distractions, we can escape to this magical world, even for fifteen minutes. The benefits outweigh the excuses.

Today is the day to take a mental break and find the peace and serenity, and as a result, we will find ourselves.

July 17

The nine-week premature little-girl fights for her life. The odds are stacked against her, yet she holds on with dear life. Today she walks out the door, a beautiful young woman going to her prom. It's a miracle, she is alive.

The dusty from the road being stirred up by the military vehicle ahead obscures the vision of the one following it. Suddenly, an explosion! The road-side bomb takes the vehicle and flips into the air like a match-box car. The soldier's legs are gone, and he is barely alive. Today he walks his new bride down the aisle of the church, unassisted with the use of new medical prosthetics. It's a miracle, he is alive.

The middle-aged man struggles with an addiction to alcohol. His life is in shambles but can't seem to break the bond with the bottle. The family has left him; he is living in his car with mere belongings. Today, he celebrated eleven years of sobriety and has a job and a place to live. It's a miracle, he is alive.

There are those that don't believe in miracles and how said that is. We should remember the great Albert Einstein's quote: "There are only two ways to live your life. One is as though nothing is a miracle. The other is as though everything is a miracle." Every so often, we need to be reminded of the miracles that are all around us. Look into the mirror and see the miracle. YOU ARE A MIRACLE! Be happy. Be humble. Be grateful. Be you, a miracle.

July 18

The grading period report cards are out. Do we dare open them? What is our grade? Some will say that they are no longer in school, while that may be true in one sense, it's not in another. We are never out of the school of life, and our graduation is at the end of our journey, so we're constantly learning as a student, but we're also the teacher.

No one else gets to grade our work. We are the only ones that fill out our report card. So what grades do we see? Is there a NI (Needs Improvement)? Are there mostly B's and C's? Why aren't there all A's? Aren't we an A student? We are an A student, but grade ourselves too harshly. Start giving A's and we will find ourselves on the honor roll.

Each day we are given a pop quiz. Each day we are given a grade in life. Here are today's pop quiz questions.

1. Did I place the needs of others ahead of my own?
2. Did I live my values as best I can?
3. Were my actions based on love?
Bonus question: Do I love myself?

We have all day to work on this pop quiz, there is no time limit. And a hint… we may see the same questions on tomorrow's pop quiz too.

July 19

We have the same number of minutes in our day. We have the same number of days in the week. Our routine is typically different from the next person, but for some-odd reason we expect others to follow our time schedule. What makes our schedule the 'Master Schedule' that all others must follow? Outside of a particular work schedule, our life's schedule is our own, and no one else is obligated to follow it.

Some will always be early for dinners, lunches or other social events, while others will be late. In both cases, it's others not following our schedule, and it drives some of us crazy. We tap our foot; we look at our watch and look around, waiting. This obsession for being on time, not early, not late causes such undue stress in our lives, yet we allow ourselves to be controlled by a mechanical device called a clock.

We all have stress in our lives, and each of us deals with it differently. If we can just remove one stressor from our day, it will allow us to enjoy the day just a little more. So let go of the fact that someone else's schedule doesn't match our own. They may be early or late. In either case, it is absolutely nothing to get stressed out over. Don't allow the hands of time take over your peace and serenity.

July 20

We may never know who or how we will touch the life of someone else. And whatever the circumstance, big or small, remains in their memory for a lifetime. We can think of someone that touched our lives and the impact they had in making us who we are today. Did we ever say, thank you?

We try to raise our children the best we can, with what we have. We may not have a lot of money to buy them expensive presents. We try to provide them with what they need first and then with what they want last. We sometimes forget that it's not about the 'things' in life, which will be broken or lost in time. It's about giving and showing care, compassion, courage, faith, and love. Those values are what, in the end, will be what they will cherish for their lifetime.

There is no better gift we can give our children, our mother or father, grandmother or grandfather or any other family member, or any of our friends is our time. Each moment we give to them is just another treasured moment that will touch their lives. It's not about 'things'; it is all about love. Every minute is a gift which turns into a memory that will never break or get lost.

Make a difference today and give the gift of time.

July 21

S ome will say their day, week, month, or year is segmented into two aspects, work and life. Isn't 'life' the total picture and not what is left over after 'work'? Of course, it is, but we want to think of 'life' as this small part of our day that is the fun part of our day. However, if we really look closely, we see our 'life' is made of many aspects that we sometimes lose sight.

If we examine our 'life' more closely we see it is made up of many parts, and 'work' is just one aspect. Let's consider these other pieces; financial, health, spouse or significant other, friends & family, personal growth, fun & recreation, physical environment, spiritual. We may have one or two more, but just looking at these few; we see our 'life' is full.

If each one plays a part in our 'life', it's time to do some analysis. How much do you value each one? How satisfied are you with them? How much time to you dedicate to each facet? Truthful answers may surprise us, and we may conclude we need to make some changes in our lives. If change is needed, what is our action plan?

Life is much more than what is left over after work and sleeping. Life is huge, and we need to make sure every day is dedicated to what is important to us, and integrated with all the other aspects of our life. We only have this life right now, so let's make the most of it.

July 22

BREAKING NEWS!!! We're human! We're not perfect! We make mistakes. Whew! Now that we got that out of the way, let's take a breath.

If we make a mistake, own up to it. Don't try to hide it, blame others, or dilute it with excuses. Take ownership, admit it, and learn from it. In most cases, we make the situation worse by telling little lies, or trying to shift the blame. We know in our heart, we made the mistake, so let's be bigger than the mistake and admit to it. When we do, those around us will respect us more and in fact, will go out of the way to help us resolve the mistake if they can. We will be a better person for it, and it's the right thing to do. Avoid the path of beating ourselves up over it for that only leads us down the path to the pit of self-pity. "Cowboy Up" as some may say and let's move on with our lives.

So now the shoe is on the other foot and someone we know makes a mistake. Remember the headline? We're human and so are they. So don't be critical, chastise them, or make them feel worse than they feel right now. Forgive if necessary, help resolve the mistake if we can. Find the compassion in our heart to help them through their mistake.

Some mistakes are big, and some are tiny. Regardless, we need to own up to our own and help others with theirs if we can. With each mistake, we become stronger and wiser. Saddle up Cowboy.

July 23

O ur journey in life has its peaks and valleys. It has dark cloudy days and days filled with sunshine. Twists and turns, up steep inclines we must climb and days when our path is soft green grass that feels so good on our bare feet. Life's journey today will be different than yesterday's journey; and today's path will not be the same as the one tomorrow, but we start each one with the first step.

There are days when we feel weighted down with guilt, shame, anger and resentments and can barely put one foot in front of the other. Then there are days when we feel naked, weak and afraid. What we need to remember is that we always have our values to help us through each day of our journey. Our values of forgiveness, respect, love will lighten our load when we feel weighted down. Our values of courage and faith will cover us and push away our fear and give us strength.

Our journey for today has begun. We have stepped out onto our path and ready for every hill, every turn, each and every challenging obstacle because we know our values are within us to meet each one. Our journey, our values... what awesome traveling adventure awaits? It's time to see what lies ahead. Safe travel.

July 24

A friend asks how we are. We simple say, fine. The tone of our voice, the look in our eye, and the lack of a sincere smile tell a different story. Now some friends will let it pass and accept our response. However, there are a few friends who will not. These friends will look into our eyes and ask again, because they know we are holding onto some emotional baggage whom we don't want to burden others. They will take our hand, or touch our shoulder and ask one more time. We feel love with their touch, their sincere words, and the compassion in their caring eyes that look deep into our soul.

The release of the emotional rocks we have carried by ourselves feels so good. Our friend has taken our heavy load and made it lighter. Tears flow as the hug of a friend allows us to release all that has weighed us down and have been carrying by ourselves. What a relief to be rid of those rocks of emotional baggage. It was our friend who took the time, looked into our eyes and did not accept our answer that we were fine.

How many of this type of friend do we have in our lives today? Some may say one or two, but sadly some may answer, none. How sad it is to feel we have no one in our lives today that can help lighten our load of the rocks of emotional baggage. There is a solution, and we can be that person to someone else. We can be that friend who will lighten the load of someone else; by not accepting their answer, "I'm fine."

Be a friend; a good, caring, a compassionate friend who cares for another person more than they care for themselves. It's about time we become the friend we needed when we were just 'fine'.

July 25

The mere sight of a small, soft, furry puppy brings a smile to even the hardened soul. It warms our heart and just for a fleeting moment all our troubles seem miles away. We watch the little puppy, clumsy with its big feet, chase anything and everything that moves. The puppy looks up to us with its sweet brown eyes and immediately warms our heart. We see and feel the unconditional love that the little creature gives us with its tail wagging and little kisses as we hold it close to our face.

The small infant, sitting quietly on the old man's lap, looks at him with their big blue eyes. We watch the grandfather hold the baby while talking softly, telling them of all the great things that are coming for them. The little baby listens intently for a minute, but then is distracted by the old man's eye glasses and reaches out to grab them. The grandfather shakes his head from side to side and tickles the little one. The baby laughs and giggles. We witness this love of a grandchild and a grandfather, and it too warms our soul, and all our troubles are far away.

It is the little things in life that make a difference, whether it's a puppy or a baby, it comes down to love that touches and warms our soul. It is love we seek, and it is love we share and in doing so, our whole life is transformed into a meaningful existence. It's time we played with the puppy or hold the baby, for each are giving us unconditional love. Each one takes us away from our perceived troubles and warms our heart. It's time we shared our love with others, warming two hearts.

July 26

*W*e expend too much energy on the negative aspects in our lives. Think back on the ugly comments and thoughts we had of others and all the nasty emails we sent. Look at all the times when we judged others and snickered as they failed or made a mistake. Did we wish ill-will on others? Sadly, the answer is probably yes. If we could just take half of that time and energy and use it for the good in life and in serving others, what a great day it would be today.

As we look into the mirror today, we are looking at the person that is responsible for our actions. We are accountable for both expending our energy on hurting others, or just the opposite and be loving and caring. The person in the mirror is responsible for that decision today and every day.

Let's be gentle in our words and actions today and not cause others around us to feel less than or unimportant. Let's not let our words or actions cause hurt and pain. Never doubt our own power to make a difference in this world. We can and we do make a difference in the lives we touch. Let's focus our energy on being of service to others today; be caring and loving. It is our way of paying back some of the good in our lives.

July 27

Our journey is filled with people, all sort of people; each one on their own journey. Their paths cross ours and ours theirs. Some are just people, while others become friends and loved ones. However, there is a special person that may walk with us along our journey that is exceptional. This person makes a difference in our lives by inspiring us, guiding us and helping us take a new path on our journey. This person is a mentor or a coach.

So what makes up a mentor? What is so special about them? There is a unique magic about them though and in almost every case, there is one common theme; to inspire, not motivate, but inspire. The mentors whom we meet on our journey are driven by their values and a deep drive to be of service to others. The selfless act of mentoring guides us on our journey and when we come to a crossroad; our mentor's words will help us make the decision that will change our life.

Our mentors inspire us to follow our heart, discover what burns deep in our soul, and follow our dreams. Mentors are teachers, coaches, clergy, or just a good friend. There are no special qualifications to be a mentor, other than a person that lives their values openly and places others ahead of themselves. We owe our mentors a deep-hearted thank you for bringing us to this part of our journey.

Do we qualify to be a mentor? Absolutely, we do, if we want to make a difference in this world, by inspiring others on their journey. Inspire!

July 28

We start our day, early in the morning and everything is a little fuzzy as we come out of a good night's sleep. We wash our face, and we reach for our glasses to bring clarity to the morning's light. If we begin our day thinking about yesterday and how we think we were wronged, or we remember the cruel words said in anger, we're starting our day as if our glasses are covered in dirt and filth. We can hardly see the beauty of the day before us because of all of yesterday's dirt and grime on our glasses.

However, if instead, we look at yesterday as just that, the past. We don't carry the resentments and anger into today, but release them and let them be part of the past. If we just take a lens cleaning cloth that is soaked in a little care, forgiveness, compassion, and a little love, and clean our glasses, our whole outlook will improve. So when we pick up our glasses to see the beauty of the morning and all that nature is laid before our feet, our glasses are clear. Our whole outlook upon the day is new, fresh and clear when we clean our glasses with a little care, compassion and love. We will see the world and the beauty in others more clearly. What a wonderful view we have.

Each morning, we need to clean our glasses, so we don't miss a moment of the beauty of today and the beauty of those who we will touch in our lives.

July 29

$\mathcal{E}$ach day we set out on our journey and follow this path we have chosen. We're not exactly sure where we're headed but what we know is, we're closer than we were yesterday. Each day is another adventure in our life, and each day may bring us challenges which we will face with courage. Our day may bring us joy and happiness which we will greet with a smile.

It's our journey, our adventure to travel. Each day we're experiencing a new day of the wonders of the world. When we face each day and each adventure with a positive attitude, we discover we can travel much further on our journey than we could if we carried around the rocks of negativity. So as the morning sun brightens the horizon, leave the negativity rocks of yesterday on the ground as we step out onto our path.

Greet the day with a smile, an open mind, and a loving grateful heart. We will make great progress today and our journey today will be awesome.

July 30

Once upon a time, in a land far away…

So the story begins, and the story could be of a prince and princess, or the story could be of an evil troll under a bridge, casting his evil upon all that cross his bridge. While many of us have heard these stories and many more, we have not heard all the stories. The fairytales and make-believe stories are just that, fantasy fiction; it's the non-fiction stories that carry the clout of the messages.

Each of us has a story, and it is ours to tell. Our story may be painful and repeating it only brings back the hurt and is the one we may keep to ourselves. Other stories are of joy and happiness, which we share freely, with a smile in our heart and love in our heart. Our story is what has happened on our path, not someone else's path and this event has been a part of what has brought us to where we are today. Our story may be one of overcoming adversity or facing a challenge. It could be the fulfillment of a dream and how we accomplished it. See? We all have stories, which truly belong to us and just us.

So as we go about our day, remember, everyone has a story, just as we do. We have no business judging others, because we don't know their story of adversity or challenges they faced or are facing still. We can share our story with others when the time is right, but do it in a purposeful manner; not bragging and boasting, but with humility and honesty.

Once upon a time, it seemed like yesterday…

July 31

The black velvet night sky is a blanket of tiny diamonds; each one twinkling its own perfect beauty. Suddenly, a shooting star streaks across the night sky, lasting only a second or two. It's then we make a wish. We close our eyes for just a moment and make this wish.

A wish is nothing more than the start of a dream. The seed of a dream is planted with each wish we make and some wishes, our dream seeds, will be nourished, watered, and cared for. The seed of a dream begins to grow, and we continue to tend to it by giving it food and water. It continues to grow. Some seeds of our dreams grow slowly, and we must care for them longer, while others will flourish quickly. Our dream garden is taking shape.

With love, we take care of our dream garden by working on making sure each dream seed is cared for and given everything it needs to grow. We spend our time watering and feeding our garden, because without our work, the dream seed would not have a chance. So we spend the time, and we give it our best care we can.

The fast-growing seeds bloom and what a wonderful sight; one of our dreams has come true with its beautiful flower. We admire and are fulfilled with this beautiful dream flower. However, there are other dream seeds that still need our attention, and we mustn't neglect them.

Our dream garden is perpetual, as long as we believe in making a wish on a shooting star in the night sky and are willing to care for the dream seeds in our dream garden. With our determination, each one will turn into the beautiful dream flower.

August

August 1

We have all heard at one point in our lives that the only constant in the world is change. The world is changing every day and there is little stopping it. While we may not be able to stop change from happening, perhaps we can be part of it. We may not always like the change that is impacting our lives or the lives around us, so what can we do to affect the change we want to see? The answer to that question is in two places. First, we seek to find the person that can make this change, and we find that person in the mirror. Yes, we are the ones that can affect change, and it starts with us.

The second place we find the answer, after we accept the mirror image as the first step, is this boiling emotion that is in our gut, in our heart, in our soul, just ready to let loose its power and that is passion. Putting these two together, accepting we are responsible for the change, so now we know who the driver is; passion is the fuel that will cause the change to happen. It's a two-part process; driver and fuel.

We need to empower ourselves with the ability to affect change, otherwise we are just in this changing world for the ride. Merely, a passenger on this journey is not why we are here. We are here with a purpose and to discover that purpose; we must change ourselves along the way. Don't be afraid of change, be afraid of not changing.

August 2

Each of us has special talents and when we use these talents to help someone else better their lives, we have made a difference. It is these special gifts that will, when we share with others freely, take "That was nice." to "That was fantastic!" If we allow our ego or selfishness get in the way of us using our special gifts to help others, our gifts and talents are not being used as they should be. We have so much to offer and when we take the time to get out of ourselves and focus on helping others, we turn 'nice' into 'fantastic'.

So, what are our gifts that we can share? We may have special skills that teach others how to do something better, and to hone their existing skills. Perhaps our talents will help someone discover a new path on his or her life's journey. There is nothing more inspiring and gratifying than watching an awakening in the life of someone else where his or her life's journey is now changed for the better.

We all have the ability to make a difference in the life of someone else. One of the greatest gifts that we can share is our time. Our time is so special and can have such a huge impact. We need to remember that the gift of our time will take "That was nice." to "That was fantastic!" Make a 'FANTASTIC' difference today.

August 3

*I*t is huge! There on our path, it just stands a great lion, with its piercing eyes, waiting for us. We stop in our tracks and stare at its massive presence. With a loud roar, we are suddenly washed over with intimidation and fear; our feet will not move any further. We are so tiny in comparison; we feel we are no match for what is waiting ahead of us. Will it rip us to shreds if we try to go around it, much less confront it face to face? Fear has paralyzed us on our journey.

Intimidation and fear are emotions that are paralyzing, and they are generated in our own mind. Intimidation is that emotion where we feel we are less than or unworthy of being part of what is around us or to be among those that are in our company. Fear is the fuel that continues to feed this feeling. What is there to fear? Really, what is so massive and overwhelming to cause us to feel this way? This is a call to action, and that action is to dig deep within our heart and soul and find courage and respect. It's when we bring courage to face the fear and respect for whatever is facing us on our journey, intimidation is replaced with self-worth.

The massive lion that scared us on our journey and caused to retreat into our shell encased with fear and intimidation, was really not a fierce as we made it out to be. It was our mind that created this ferocious creature, when, in reality, it was a small kitten. A little furry creature that's voice was a timid meow and not the loud roar we imagined we heard.

It's when we face adversity on our journey with our values of courage, and respect do we make great progress on our path. We have them within us; it's time to call them into action.

August 4

I t's just a matter of time. When we hear these words, our mind immediately goes to expect some event with negative consequences. Perhaps that's because people only say those words when there is that possibility. What if we could use those same words with the intent of positive outcomes? While we may not be able to change the world's perspective on those words, we may be able to change one person's thoughts of a negative outcome to a positive one. For example:

It's just a matter of time… when we realize our true potential.

It's just a matter of time… when we find serving others with love is one of the greatest gifts we can give away.

It's just a matter of time… when we feel the deep connection with another's soul, so deep that we are one with them.

It's just a matter of time… when we push away our defects of character and replace them with the good personal values that are within us.

It's just a matter of time… when truly enjoy the breath-taking sunrise and feel we are one with all of nature.

It's just a matter of time… when we see the beautiful light ahead on the somewhat dark path we have traveled so far.

It's just a matter of time. It's just a matter of our time and how we look at it. It's our time to live a life filled with joy and happiness. It is a matter of time, and we can make a difference with this time of ours if we choose to do so. The next time we hear someone say, "It's just a matter of time.", finish the sentence for them with a positive ending and see what happens.

So it's just a matter of time… where will you go with it?

August 5

Some things are black and white and when we acknowledge these as such, we are imposing strict and disciplined belief. This decision is a very distinct line between this and that, black and white, with no room for compromise.

If we are living in a black-and-white world, we are missing so much of what life has to offer us. We're missing the beauty of colors. The bright-red apple sitting on the table, the fresh bloom of a yellow rose in the garden, and the light pink break of dawn on the eastern sky are the beauty of color we miss when we see the world as just black and white.

So how are we living our lives? Are we living a life, void of care and compassion? Do we miss the chance to have a life filled with love and serving others? These are the colors in our lives that make our life a beautiful rainbow of color. It's the opening of a new world, filled with bright beautiful colors when we simply let our values become part of our life.

There is more than black and white in this world. There is a beautiful flower within our soul, yearning to blossom and share its beauty with all of the world, and that flower is our whole existence. That beautiful blossom is our self-worth and our loving values.

Let's stop seeing the world as black and white and recognize the beauty in everyone we see today and every day from this day forwards. The colors of life are gorgeous, enjoy!

August 6

We et, cold, and scared, our journey has been stormy and dark. We have gone through drenching rains, fierce bitter cold winds and pitch black skies, and we have come to rest for a moment. We are beaten down and feel alone and somewhat lost as we rest to gain strength to go on. Our mind slips into feeling sorry for ourselves, and that we question the need to continue.

Suddenly, a flash of lightning turns the dark sky into daylight for just a second and in the second; we see a small creature, trembling beside our path. Its fur all wet; it shivers as it looks up to us, silently asking for comfort and help. Not fearing the creature we slowly bend down and begin to stroke its fur. It is not afraid, so we pick it up, open our jacket and place it against our warm chest. We give it a tiny morsel of food from our pocket and within minutes the small creature, now warm and dry, sleeps against our chest hearing our heart beat a soothing rhythm. It is time for us to rest too, so we sleep, comforting the tiny creature in our jacket.

As we awaken, the storms are gone, the cold wind is replaced with a gentle breeze and the sun peeks through the clouds. We feel the tiny creature stir against our chest, and we open our jacket. Its eyes look to us as to say, thank you for your comfort and care. We take the creature out of our coat, place it on the ground, and it begins to crawl away. Looking back one final time, it seems to say, thank you one final time before it disappears from sight.

So, it's not all about us. When we can get out of ourselves and bring care and comfort to someone or something else, the dark stormy path we imagine is replaced the gentle wind and sunny skies fueled by love. Help someone else through their storms and our journey will be brighter.

August 7

*I*magine the elation that overwhelmed the person who had a scientific breakthrough that potentially would change the world. Think about the sense of accomplishment the medical professional feels when they watch their patient walk for the first time after an accident, when they were told they would never walk again. The student struggles with the word problem, but the teacher's aide sticks with it and helps work through each step in the process until the 'click' happens in the student's mind and then it all makes sense; like a piece of the puzzle is put into place and we see the whole picture.

Huge scientific discoveries in making the world a better place to live, or small steps in helping make the world better for one person, they are all making a difference. Each day the world is a little better because someone made a discovery, performed a miracle, or simply put the last puzzle piece in place. We are these people. We are the ones that are making miracles happen and are making a difference in the world. We should never underestimate our impact on others, because it will be that one word, or one action step, or that simple act of kindness and the world will be changed.

The world is just a little better because we are here serving others. It is when we focus on the needs of others, do we reap the overwhelming wave of accomplishment and satisfaction in serving them. We are here with a purpose, and we must discover that purpose so that we can change the world, even if it is one person at a time.

The time is now, and the world awaits; greet it with a smile. Make a difference by inspiring others.

August 8

$\mathcal{M}$ any roads we drive are made up of two lanes or more. There is the regular traffic lane, the right lane and there is a passing lane or the left lane. Just as roads have two lanes, our path on this life's journey has two lanes also, but have different meanings.

The right lane on our path is a regular lane where many of us just trudge along, sometimes getting into bumper to bumper "I don't wanna's." or "It's too hard." This lane is also filled with speed bumps called excuses and with each of these speed bumps, we hit, our progress slows. We also need to watch for the detour signs called blaming others; for that will really take us off our path. This is lane where we see, not "Construction" signs, but "Destruction" ones. It is so easy to allow all these obstacles on this lane to take us off our given path and slow our journey.

Now for this other lane on our path, it is the action lane. It's like the HOV lane with no passenger rules. This lane is free from the speed bumps of excuses and detours. It is the fast lane, avoiding the "Destruction" zones and the bumper-to-bumper traffic. This lane is where we are driven into action, and our speed is of our choosing, without regard of law enforcement giving us a ticket. The action lane is where we see our dreams come true, our lives enriched, and meaning is added to our life.

We have the choice of the two lanes in which to travel our journey. If we find ourselves in the right lane, the lane of obstacles, then we need to turn on the blinker to the left and let's get into the action lane. Our action lane is open, let's go.

August 9

A chill comes over us. Goose bumps pop up on our arms, traveling from shoulders, to our elbows, and down to our wrist. What has just come over us? It is as if we felt a cold image passed through us, invisible but present. Waves of these tiny goose bumps flow over our body. The cold shiver flows by, even though moments before we were comfortable. What has just happened to bring this change? Maybe it was a ghost.

The ghost of our past may unexpectedly revisit our lives and may bring with it bad memories of our past. Our ghost brought with it events of yesterday, as well as events of years gone by, all of which are a part of our past life, but obviously, our ghost wants us to remember them again. What is the lesson our ghost wants us to learn? Is it something we need to use today or tomorrow?

We shouldn't fear this ghost, nor resent its presence. Simply look for the message that it brings and find how we can use our past to create a better today. We cannot change the past, but we can learn from our mistakes that are there. Our ghost merely brings with it a gentle reminder that we can change the present, by learning from our past. Once we realize this, our ghost of the past will fade away, for now at least; until it's time to learn another lesson for today.

We can be great teachers by learning from our past and not completely shutting the door in it.

August 10

*I*nside or outside? It's funny how many of us may think how our mother would be saying these words to us about either staying inside or playing outside and quit running in and out. We may also be accused of trying to air condition the entire world with the door being opened so frequently of coming inside and going outside.

An even more egregious fault of 'inside or outside' is when we judge our insides with someone else's outsides. Now the scales can tip in one of two ways. It could be that we judge someone else negatively and look down upon them. Here is an example where our ego is boastful and condescending; judging another person when we have not walked in their shoes on their journey. We're making unjust judgments. The scale could tip the other way, where we're holding someone else on a pedestal and admire their mere presence; while we are holding a low opinion of ourselves. Here our ego is deflated, and our self-esteem is very low. Again, we're judging our insides with their outsides.

We can admire others for their success, or have compassion for those that may be less fortunate, but we should never allow our boastful ego or our deflated self-esteem defines who we are. We need to stop comparing our insides to other's outsides. Appearances are deceiving, and we have no right to judge in the first place. Once we get real with ourselves and be brutally honest, we can find our true selves. Our true self is what the world wants to see, and when we remove our masks and can be authentic, we then realize the true value of our existence.

Just be you, that's who we're looking for... just the beautiful and loving you.

August 11

$\mathcal{M}$ any of us use a to-do list, which makes sure we accomplish certain tasks in a given time period. Even if we don't write one out, we capture a list in our mind, and we check the tasks off as we get them done. Here is a to-do list we all should have.

___ Begin the day with a smile.
___ Walk for 15 minutes.
___ Give someone a hug.
___ Call or email a friend to tell them you're thinking of them.
___ Let the words of kindness and compassion override the words of anger.
___ Only drink one soda.
___ Be grateful for what we have.
___ Look in the mirror and give yourself a pep talk.
___ Hold a door open for a stranger and smile.
___ Say, "I love you."
___ Say a prayer for someone who is struggling with an illness or another conflict.

The last item on the to-do list is reserved for tonight, just before bed time. Review today's to-do list and see how many on our list we accomplished. Now the final To Do...

___ Commit to do better tomorrow.

August 12

*J*oy... Sadness... Love... Anger...Serenity... Stress... Resentments... Forgiveness... the list goes on. These are feelings, just feelings. All of us will experience all of these and more, as we walk our journey. Feelings are a part of our life, and we should be happy we have them. If we didn't have them, it would be like the injection of Novocain, it deadens the area so our nerves are numbed, and we cannot feel the discomfort. Without feelings, we're numb to the world; we are numb to our existence and how sad that is.

It's easy to share with others the feelings of joy and happiness, but some of us will bottle up our negative feelings and not share them with others. We add these massive burdens to our backpack, and they weigh heavy. It's when we share all our feelings, honestly and openly with another human being is the burden on our heart lighter.

Feelings are good because they tell us we're alive and not numb to our existence. Feelings, good and bad, are best shared with a friend who can enjoy the pleasant ones with us and lighten our load with the ones that are not so good. It's time we open up these bottled feelings and let them out; like seeing butterflies being released into the air, our heart smiles. What a relief... to feel... to share... to be alive.

August 13

The sun has not yet broken the horizon. The night's blanket still covers the early morning's birth. However, there is a hint of the new day coming on the eastern sky, and we are ready to meet it. We don't know what the day will bring, but whatever it may be, we must be ready to face the day ahead.

Our journey today is uncertain. We may find storms on the horizon, or a sunny stroll on our path. Regardless of what we may encounter, we must not hide. We must face today with faith and courage. We cannot allow our fear to get in the way of our journey today.

Accept the gifts of today with gratitude and humility and face every challenge with confidence. Greet other travelers with respect and serve others with love. And when we do all this today, we can rest tonight, knowing we made a positive difference in this world. It will be a good day after all.

August 14

We're in it for the money. Everything has a price some may say. "I'll do it for $." Cold and greedy is that that money is the bottom line, and nothing is pro bono. Agreed, most of us cannot live without some sort of monetary income, but that doesn't mean we have to be compensated with money for everything we do. Whatever happened to the freebie? Is nothing truly free?

Now this applies not only with monetary compensation, but also with compensation in trade. If we do something for someone else, we may agree that this other person does something for us. This seems fair, doesn't it? It does when both parties are clear with the intentions. It's when we do something for someone, appearing to be free in their mind, but not our subconscious intent. We expect them to "owe us" something in return. In fact, we can get so bad that we have a running tab in our mind. This running tab will build a wall of resentments and can possibly destroy a relationship.

The approach we should take in doing something for someone else is that we should not expect anything in return. Nothing! We give ourselves in service to others, and we don't add it to a running tab. When we do this, it is a true service to others; given with love and care.

It's freebie time… truly free of any payment in return. What a wonderful feeling deep inside, for we have given ourselves to others and made a difference in their lives. Our payment is the warmth in our heart, knowing we helped someone. And there isn't any better compensation.

August 15

The Olympics are in full swing, and we watch as one competitor pushes themselves to give it everything they have against another competitor. Each race, each event they give it their very best, for this race may be their last chance to win gold. Some races are so close, hundredths of a second, while others are won by a much larger margin. However, the winner is unknown until the sound of the starting gun pops, and the race is on. Each runner is racing in their lane to win the gold.

We are in our own race; in fact, we have several races we're competing in each day. Here's the lineup. In lane one, we have fear running against faith in lane two. Lane three is ego running against lane four, humility. In lane five we have guilt and in lane six is self-forgiveness. And wrapping up this race, in lane seven is anger running against compassion in lane eight. This is the set up for today's race, and the starting gun pops when we start our day.

The race is on. This is not a sprint; it is an endurance race and will last all day until we close our eyes. Each runner in each lane will have the lead at some point during the race. It can be a very close race at times with the lead changing over and over. Who will cross the finish line tonight as we rest our head on the pillow?

There is good news and bad. The bad news is, the race is fixed. The good news is, we control the outcome and the gold-medal winner. Who will win in each of the respective lanes is of our choosing, but even then, the race is not easy. We must remain focused and determined to bring our best game to the track. Remember, we control the outcome of our race.

August 16

When playing poker, it is important not to give away your hand with our expressions on your face. A little up turn to our mouth, even the smallest smile will tell others we have some good cards. Scrunching of the forehead may tell the tale of a losing hand. So a poker face, void of emotion, is essential when playing cards to win, so that those around the table cannot read the hand we're holding.

We also try to apply the same principle in life, in that we try to hold back expressions or emotions to the outside world. We bottle up so much inside that it is very difficult to have a poker face all day long. It will be that twinkle in the eye, or slight frown on our face that will give us away to those around us. Now ask ourselves... so what? What if we didn't work so hard on maintaining a poker face and just allowed our emotions to be other there? What if we just laid our cards on the table for all those around to see? Lay out the good hands when we feel joy and happiness as well as the bad hand of sadness and pain. It's okay; because regardless of our hand, our friends are there to help play our cards. They are not going to fold or try to raise the ante; they are there to make us a winner.

Keep the poker face to the poker table, but let's reveal our hand so that others can make us a winner. Stop bottling up all the emotions that are inside and lay our cards on the table. We will be a winner in the long run. Now it's time we helped someone with their hand. Watch for the poker-faced people and find a way to have them lay their cards on the table.

August 17

The tiny flower closed its colorful pedals the night before, now waits for the first glimmer of the dawn to unfold its beauty to show the world. Little does it know that other flowers are there, waiting for the same dawn, with the same purpose. With the dawn comes a fresh beginning, a new life. All the flowers begin to open as the sun breaks the horizon, and the flower bed comes alive. The pedals unfold, and face the eastern sky, waiting… waiting for the sun to shine upon them and give them fresh life. The garden is vibrant with so many colors and is just another example of how wonderful nature's beauty is and that today is a new beginning.

Just as the flowers in the garden, we awaken and look for the sun to brighten our day. The dawn brings to us a new day, new opportunities, new friends, and new beginnings. Our colorful pedals are how we will find ways to fulfill our life's purpose with the values, we hold dear to our heart. Each pedal of our blossom is a value, and together they form our flower, which is who we are. It is the flower within us, our values, which others will see if we allow our flower to blossom to today's new beginning.

We are not alone in our garden. We have many others that make up this beautiful flower bed, and each one is experiencing new life with the dawn. Side by side, we add so much to the world's flower bed of life. While we may think, we don't make a difference, if our flower did not bloom in this vast garden, the world would have one less beautiful flower and would not be quite as pretty.

Today is a new beginning. Today is a day to blossom and show the world who we are, and that we add beauty to this garden of the world.

August 18

What will it be today? Will it be a single word? Or will it be a few words in a phrase or sentence? Will it be the handshake as we meet a new friend? Perhaps it will be simply holding the door for a stranger. Could it be the hug with a friend, where we create, even for a few seconds, a oneness with their soul? What will it be today?

It is each one of those that will make a difference in someone's life today. It is each word, each act of kindness that will touch a life for the better. We go about our day thinking about work, the report that is due, or the grocery shopping list in our head. Our waking hours are consumed with our little world, but it is when we leave our little world, even for a few moments and speak loving words or do an act of kindness for others, does it make our world just a little better.

One of the greatest gifts we can give away is just a little of ourselves. When we take the time to reach out to someone else and try to make their day just a little better is what life is all about. And the greatest payment in return is when that person does the same for someone else, and the domino effect begins.

So, what will it be today? A kind word? A random act of kindness? A hug? Whatever we choose; it makes a difference and never doubt that we can't change the world.

August 19

Imagine the blackest of black. Darkness so intense and so extreme we cannot see our hand in front of our face. Now imagine being weightless in this blackness. We cannot tell if we are upside down, spinning, or moving in any direction. Lastly is the silence. We shout out, or we think we do and hear nothing; completely void of sound in this silent, black, motionless world. Where are we?

This place and time in our lives are very rare and in fact, many will never venture here. We have lost all touch with the outside world and have fallen into this deep dark abyss called oblivion. We have collapsed into ourselves and think only of ourselves and nothing else matters. We have fallen into a world where darkness consumes us, and we have lost touch with everything and everyone around us. Oblivious to what is important; we simply fall into an existence and can hardly call it a life.

There is a way out of this dark silent world. There is light and music at our fingertips, if we simply get out of ourselves and look around. Step up and do something for someone else today. Get out of our self-imposed darkness by reaching out to help a friend with a kind word or gentle touch. Wake up to the world that is all around us and see the wonders and beauty of life. Awaken the beauty within and see how we are an important part of today. Believe we make a difference when we venture out of self-oblivion and into the world of light and beauty.

Welcome to the new light, the new world of a wonderful and bright life, filled with love and joy.

August 20

rrands to do, places to go and people to see are the agenda we're facing today. And as we go about our day, running here and there, we come across a white envelope. Written on it by hand is "Please Open." Now we may have found this on our car's windshield as we came out of the store, or we may have found it on our desk at work, regardless of how it came to us; it's now ours. Our curiosity gets the best of us, and we open it. Inside the plain white envelope is an ordinary white piece of paper and a single penny.

Handwritten on the paper is this:

Dear friend,

Thank you for opening this envelope. You may know me or I may be a stranger, but in either case, I want to wish you the very best day possible. I hope you find peace, prosperity, love and happiness in your life. I give this penny to you to make you a little richer than you were moments ago, but if you want to be even richer, put this letter and the penny back in the envelope and leave it for the next lucky person. For you see, we are fortunate and rich already. Simply think of one thing you are grateful for right this moment. What is it? Think of it one more time. Can you see how rich you already are?

Now you have a choice. You can keep the penny and throw away this letter and the envelope, or you can put the penny and this letter back into the envelope and pass on this gift of love. Whatever you decide, I wish you well for the rest of your day today.

Anonymous

Our life is now just a little different as a result of the envelope and its contents. We can be cynical and toss it in the trash, or we can take a moment of our precious day and make someone else just a little richer. We can share our wealth in more ways than money; we can share our values of care, compassion, and love. By doing so, we have made a difference, one envelope at a time.

August 21

A new life came into the world this morning. A new baby drew its first breath, and today is their birthday, so happy birthday little one. Welcome to the first day of your life. This new living creature has stepped onto their path for the first time, and their journey has started. They will need our help along the way, just as others helped us, so we need to share our wisdom, so they may learn the importance of life and the joys that come along.

This new baby, born just hours ago has already begun to learn. Held against their mother's chest hears the rhythm of a familiar heart beat and is comforted. Today's lesson is love and this lesson will be repeated over and over, for we never stop learning how love is one of the most important values we possess. This lesson to this new child is the beginning of many more to come.

We are the teachers and also are the students. We share our wisdom, and we learn from others. Sadly, we teach, not intentionally, bad habits and character defects along the way too. Our values are suppressed by these negative aspects in our lives, and we begin to allow them to control our life and in doing so, we are teaching and demonstrating them to others. Just as the new child gets a lesson in love this morning, how soon will it get a different lesson?

We need to be aware that we are teaching, through living our life. If we are negative, we will teach others how to be negative. If we live a life of values, we will teach the importance of them. Courage, love, compassion, faith, truthfulness are the lessons we should be teaching, and we do this by living these values. What will we teach today?

August 22

The bully leans against the ladder to the playground equipment. His arms are crossed his chest and has a mean look about him. We have seen him in action in the past, where he will trip or push anyone as they try to play on the swing and slide. He also has a weak following of wanna-bees, standing close by to give the appearance of a small army, ready to pounce on the weak and timid. We think this is unique to children, but we see it in adult life too. While it may not be the physical bullying, the verbal intimidation is just as powerful. In both cases, the bully has an influence over those around them.

In contrast is the child on the playground that encourages others to come and play. She helps them climb the ladder or pushes them on the swing when they need a push. It is laughter and joy we see and hear when this person is on our playground. So many others want to be part of this group because there is fun involved. We have these type individuals in our adult life too. They come into our lives to help us, to reach down with their hand to lift us up, or to give us a hug just because. This influence on us and others that witness it, is positive and loving.

We carry around with us a sphere of influence. It can be one of intimidation and verbal abuse, or it can be one of caring friendship and love. This invisible sphere of influence is not so invisible. Which one do others see us portraying? Let's all play on the same playground and have some fun.

August 23

*F*rustrated and disappointed in our progress on our path, we wonder why life has been so hard for us. It's one setback after another, and our progress on our journey seems to have come to a standstill. Could it be the education choices we made? What about life's choices? Are these the reasons we have fallen behind and not where we want to be? Of course, we have tried hard, yet we have stumbled, fallen, and virtually fell into mud and mire, getting nowhere. Why is this happening to us?

WAKE UP!!! It's time to stop making excuses and start making a difference, not only in our life, but in the lives of those around us. Many of the perceived obstacles are of our own making, and so we can fix those. We stumbled because our shoelace was untied. We're in the mud and mire because we didn't see the foot bridge a few yards away. It's time we start taking control of our lives; stop making excuses of what we think is holding us back on our journey.

So the question is this; when did I get in the way of myself? Once we push away the self-generated excuses, we will begin to live life. We will begin to see miracles come true. We have to have some faith and belief in ourselves. It is then; excuses slowly fade away as dust on our path. Get ready, here we come.

August 24

The concert is about to begin. The crowd has been gathering for hours, and it's time for the headline act to come on and perform for the massive crowd. The crowd chants and screams, over and over as the time gets closer and closer for the rock star to make his appearance. Then the crowd goes wild as he comes on to the stage to play his music. Wild and excited, the people spend the next ninety minutes listening and singing, truly enjoying the experience. Wow!

Are you a rock star? Do you have thousands of people screaming your name? Most of us would answer those questions as, 'no', of course not. The truth of the matter is, certainly you are a rock star. While we may not have thousands screaming our name, we are special.

We touch lives each day and leave a little of ourselves behind with each action and each word. We can never tell how many lives we touch by simply being ourselves. When we are authentic in our words and actions, our true self is revealed to those around us, and they can see it is okay to take away the mask and let the real inner self be revealed.

Are we a rock star? Of course, we are. The difference between us on the one that the crowd screams about is that we don't have make up, perform on a stage, or rely on others to make us look good. We simply need to be ourselves, with the dream to make a difference in the lives of others by living our life with courage, truthfulness, compassion, authenticity, and love. Can we do this "Rock Star?" We can and do each day. Make a difference today and every day.

August 25

*C*an we handle the truth? Maybe the first question we should consider; what is the truth? The truth is typically one person's perception of an event, concept, or idea that they believe to be factual. It doesn't mean it is actually true. There is one truth, and it is the 'absolute truth' which may be beyond the grasp of mankind. We will take 'our truth' and spin it slightly by our words and articulate it the best way we can. While it may be very close to the absolute truth, it remains our truth. So... can we handle the truth when someone tells us their truth?

Next, can we find enough courage to tell our truth? It does take courage to speak our truth because sometimes we doubt ourselves and the accuracy of our truth, or we don't want to hurt someone else's feelings. Our truth is just that, our truth, and we should feel embarrassed about telling it, but how we tell it is where the challenge comes in. The term, brutal honesty is just that, brutal, hurtful, or vengeful perhaps. We should consider replacing brutal honesty with loving truth. When we speak our truth, do it with our heart and not with hurtful words. If we speak our truth with love and compassion, our truth will come from our heart.

Welcome the truth, for lies and dishonesty are ever changing, but the truth is the truth.

August 26

In the science of physiology, it has been told that one of the strongest muscles in the body is one that comes from the Achilles tendon and is under the calf muscle. While it may not be the largest muscle, it is one of the strongest. We use our muscles each day to move around, work, and play. Muscles are connected to one another and when working in unison, they are stronger. We use them for all sorts of activities and when we strain them, we learn of new muscles we didn't know existed. Muscles must be used and if not, then they simply grow weak and die.

There is one muscle we use, and it is so strong it can move mountains, or beat our strongest enemy. It is as durable as steel and sharp as a razor. It is our tongue. When we lash out, the sharp tongue cuts through and cuts deep. It can rip to shreds in mere seconds, what has taken years to build. Working alone, our tongue can destroy relationships, burn bridges, and utter words that cannot be taken back.

We also have another muscle that works for us each day, our heart. Physiologically, our heart pumps blood throughout our body, but there is also a magical component to our heart. Within our heart live our personal values. And when we use this muscle, our heart, in conjunction with our tongue, we build bridges, not burn them. We mend wounds with words of forgiveness and love. When we use our tongue as an extension of our heart, we serve others and make a difference in the lives we touch.

It's time to exercise our muscles in unison, to express our values and change lives.

August 27

The young single mother finishes up the dinner dishes, and she sees her fourth-grade son working on his homework at the dinner table. Diligently, he works on writing on his lined paper, trying not to make a mistake on this very important assignment. He has to erase a word or two, and that's okay. He closes his notebook and packs his books in his backpack. His assignment is done.

The young mother walks over to the table and asks her son what was the homework assignment he was working on? He tells her it is a writing assignment titled, "Who do you admire most?" She asks if she can read it, and he hands it to her. She reads…

My mom because my mom hasn't lied to me. My mom is there for me. She goes to my games. She goes to my practices.

I love her and she loves me to. My mom and I joke around. She said that she would go around the world to find me and my sister. I will miss her when she dies.

Tears fill the young mother's eyes, and she asks, "Why'd you feel the need to write that last sentence? Do you think I'm that old or what?" His response was, "…most of all you are the best mom a boy could ever ask for, and I know you will always love me and be my best friend no matter what, which is why if or when you die, I will lose both and it will break my heart."

Tears streamed down her face as she laid the homework on the table and hugged her son as tight as she could. No better gift could have been given to her that night.

This story is real. This story is a living example that we teach our children values by living them ourselves. This mother taught her son love, compassion, service, and honesty. These values are from the heart, and if we can find ways to teach our youth these values, the world will be a better place. Living our values, just as this young mother does, makes a difference in the world. This is our homework assignment. [3]

---

[3] This true story has now reached hundreds of people, maybe thousands... and has made a difference. This story was told with permission of Ashley W. of Oklahoma and her son, William. Thank you for allowing me the honor to tell your story. You both inspire me.

August 28

*T*rust is that confidence in someone or something will meet some set of expectations, whether or not these are clearly outlined. Trust is the reliance of someone's integrity, confidence to be unwavering and true. It's when the actions of others, failing to meet the expectations of the trust we gave them, are we hurt. It hurts because we have a level of honesty and integrity which we're measuring the actions of others.

Some may say they longer trust anyone because of all the hurt they have experienced in life so far. Going through this life, traveling on our path, trusting no one is such a sad journey. It is the actions of others that have caused us to feel this way, and we can blame them, whoever 'them' are, or we can choose not to let 'them' cloud our trust in others. We should not allow this distrust of everyone be the result of a handful that had wronged us in the past. It's time we find forgiveness for them and move on with our journey. Trusting others should not be blind, but judging and condemning everyone by not trusting them is far too cynical to those we will meet on our path.

We need to trust ourselves to make right choices, to live a life of integrity, compassion and forgiveness. Trusting no one is a sad and lonely journey. We need to find faith in mankind, faith in ourselves and to learn to trust both. Trust is hope, faith and love; we shouldn't cast it aside.

August 29

Ann, Bill, Lisa, Bruce, Linda, Dave, Barbara, Lance, Kelly… are names of people, not just proper nouns, people, living human beings. These words are not necessarily unique, but are associated with one or two people we may know. These are people that are in our lives and are walking along side of us on our journey. We should be grateful for each of them.

How does it feel when someone we may casually know remembers our name and uses it to greet us? Doesn't that make us feel special? Of course, it does. To show the proper respect, let us remember the names of those who are part of our journey. We honor the stranger we just met by remembering their name. This stranger is possibly our new best friend. So the next time we see them, greet them with a smile, extend our hand, and use their name. We just made them feel special. We made them feel they are important to us and in doing so, we have made a difference in their lives.

Using a person's name is a subtle way of saying, "I respect you and honor you, for who you are."

August 30

The art museum is filled with beautiful works of art. The art, some detailed, others wild an abstract is viewed by many. The paintings are filled with color, and the artist has portrayed a beautiful aspect of life. Each color from his palette has expressed what he was feeling or an image in his mind. His life, his dreams and the things he lives for are painted on this once blank canvas. His art is admired by many for its beauty.

Each day we start with a clean canvas. We pick up our palette, and we begin to paint our life, our dreams, and what we have in our heart. Our brush is our words and actions, and the colors are the bright vibrant colors when we paint with our personal values, or they could be the dark and depressed tints of character defects. We have our brush in hand. The color palette is prepared. The blank canvas stands before us. It's time to paint.

With each stroke of our brush, we add to our blank canvas throughout the day. At the end of our day, our painting is done. Did we create a beautiful piece of art? Or did we paint a dark, void of bright colors canvas? Which piece of art do we want others to admire and talk about?

August 31

The night slowly comes to an end, and morning is making its way into our day. We wipe the sleep from our eyes, and we lie there, remembering we had a dream. The pleasant fantasy of the night is a little cloudy, but we still remember little parts of it as we begin to gain consciousness. Oh the night with its sweet dreams and times for rest. The dreams begin to fade as our mind starts to focus on our day.

As sad as it may be, many of us let our dreams fade into a distant memory as we go about our day. We allow our dreams only to exist when we sleep, when, in fact, we need to have our dreams more real when we are awake. Our dreams can be that lake house overlooking a beautiful pristine lake, surrounded by tall trees. Our dream may be to create a business and serve wonderful pastries and exotic coffee. Our dream may be to travel to distant lands and see all the wonders of the world. It is these dreams that are closer to reality than those we have while we sleep.

A dream is a dream of a dream. And this is the first step in fulfilling our dreams. We must dream while we are awake. Write these dreams down on a little piece of paper or in a small journal. We can't simply stop there. We must revisit each one and see what we are doing in our lives to make these dreams turn into reality. It is up to us, no one else to make these dreams come true.

Dreams real or imagined... we determine their reality by our actions.

September

September 1

As we walk on our path, we will find others walking theirs, and we will travel with many along our journey. Some of these other travelers are not always good traveling companions. They will try to take us off our path and onto another one that leads us into some troubling territory. Some of the people we meet along the way may be abusive and cause us physical and emotional pain. Some may say to turn the other cheek and forgive, but the answer may be to turn away, get back on our own path and forgive; wishing them no harm, but we need to take accountability for our travels.

We will also meet some on our journey that are good for us, support us, and help us carry our load. They will love us when we find it difficult to love ourselves. They will lift us up when we stumble and will hold our hand through the rough spots on our path. A few of these special people will walk with us all the way to the end of our journey, our destination, yet their path and journey continues. Some may say these are our traveling angels, human in form, and angel in spirit. There is just something special about these traveling angels that walk with us. We may not see it right away, and perhaps we may never see it until it is too late, but rest assured; we have them in our lives.

Turn away from those that lead us in the wrong direction and abuse us, and welcome the traveling angel that seeks only to help us be a better self and to enjoy this life we have been given. Be grateful for each traveling angel that walks with us on our journey, for they are very special.

September 2

"It's impossible." The moment we say that or think that, we have accepted defeat and will not try any more. Others may come back and say, "Anything is possible." It's the battle of the glass half full or half empty, and it is the one we choose that takes us on our journey. We can be quick to accept defeat and surrender, or we can use every ounce of our energy to make things happen; accepting the daunting tasks and challenges head on.

We may be also quick to doubt ourselves too. Our surrender to the 'impossible' are "I'm not smart enough." Or we may think, "I'm not handsome or pretty enough." The excuses for surrender go on and on, but few, if any are really true. When we give up quickly we miss the opportunity to see the miracle. That miracle is not someone else doing for us when we give up, it is us doing it for ourselves. We have the strength and determination to face whatever challenge comes our way and not let it defeat us. We can be more, do more, achieve seemingly impossible feats, when we believe in ourselves and not let the 'impossibles' get in our way.

Our limits are in our mind, so anything IS possible. With a simple punctuation mark and a single space, we take 'Impossible' and make it, "I'm possible."

September 3

O ur journey has not been perfect. We have made some mistakes along the way and our actions have caused us to hurt others, maybe not intentionally, but none the less; we still hurt them. We truly do not know how much pain we caused them, but we need to find it within ourselves to seek forgiveness and admit our wrong doing. Simply saying, "I'm sorry" is usually lacking true sincerity. It's when we admit to this person that we were wrong, and do not continue the sentence with the word 'but'.

When we use 'but' in our amends, we are saying, ignore what I just said, here's my excuse for my actions. We need to acknowledge that we were wrong regardless of the circumstances. We need to take ownership of the pain we caused and find ways to make it right. No excuses, no 'buts', simply ask for forgiveness. Depending on the way we seek this relief of our wrongs, the other person may find compassion in their heart, or we may discover the pain was too deep and hurtful so forgiveness is not coming. A sincere amends is what we need to try to do. Acceptance of it is not our choice; it's theirs.

There is one amends we can control the acceptance; it is the amends to ourselves. There are not 'buts' in this amends, for we know the truth in our heart. We need to seek our own forgiveness for the guilt and remorse we carry. Easy? No way! It will be one of the hardest apologies we will ever make, for we know, deep inside, what we did and the hurt we caused. Self-forgiveness is one of the keys to help us find our way back onto the path of joy and happiness.

Be gentle on ourselves and find the love in our heart to forgive and love ourselves for who we truly are; a good and caring soul.

September 4

Our path brings to a beautiful pond. The morning fog hangs just above the water, and the only sound is a bird in a distant tree. It's so peaceful and serene; we just want to take a moment and take in all this serenity. We sit on the grassy edge of the pond, and we reflect on yesterday and the day before. What were the lessons we learned? We learned hatred can be eliminated with love. We saw how ambivalence is overcome with compassion. We learned fear is removed with courage and faith. We discovered life is worth living and not merely existing. We find the answers to our early-morning questions, not in analyzing with our mind, but listening with our heart.

The sun has now topped the trees across our serenity pond, and the fog is slowly dissipating. This is our sign; it's time to leave and get back to our journey. As we stand, we pick up a small flat rock. Placing it in the curve of our fingers, we skip it across the glass-like surface of the pond. Seven skips we count before it sinks into the peaceful water. The small ripples of each skip show us that our actions will ripple out and will touch the lives of others. The seven skips tell us we will touch seven lives; we just don't know who. Remembering the lessons we learned, as we sat by our serenity pond, we can cause our ripples to be courage, faith, compassion, living life to its fullest, and most importantly, serving others with love.

We make a difference and have a ripple effect on others when we live our personal values.

September 5

S ome of us have been known to fall, skin our knees, fall on our elbow, or twist an ankle, nothing really serious but a bruise or a scrape. We put an ice pack on it, maybe a band aid, and it will be fine in a few days. We're sore and may limp a little, but it is certain we will survive our injuries.

But what about the bruises that are not visible, the ones inside? The bruised ego, the scraped up self-worth, what about those injuries? How did we sustain these internal bruises? In some cases, we may have let someone inside, and we allowed them to use us as a punching bag. The injury is more than hurt feelings; it's deep and painful. So where do we find the first aid for these bruises? Ice packs, and band aids will not work. We find our treatment in the comforting touch of a friend's hand and soft voice reassuring us. We discover healing within ourselves, by our own voice telling ourselves that we are who we are; no less and no more. Humility and gratitude for our lives heal the hurts. When we can be right-sized, not too big and not too small, we rediscover who we are and our bruised egos and scraped self-worth start healing.

Just as with the twisted ankle or scraped up knee, we will survive these other bruises too. We have a beautiful flower within our soul, and we need to nourish it with a belief, we are worthy of its beauty. It's time we looked into the mirror and see the swan and not the ugly duckling. See it and believe.

September 6

We carefully map out our course; each detail planned out. We have done our homework; we know what needs to be done before we venture out. We have our map and all our supplies for our journey today. Confident of success we set forth on our path, knowing we have not let off any detail.

It's within minutes, we are facing some unexpected turn of circumstances. This has never happened to us before, so it didn't even enter our mind to plan for it. All our plans, all the details we so carefully mapped out are now in jeopardy. How did this happen? Why us? We did our best in outlining the steps for today and now this.

We have some choices now. We can just fall down and sit on our butt, beating ourselves up about not thinking it through enough, or we can accept this turn of events and make a new plan. The choice is simple; pity-pot or action ladder. If the journey is as important as it was when we did all the initial planning, then the only option is the action ladder. Look at the new situation; take what we learned in the initial planning and come up with a new plan. The path is still there, though it may take us in a direction, we didn't plan. Our journey seldom goes as we planned each day, so we need to be prepared to be flexible and adapt to changes. The choice should never be to give up and fall into the pity-pot.

A new journey lies ahead, and it will be challenging and rewarding. We need not to dwell on the little bumps along our path, but look ahead to the beautiful journey that awaits us.

September 7

Our handouts are neatly sorted, stabled in the upper left-hand corner, three-hole punched. Perfect we think for our presentation at today's meeting. Twenty-five slides in the deck; already loaded and primed with the first slide. We rehearsed our script over and over, making notes in the margin to emphasize important points. We're ready. We're prepared for the hour long meeting to begin.

The crowd assembles, taking their seats in the tall leather chairs surrounding the large mahogany table in the boardroom. We're given the nod to begin. Slide one comes on the screen, and we begin. The hour passes quickly making one point after the other; right on track and it comes to the end with five minutes for questions. The first question is totally out of left field, and the question has missed the point completely. The next question is equally out of the blue and not relevant to the presentation. How could they miss the point? We went rehearsed this over and over. We knew the material, and we thought we presented it well, yet the last hour seems to have been a waste of time. The impact of our message was lost. Where did we go wrong?

We can pick up that huge rock of guilt and carry it around, blaming ourselves for our perceived failings. Or we can accept the fact that we were prepared and presented the material well. Those that missed it were either answering emails or playing games with a little bird on their phones. What we don't realize there were people in the room that understood the message and learned from it. We need to drop that rock of guilt and feelings of failure. We need to hear that voice in our head, "Stop beating yourself up. You have nothing to feel guilty about." That rock weighs heavy on our heart. It's time we drop it and move on, with the promise to ourselves to try harder the next time.

September 8

$\mathcal{W}$hy do we get up in the morning? Many of us may answer this question with the fact we have to get up and go to work; to earn a paycheck, to pay the bills. Yes, that's true, but what are the other reasons we get up in the morning? Isn't there more to life than simply following the same pattern?

Our path seems to develop a rut and over and over, we follow it, making it deeper and deeper. The groove in our path is now over our head, and we cannot see over the walls. We are on a path; the walls of the rut block our view; we can only see what we left behind, and the path in front of us appears to be a single path leading to who knows where. We have set ourselves up to a single path to a destination, leaving all the beauty and joy of our journey above the walls of our rut.

Obscure and almost invisible we discover a narrow set of stairs on the side of the walls of our self-worn rut. Here is our chance to escape our monotonous path. We climb the stairs and as we get close to the top, we see sunshine and feel a gentle breeze. We reach to top of our rut, and we see beautiful fields of flowers, and hear birds singing their morning song. The smell of fresh air fills our chest as we take a deep breath. We have been missing all the beauty of nature has to give us.

The blinders of the walls are removed, and we can now answer the question differently. We get up this morning to take in all of life as we can. We experience the beauty of nature and share in the joys of our fellow travelers. Our journey is too short to be stuck in a rut. Find the stairs and climb out; there is so much waiting for us on the top of our path. Enjoy the journey today.

September 9

*I*t's early morning, and the house is quiet and still. Nothing is stirring this early in the morning; yet we're wide awake. We climb out of bed, walk down the hall and peek around the corner into the living room. The Christmas tree lights are off, but the ornaments on the tree twinkle from the street light shining through the front window. Gifts, all neatly wrapped, cover the area under the tree. The wrapping paper is colorful and bright. We can hardly stand it. Our heart is racing, wanting to know what is in each of the pretty packages. Our eyes are wide open, taking in all the colors and twinkles of lights. We are excited about today.

Why do we hold back all that joy and excitement to a single day? Each day we are given a gift. It may not be wrapped in colorful paper, or under a beautifully decorated evergreen, we still receive a gift. Today is that gift. Today is wrapped up in a beautiful sunrise of the morning and the early-morning sounds of bird's singing. Today is a special gift because we are given another day to talk with a friend and share laughter. Today is a gift of sharing a smile with a stranger or helping someone at the grocery store find which aisle something may be found. This gift of today is more valuable than we give it credit. The gift of today is wrapped up with a beautiful bow called love.

We need to get giddy and fill our heart with joy and happiness, like a child on Christmas morning, with this gift we are given today. Share this gift with others and don't hold back the joy and excitement to a single day, celebrate it every day. Today brings us a life and for that we should be grateful, joyful, and happy. Don't wait until Christmas, celebrate today and get giddy with life.

September 10

The small boy plays with his wooden blocks; stacking one on top of the other. Connecting a longer block to the two stacks, it creates a peak. In the little boy's mind, he sees a tall skyscraper, towering over the city below. His mind sees perfection in his tall tower-like building, yet the blocks are not straight, and it teeters, slightly unbalanced. The child sees none of this; he sees his dream of building a tall structure.

The little girl plays with her dolls, dressing them in one outfit and yet another. Holding them around the waist, she pretends to dance them across the floor, like a princess at the castle ball. She sees herself in that pretty dress, beautiful and perfect, dancing and being in the spotlight. She is the princess even for just these few minutes.

Imagination... creativity takes us from our self-imposed box into a world of limitless opportunities. We can take the approach that the wooden blocks are not straight and in perfect alignment, or we can see our dreams of a beautiful home, or mansion on a hill. We can look in the mirror and see what appears to be the Cinderella in his work clothes, cleaning the floor, or we can dream and see ourselves as the Cinderella on the dance floor with Prince Charming.

We have dreams, and we have the power of imagination and creativity. It's time we left our self-imposed limited box and dream, and since we're dreaming, dream big, really big. We hold ourselves back from dreaming, and we never see our full potential. Remove the barriers and get on with life and live it to the fullest. Imagine, living our wildest dream. Wow! It starts today. Imagine! Dream! Believe!

September 11

By now, we have all seen many remembrances of the most tragic event the United States has gone through in modern history. We are sad for the losses that many families have suffered. We are sad for all the innocent victims of such an act of cowardice. We are sad that such a horrific act has happened, but we need to see how this day has brought Americans closer and more united. Yes, our travel has been interrupted by additional security, and we are more aware of our surroundings. This day, now years ago, did not defeat us, but made us stronger as a nation.

The toll of September 11, 2001 continues today in the loss of American service men and women serving in harm's way today, protecting us from future acts of terrorism. Each day we go to work, take our children to school, take a vacation, or celebrate a holiday, we owe a huge 'thank you' to all those that are protecting this freedom. We have the freedom to live in a country that is filled with hope, joy, and love.

While we made shed a tear today and have a solemn heart as we remember as we watched the horror unfold, we also need to share our love with others. Hold someone's hand, place your arm over someone's shoulder, and hug someone who is having a rough time. We are a nation of compassion. We are a nation that wants to comfort others. We need to share the love that is in our hearts with others. Today is a day to let others know we care, because, we do.

September 12

he statue of a man, his elbow on his knee and his chin resting on his hand is the statue we're all familiar with, the great Thinker. Perplexed and serious in his facial expression, it depicts a man, in deep contemplation, thinking of what? What is the Thinker trying to solve or is he just dreaming of great things to come? The artist leaves all these questions to be answered by those that view his art.

So we find ourselves in deep contemplation too at times. We are thinking of all sorts of things; our plans for today, which path to take and perhaps even deeper thoughts into our life's purpose and why we are where we are. What is the big picture? What is the big plan for us in our lives? We ponder these questions and many more. We think about what is immediately before us on today's agenda. Perhaps we think about how we can comfort the sad, or add joy to someone else. We think about how we can serve and love others better today than we did yesterday. We think and think.

It matters not what we think, but what we do. Doing for others is really what matters. We can be frozen in thought, just as the Thinker, or we can find our way into action and begin to make a difference. If we spend more time in doing than thinking, we touch the lives of so many and our purpose of life will reveal itself, we don't have to ponder it. The great Doer, or Giver is the statue we should look for to find within ourselves.

September 13

T.G.I.F. What a minute. It's not Friday yet. What's up with today's Thought of the Day? We use this abbreviation for giving thanks for a particular day, probably because it is at the end of a workweek for many. Yes, it brings a level of gratitude for surviving (for some; it is just surviving) to the end of a week and beginning a couple of days off for some. However, our life is just not getting through a Monday through a Friday; our life is much more than that.

Our life includes components of career, family, fun, friends, personal growth, health, financial, spiritual, and more; yet we only celebrate one day. Each day we are involved and working on one or more of these components, and each day is another day to improve our level of satisfaction, our level of improving each one. This is life. This is what we do each day and some days we focus on one component more than the other, maybe it's the weekend, and we're focusing on family and fun. Maybe it's Tuesday, and we're celebrating with a "Take Out Tuesday." Each day is as important as the next one, or the last one. Each day we grow, we learn; we live our lives; we serve others. Today is special, in one way or another; we may just have to open our eyes to see how special it truly is.

So, T.G.I.T. ~ Thank God It's Today.

September 14

Serving others is a wonderful purpose in life and for those that share this purpose, we touch the lives of so many. We feel good about ourselves when we do something for someone, and his or her life is a little better as a result. Not an ego booster, but self-satisfaction that we were able to get out of ourselves and make a difference.

Along with that purpose, a dark cloud may appear. This dark cloud is fear; fear of failing to fulfill our intended purpose of serving others. Fear of not meeting the expectations of others, leads to a fear of disappointment in ourselves. Fear, what a wicked foe, for it beats us down and draws the energy from us; causing us to question our purpose of serving others. We ask, "Did I serve this person as best I could?" Fear answers, "You didn't. You failed to meet their expectations."

Fear causes us to carry too much of this burden of expectations, failing promises, not living up to the standards we set for ourselves, or the burden of disappointments. These weigh heavy, why?... because we care about others. Eliminate the fears by reminding ourselves that we're doing the best we can, with what we have and when we see that we have, we don't allow that fear to weigh us down. We can stand tall, knowing we did our best in serving others. As we reflect this evening on how well we lived our purpose in serving others, we will take that inventory and then, we will promise ourselves one thing, we will try again tomorrow. With that promise, fear will not dog our sleep.

September 15

Sunday dinner at Grandma's home is always extra special. It's not only the special dinner she makes, the fabulous dessert afterwards, but it's the little stories she shares; imparting her wisdom to all that will listen. Walking into her home, we are once again not disappointed by the aroma coming from the kitchen. The smell at Grandma's home is a smell that is comforting, safe, and peaceful. Is it just the smell that overwhelms us as we come in, or is it something else?

We always try to get Grandma to share with us her secret ingredients in whatever she prepares. She simply says, it nothing, just a little of this and a little of that. We know better, there are secret ingredients. Enjoying dessert, Grandma shares her stories of when she was a young girl and each one we sit intently, mesmerized. Recounting each one, we feel as if we are there. Each one told is a special way, sharing her wisdom. Another secret ingredient can be found in her wisdom.

Just as our Grandma makes a difference in our lives by her wonderful cooking and telling her stories, each one with its own secret ingredient, we too have the same secret ingredient available to us. It's not on the pantry shelf or in the refrigerator, it is within our heart. The secret ingredient grandma uses in all her wonderful recipes and her fascinating stories is love, and love is within our heart too.

That sense of comfort and peacefulness that we found in Grandma's home, is a safe sanctuary, built on family and personal values. Respect, truthfulness, kindness, compassion, forgiveness and so many more are foundation, the secret ingredient. We have the secret ingredient too, and we can make a difference in the world by using it in all aspects of our life. These values are within us, sprinkle generously.

September 16

S lightly under five feet tall, the little guy is wearing his football uniform; pads, helmet, the whole works. He is virtually lost inside all that equipment, but boy does he feel proud he's wearing a football uniform. The coach leans down and tells the potential Heisman Trophy recipient which play to send into the quarterback and that he is to do his best in the next play. The little guy runs onto the field and reaches the huddle with the other players and tells them what the coach said. They line up; the ball is snapped, and the quarterback hands it off to the little guy and he runs. He dodges one tackle and then another; the goal is just yards away when, for out of nowhere, he is tackled. He ran thirteen yards, but not enough to score.

The coach waves him over to the sideline and tells the little guy that he did great. The little boy says, "But Coach I didn't score the touchdown." The Coach asks, "Did you try your best?" The little football simply nods, yes. "Then that's all I ask, just try your best. Now get back out there and let's try again." The little boy runs back to the huddle, and the game continues.

It's not always winning or scoring a touchdown, it about honestly trying. We all have coaches in some form in our lives, giving us guidance and pushing us to do and learn new things. That's how we have grown. These are sports coaches, spiritual coaches, life coaches, or just best friend coaches. Each coach plays an important role in our game of life.

Who are you coaching? Let's go Coach…What's the game plan?

September 17

*T*he early-morning silence is broken by the sound of a distant train whistle. The long blast of the train engine's whistle echoes a long and melodious sound, warning others ahead that it's coming. The train sounds its whistle to protect those ahead and keep them from harm's way. We pause for a moment and wonder, where is this train headed? Is it pulling a long line of train cars, each one with its own destination? Down the rail it goes and the sound of the train's whistle simply fades away and again, silence surrounds us.

Where is our train taking us today on our journey? Our destination may be uncertain, and our path is not restricted to the parallel steel rails of a train. We have choices on the path to follow, and can take a turn without the restrictions of the rails on the ground. Unlike the train, we needn't blow a whistle to warn others ahead of our pending passing through, protecting them from our journey.

We have a whistle to blow, but when we blow our own whistle, it isn't to let those ahead to stay clear; it is merely to bring attention to ourselves and has nothing to do with others. Tooting our own whistle is a sound that is anything but melodious.

So when we hear others blowing their own whistle, it is a warning to us, beware of this train, for it has a long line of train cars filled with ego. Be warned; stay clear, for that train is one headed for a wreck somewhere down its rail.

Let's silence our whistle and learn to find ways to serve others as we travel our journey of our life's purpose.

September 18

Many of us subscribe to the local newspaper. With that subscription, we expect a newspaper to be delivered to our home, usually in the morning. Those are the minimum requirements. However, a wet newspaper thrown on the lawn while the lawn sprinklers are watering our grass is virtually impossible to read. A paper lost in the bushes somewhere is impossible to read, or one that is never delivered. We have certain expectations with our subscription and when they are not met, we usually end up calling the subscription office to complain and threaten to cancel our newspaper delivery service.

But then... what about the newspaper that is wrapped in a plastic bag every day and in fact, double bagged on days when rain is forecasted? What about when the newspaper delivery person is willing to get out of their car to place the paper on the porch when they know there is a need? What about the paper being delivered by 4:45AM each day? Do we call the subscription office then? Probably not... why not? Why not give some accolades to those that go beyond the standard requirements?

We get so wrapped up in our own lives that we sometimes fail to see that others are serving us beyond what is necessary, and we don't take the time to acknowledge it and thank them for what they are doing. We should not accept double-bagged newspapers, or carefully placed on our porch as the norm. Be grateful and find a way to thank them.

What are we doing today that will go beyond the expectations of others so that we may serve them better? Double-bagging today?

September 19

As we walk into the building, we see an escalator, elevator, and stairs. We only have three flights to go up, so it's a simple choice. If we have a physical handicap or are loaded down with 'stuff', then the choice is obvious, either the escalator or the elevator. If we're physically capable of climbing the stairs, and not carrying a bunch of stuff, why do we avoid the stairs? Using the stairs would give us a little exercise in our day, and that's a good thing. Using the stairs is not taking the easy way, but it is a good way.

We tend to follow the path of least resistance and most of the time it is the escalator or elevator. We rationalize our decision of not taking the stairs in that we're in a hurry, or the doorway to the stairs is 30 steps out of our way, and even a self-made promise that we will take the stairs the next time. We go through life looking for the "E"-Way (escalator or elevator) or easy way, and not the way that may benefit us. If we go through life looking for shortcuts, and always take the "E-Way", then when we're faced with only stairs, we're stopped in our tracks. What do we do? We look around for the escalator or elevator, and they are not there. We don't see the stairs because we are only focused on finding the "E-Way" and we become stagnant.

There are many paths on our journey and not all of them will have elevators and escalators. We need to take the stairs more often, so when we're faced with challenges and there is no "E-Way", we still overcome the challenge, and our journey will continue. Going up?

September 20

*H*e or she is wearing a business suit straight from the cleaners. The shirt or blouse is pristine white, and shoes are highly shined, and yet there is something that seems to look a little out of place. What is it? They appear to be ready to walk into any boardroom and make a profound entrance and powerful presentation. Still, there is something not quite right.

IT'S GOOFY HAT FRIDAY!!! Yes, adorned on the perfectly combed hair of each one is a crazy hat. It may be a pink princess hat, with fuzzy trim and flowing white lace coming out of the top, and that's on the gentleman. The business lady sports a brass Viking helmet with two horns coming out of the sides, pointing upward. Yes, we smile as we imagine such images, and it's not even Halloween.

We take ourselves too seriously sometimes, and we need to let go of the starch and rigid lifestyle and have some fun. Today will be over before we know it, and if we didn't smile and have some fun, we sure missed an opportunity to make today special. So as we go about our day today, and we see a business man or woman, all dressed up and professional looking, imagine the princess hat and Viking helmet and a smile will come to our face. Or if we're stuck in bumper-to-bumper traffic, look at the driver on either side and imagine them wearing a rainbow-colored wig. See? A smile…

Happy Goofy Hat Friday!!! Don't forget to smile today.

September 21

We walk by the vendors' tables at the big event and look for the 'free' stuff. We may have some interest in what they are representing, but if there is free stuff, we suddenly become more interested. It could be a simple plastic tote bag, a pencil or pen, a letter opener, or a ruler; each one with the logo and contact information of the vendor. So we take each piece of free stuff, not because we're interested in their product or services, because it's free.

We spot some really nice books, or canvas tote bags and our 'free' radar zooms in for the kill. It's not as free as the other things we have gathered so far, we must fill out a survey card with our name, address, email, and phone number to sign up for their mailing list. We know we're going to get unwanted calls or emails, with no intention of buying, but what the heck, we get more free stuff. We get all this stuff home, and it gets piled up with all the other free stuff from the last event.

Nothing more than a form of greed, we get into a mindset that we expect things be given to us for free, and that we don't have to work for them. These thoughts of entitlement don't teach us responsibility. We think the world owes us a free ride, well; it doesn't. If we think along these lines, we are self-centered and ungrateful, because we constantly want more free stuff.

It's time for us to give away free stuff. Give away our time in serving others. Give away our care and compassion with a listening ear. We have some much free stuff to give away, and when we give it away, we receive so much more in return.

September 22

Many days we focus our energy on serving and helping others. Today it's about YOU!

It's about YOU because YOU give and give and ask nothing in return.

It's about YOU because YOU are beautiful and brighten each day with a smile.

It's about YOU because YOU are powerful and make a difference in the world.

It's about YOU because YOU are grateful for all the glorious things YOU have in your life.

It's about YOU because YOU dream dreams and don't let the past hold YOU back.

It's about YOU because YOU are wise and share your wisdom with humility.

It's about YOU because YOU love unconditionally.

It's about YOU because YOU are here with a purpose and the sooner YOU discover it, the sooner YOU will make a bigger difference in the world.

It's about YOU because YOU inspire others.

It's about YOU because YOU because there is no one like YOU!

Just continue to be YOU because we all need YOU!

September 23

Sadness, anger, joy, love, and so many more are feelings we experience in life. These feelings become so strong sometimes, we don't think we can bare the pain of sadness or anger, and we choose to chemically suppress it with alcohol or drugs. We take a pill or take a shot, followed by another because the feeling is still there; it's not gone away fast enough. We know better than to try chemically erase these feelings, but some will try. Feelings and emotions are okay. They are part of life, and we can survive them.

Like a pendulum, swinging back and forth, so are our feelings. Sad and depressed at one point of the swing, we feel joy and happiness on the other. The more extreme the swing, the greater the emotion has an impact on us. With the deep heartfelt sadness of the loss of a family member at one peak of the pendulum, it will swing back to the other side, and we will know joy and happiness like we never have felt before. The pendulum swing of anger and resentments will be replaced by a love and compassion that we could not have dreamed.

From one extreme to the other, we experience life and our feelings are part of it. If we try to suppress them, then we don't get to enjoy the full effect and power of the good ones like joy, happiness, faith, compassion, and love. Feelings are meant to be felt for when we feel, it means we're alive and experiencing life. Feelings are not the end of the world; they are just part of our journey. Embrace the fact that we can feel emotions, from one extreme to the other. Life can be an extreme sport sometimes, hold on; get the full effect of the ride. When we swing to the bright side, it will be brighter than we could have ever imagined.

September 24

"Go this way." We say to our friend. "No, this way is faster." Our friend says back. They insist they know what they're going and before we know it were stuck in traffic. The 'I told you so' is running around our mind and we so badly want to say it. We can feel the blood rushing up our neck as we sit in traffic. The movie starts in fifteen minutes, and we're going to be late. We hate being late and we think, if they had only listened to us, we would be pulling into the parking lot by now.

So we pout and sit silently in the car, which is not moving in this traffic. Disappointment, anger, frustration are all spinning around and the tension builds. If they had only listened to me…

NEWS FLASH!!! Not getting our way is NOT the end of the world. Yes, it is true; the world will not stop because we didn't get our way. Yes, we will be late for the movie. It's not a big deal. It really isn't. The situation caused us to develop anger and tension with our friend for what? A movie? Really? Is our friendship so cheap and weak that we allow a movie, or not getting our way cause a friendship to be put into jeopardy? What we should be sad about is the fact we missed the time we could have spent talking and sharing stories with our friend, while stuck in traffic. We could have laughed about the situation, instead we pouted because we didn't get our way.

Not getting our way is just not that big of a deal. We allow our ego to think we have all the answers, and it must be our way. Well, we may have good ideas and make suggestions, but if it doesn't go our way, tell 'ego', it's not a big deal.

September 25

The day starts just as most mornings with the alarm going off, or the kids waking us up wanting breakfast. Our routine is set in motion, and our day begins. It seems as though we have little variance in our start of the day, but in reality, we have more control of our day than we appreciate.

The day will be as good or as bad as we decide to make it to be. We can see the rainy skies as dreary and depressing, or we see it with the excitement of seeing a rainbow later that day. We can view the tasks that lie ahead as drudgery, or we can see how what we do making a difference in the lives of others. Look forward to find the beauty in the day ahead, not the ugliness that seems to creep into our mind. See that we are one of many not wallowing in a pit of darkness, but are with others that share in a state of gratitude.

We get to choose the see the good or the bad as we begin our day, and by that choice so will go our day. Which is better? The frown of the depressing thoughts of how bad today will be, or the smile that we have been given the gift of another day, and we plan to make it the very best day we can.

Find the good at the start of the day and cast away the bad and the ugly. By doing this, our day today will be fantastic, and we will smile throughout each moment.

September 26

*I*t is somewhat human nature to judge others because we're comparing their actions and what they are saying with our beliefs and feelings. We're looking at their external being and comparing it to our internal one, and by doing so, we're judging them. Now this judgment does not always have a negative aspect; it could be just the reverse. We could be looking at this person as a hero or some superior being. Again, we're comparing their external with our internal, which could be a feeling of low self-esteem.

Placing a person on a pedestal, towering above us, some sort of god-like entity is setting ourselves up for disappointment. If we do, and for some reason, they fail in our eyes, we don't see them as human, but as a superhero that can do no wrong, and our "hero" bubble is burst. But they are human, just as we are.

If we judge a person as inferior and we cast them aside in the gutter, our internal is being fueled by ego. We are not really looking at our internal being very closely. We are not seeing our faults in life, only theirs. The only time we should look down upon someone else is to give them our hand to help them up.

Those that find fault in others, should find a mirror and look to see theirs first. And those that place people on pedestal should find a mirror and look to see their value and self-worth. Our mirror will guide us to the right answers when we begin to compare someone's external with the internal we see in the mirror. We need to look closely in the mirror and see our true ourselves.

September 27

We elbow our way through the crowd, being a bit of a bully, just to get to there, wherever 'there' is. We are on a mission. We push and push, causing anger in some along the way, pushing and shoving. Our adrenaline is pumping and our energy is focused on one thing, getting through the crowd and getting whatever is causing this mass of humanity. We successfully have now reached the destination, bullying our way through, pushing and shoving, having little concern of others in the path of destruction we left behind, only to find... whatever it was we were so adamant in getting wasn't there. We turn around and face the crowd we so cared little for and simply walk back through the mass of people, wondering why we had such a little concern for others to allow this event to take over our life for that moment.

There are also times when we bully our way into the lives of others too. We seem to be on a mission of a different sort. For whatever reason we think we know what is best for someone else, and we push and shove our way into their lives. Reaping havoc along the way, we have blinders on, not seeing the damage we're leaving on the side of the path. We do this with a false sense of 'we know what's best', or 'we're doing it because we care'. Pushing and shoving our opinions into someone's life can be counter-productive. Who says we know best? Who left us responsible for someone else's life?

Sometimes the best thing we can do is leave the other person alone. We need to make sure they know we care about them, and that we're there whenever they need us. It's their journey, and they must walk the path that is before them. We can walk beside them and help, but we should not bully our way into their lives.

September 28

It just takes one hand to help someone up.

It just takes one eye to look into the heart of a loved one and make them feel loved.

It just takes one smile to make a new friend.

It just takes one heart to touch the life of another.

It just takes one thought to create a dream.

It just takes one step to follow that dream.

It just takes one handshake to build a bridge of trust.

It just takes one glimmer of faith to clear away the clouds of fear.

It just takes one act of kindness to be worth a million dollars.

It just takes one kind word to show care and compassion.

It just takes one laugh to lighten the day.

It just takes one hug to for two people to feel as one.

It just takes one whisper to sing a beautiful love song.

It just takes one friend to lighten the load of the rocks of burden of a friend.

It just takes one beacon of hope to light up the darkest path.

It just takes one service to others to make us rich beyond measure.

It just takes one day of living our personal values to create a legacy worth more than any bank account or mansion on a hill.

It just takes one minute of our day to make a difference in the world.

It just takes one, just one of us. Are you that one?

September 29

$\mathcal{M}$ any of us have a boss we report to, while others may be self-employed or unemployed and do not report directly to another individual. Our boss gives us projects and tasks to complete and in return, we are compensated each pay day. All these efforts are for the end result, keeping our employer in business, and we're a part of that whole process. We are part of the organization that is providing something for someone, and we're helping make a difference.

Now our boss may come in and may attempt to motivate us to work harder or complete a project faster with the promise of a bonus or pay raise, or something else that is above and beyond the normal compensation system. So we work a little harder, now motivated by the carrot that dangles at the end of the bonus pole. This type of motivation is if we do something extra, someone else benefits from our efforts. Yes, we are rewarded with the bonus, but in the overall scheme, it's about the company's initiative. There is nothing wrong with motivation; it has its place in the world.

However, let's consider another concept, inspiration. Would we go the extra mile, or put forth the extra effort if there were no additional compensation? Would we do it for free? In some cases, we will say 'yes', and it's this situation where we're not motivated, we're inspired. We feel in our gut that doing the extra work we will make a difference, and we feel good, no… we feel better, knowing our work goes to the greater cause. We do this because we're witnessing others and their actions. We're inspired to step up and go that extra mile.

Motivation is in the mind; inspiration is in the heart. Motivation is short-lived; inspiration is a life-long passion. We can make a difference in every life we touch if we are inspired. Be inspired and inspire others.

September 30

*I*t is a wonderful morning. The sun has just made its appearance on the eastern horizon. The sky is filled with beautiful warm colors, washing away the darkness of the night. We are ready to begin another day of our journey and look to see what wonders lie ahead. It's not too far along our path do we see a beautiful flower bed, filled with bright red and yellow flowers. We take a moment to enjoy its beauty when we suddenly notice a humming bird silently flying around each blossom, taking the nectar for nourishment. The hummer seems to float in air, and we simply watch in amazement. As we watch it go from one flower to the next, we think for a moment that it looks at us, and there is a connection for just a second. Then we see another one, flitting around, and it hovers and seems to look at us too. It's just that second we connect, as if it were an angel, hovering so close, letting us know it's there. In an instant, they disappear.

We may not see another hummer along our journey today. We may get so wrapped up with our day we forget about the hummers, our little angels of nature, but they are there. There are other angels in our lives too. These angels don't have tiny wings, hovering effortlessly, flying from one flower to the next. These angels are not so recognizable either, yet they are there, just as the hummers. Our friends are our angels, walking with us on our journey, protecting us along our way. Sadly, we don't see our friends as angels, our little hummers, and we take them for granted.

So as we travel on our path today, and we're lucky enough to see a hummer, see it as an angel watching over us and letting us know it's there. When we see that friend that has stuck with us through thick and thin, see them as a tiny hummer, our angel, and be grateful.

October

October 1

*T*he A, B, C's of life are as basic as the A, B, C's were in first grade. These A, B, C's of life are not complicated, actually quite simple. As a child we learn our lessons in school, and we learn the alphabet from A to Z; then in living we learn life's version of A through Z.

- A is for authentic. In life, we don't need to hide behind a mask. It's okay to be who we are and not pretend to be someone we're not.
- B is for benevolence: An act of kindness and the giving of the gift of our time leave a legacy that is worth more than all the gold in Fort Knox.
- C is for compassion. Life's lessons are not always easy and when someone close to us struggles through their challenges, we need to show compassion to help alleviate some of the pain.

Sometimes we learn certain letters of the A, B, and C's from the wrong teachers in life. These lessons are sometimes hard to forget too.

- A is for arrogance. Our ego rears its ugly head of presumptuous superiority.
- B is for belittling. Voicing our opinions of others that they are less than, with no basis is nothing more than an ego monster.

- C is for cold-heartedness. The lack of sympathy or care for another being is almost being void of a heart. Cold and callous, we serve no one.

Learning the A, B, C's of life is part of life, and our teachers come in so many forms. As students we put these lessons into action each day, and then we become the teacher by living the A, B, C's. Which version of the A, B, and C's are we teaching?

October 2

O ur path today takes us along the edge of a park. A small lake is surrounded by trees full of green leaves. Swans slowly glide over the still water, and children play nearby. We see couples holding hands as they walk slowly along the path around the lake. The warm sun and gentle breeze set the stage for a wonderful and pleasant part of our journey today.

Our path brings us to a bench facing the lake and an old man is sitting there, looking out to the lake. There, by his side, is his dog sitting quietly, occasionally looking up to the old man. We have been walking for a while and could use a short rest, so we ask the old man if we could join him on his bench. He turns, and gestures that it would be fine. Still no words spoken, we sit with the old man and his dog enjoying the scenery too.

"That is a pretty dog. What is its name?" we ask. The old man reaches down and pets his dog behind its ears and says, "Her name is Love."

"That is an unusual name for a dog, but I like it. How did you come to that name?" we ask. Smiling, the old man doesn't look at us; he simply continues to look into his dog's eyes, scratching her fur behind her ears and says in a low voice, "I give her food and water. I bring her to the park for a walk. In return, she greets me with her tail wagging as I return from the store, and she sleeps at the foot of my bed at night. We nap together in the afternoon, and we share a cookie later. She gives me unconditional love; so pure and real. There isn't a better name for her, than Love."

We see it in his old eyes and the eyes of Love that these two are bonded together, and their love for each other is strong. "There is too much anger, hatred, people holding grudges, and harboring resentments in the world today. We don't to add to it ourselves. What we all need is a dog named Love." The old man explains. We smile. As simple as his words are, we hear his wisdom and agree. "I would like to hear more about your life. Will you and Love walk with me on my journey and share your words of wisdom?" we ask. A tiny tear forms in the corner of his eye, reaches down and pets Love again and says, "Thank you, but I have reached my destination, and I just want to spend the rest of my day with Love. I wish you safe travels on your journey and that at some point along the way; you find your Love."

We get ready to leave. With a tear in our eye, we thank the old man, and we reach down and pet Love. Her beautiful brown eyes look up at us, and we can feel her love. As we walk away, we stop for a moment to look back to the bench where the old man and his dog sat. The old man is gone, and Love is still sitting beside the bench. We're sad, but hear the old man's wisdom of how the world needs more love and less anger and hatred. Love is still there, just waiting for someone else to accept what she has to offer; unconditional and ever-lasting love.

October 3

It would be easy to step it down on the exercise bike today; it's just one day. Instead, we step it up a notch, a little higher resistance and set the timer for 5 minutes longer than normal. It's almost like our hands are not our hands setting the controls on the bike. We push through the morning exercise.

Walking through the break room a work, we see a box of fresh doughnuts and a bowl of fresh fruit. Without hesitation our hand reaches for the fruit. Again, almost like our hands are not our hands. These invisible hands are taking over and making choices for us.

We go about our day, and these invisible hands continue to keep us on track. We're driving to somewhere for lunch. Instead of the burger barn, our invisible hands take us to a salad smorgasbord. What is it with these invisible hands?

Each day we're faced with decisions. Some decisions are easy, but not always the best choice. It's our invisible hands who help us through some of those tough decisions on what is best for us.

These invisible hands are the hands of self-discipline; driven by our conscience, these invisible hands know what the right choices are for us. We tie our invisible hands sometimes with the rope of rationalization; justifying wrong decisions with fabricated facts. It's time we untie our invisible hands and let our self-discipline take over.

Have we untied our invisible hands yet?

October 4

*F*ruit is an interesting food product, in particular, fruit that is seedless. We have seedless grapes, oranges and other fruit. We also have fruit that is not seedless, such as apples. So if seeds are what perpetuate another plant, how does seedless fruit grow another plant? Do the growers genetically alter the plant?

Are we seedless? (Not in a biological sense) Have we been altered by the growers in our lives? Those that have nurtured us, helped us grow, planted seeds in our lives that allowed us to grow into who we are today. Many seeds taught us right from wrong, while other seeds were ones of anger and resentments. Seeds flowered into beautiful flowers of self-worth, care, compassion, and love. Yet, the seeds that caused the weeds of guilt, selfishness, and low self-esteem also flourished in our garden.

We are not seedless. We plant seeds, not only in our own garden, but in the gardens of others. Our seeds are cast, and the even the slightest breeze will carry them to gardens far away. Are the seeds we plant in our lives and in the lives of others growing beautiful flowers filled with gorgeous blooms? Or are the seeds we plant grow the prickly ugly weeds of life?

We are our own gardener, and the seeds we choose are the ones that will grow. As we plant ours, so do we plant seeds in the gardens of those we will touch today. Pick out the seeds that are rotten and put those away and plant the ones that will grow and make all of us better gardeners.

October 5

The hometown football team scores a touchdown and the crowd cheers. During the team's next possession, the quarterback fumbles the ball and the other team scores a touchdown. Our team is down by one point as the game played out. It's the fourth quarter; our team has the ball on the twenty-yard line, with only four seconds in the game. The ball is snapped to the quarterback; he goes back to pass, and...

The conclusion of the game is not important. Win or lose, who was responsible? Was it the coach? The quarterback? Any of the other players? So during the postgame interview, if our team had won the game, the quarterback gives full credit for the line holding the other team back and gives credit to the receiver for his agility in catching the ball in the end zone. If our team had lost, in the same interview, the quarterback accepts the blame for his poor pass or for the fumbles during the game that caused his team to lose.

A true leader in life accepts no credit for when things go well, but accepts all the blame for when they don't. We give credit to the production team for meeting their goals; it wasn't us that did it; it was our team. We acknowledge others for their accomplishments and take no credit. However, if the project fails, we must step up and accept all the blame. True leaders inspire others by praising them for the good things in life, and takes on the burdens of blame for the not so good that happens.

Taking no credit, but all the blame is a hard pill to swallow, but how many have done that for us? It's likely we didn't see it, for a true leader just takes care of it.

October 6

We pass by people every day; never knowing who they are or what is going on in their lives. Making very little eye contact, if any, with these strangers in our day, we simply go about our day, doing whatever is on our agenda. In our own world, and them in theirs, we simply scurry from place to place, like mice in a maze.

Then it happens. Our eyes meet the eyes of a stranger and for some unknown reason we get a glimpse into their heart. It could be the single mom that carries one child in her arms, while another stands close by in the grocery line. The single mom just was laid off, and the former spouse is not providing any financial support. She can't afford to go to court and the rest of her family is hundreds of miles away. We can see it in her eyes; the despair, pain and the sense of helplessness. The groceries on the counter add up to more than she can cover with little cash and state supported coupons. We look and see it nothing special or out of the ordinary; diapers, milk, cereal, peanut butter, jelly, and one special treat for her girls… simple staples for this young mother and her children. Embarrassed, the single mother must start making choices what not to buy. Item by item the cashier removes it from the total.

We step up a little closer and tell the cashier; put those items back on the counter, we will pay for her order. The young mother looks into our eyes, a tear forms in the corner, and simply says, "Thank you." The little girl looks up to us and smiles. We smile back. The young mother and her children take their bagged groceries and walk out. The cashier says to us, "That was very kind. Thank you."

A simple act of kindness that was only $40 or so, yet it touched the lives of five people. So are we little mice scurrying around in a maze, oblivious to those around us today? Or are we looking into the eyes of a stranger to see who they are and maybe touch their life with a simple act of kindness as simple as holding the door open.

October 7

*O*ur early-morning run starts out great. The air is cool, but not cold. The eastern horizon is slowly coming alive with color. We're on a good pace, and it looks like we will meet our goal today in making our miles. Our stride is good; our breathing is now in a good rhythm. This is going to be a great run.

We didn't notice our shoelace was coming untied. We were focused on the run and making our time. One foot strikes the ground; the long shoelace dangles off the other shoe, and our retreating foot is now suddenly stopped as it leaves the ground. We stumble forward; throwing out our hands to break our fall. Our palms and knees strike the ground, and we stumble forward. Pain is now shooting up our arms and legs… we gather ourselves for a moment. We see our knees and hands are scraped up and a bleeding, but we're really okay.

We get up, evaluate our injuries, and then realize; it was no one's fault but our own. We failed to tie our shoelace tight, and we simply tripped over our own shoelace. We can beat ourselves up over our clumsiness, or we can tie our shoe again, get back up, and continue our journey.

As we walk our path on this journey of life, we will stumble over our shoelace, fall, scrape our knees, and feel embarrassed. We can never allow the power of a simple shoelace stop us from our given journey. We must get back up, brush ourselves off, tie our shoe, and continue. Whatever the 'shoelace' may be; we are stronger and determined to follow this path that lies before us. We will get in our miles, and we will make our minutes, never letting a 'shoelace' stop us.

October 8

We go about our day, walking on our path, not a care in the world. Suddenly, without warning a huge hairy creature jumps out from the bushes and is standing in front of us, blocking our way. It growls and snarls, showing its teeth. The words coming from this ugly creature are words condemning others and spreading half-truths, trying to convince us these others are evil and are not worthy. Casting false accusations, our hairy monster continues to banter with pure ugliness of others, people we don't even know.

This monster is the ugly and vile creature called gossip. It comes out of nowhere and tries to take us off our path and follow it into the darkness of judgmental and character assassinations. It pulls us into its grip with little white lies, and soon the poison will enter our system, and we begin to feed on its vile words. The monster is a monster of sorts, but in reality, it is a mask, covering up an ego-filled, self-centered weak creature. The mask hides the insecurity and weakness but casting harsh and cruel words about others; trying to make the gossip monster look better than it truly is.

How sad that the monster, with its ugly mask, has to stoop so low as to spread rumors and hurtful words about others, just to feel better about its self. We have a defense against this monster who has stepped onto our path, trying to take us into its den of darkness; we simply not engage in a conversation with it. Its evil words are not worthy of a verbal exchange. We simply look into the evil gossip, walk around it, and continue on our journey.

Gossip is evil, hurtful, and has no business in being part of our journey. Our journey should be filled with our values of care, compassion, courage, and love. With these values as part of our everyday journey, life is good.

October 9

You are one of a kind.

You are one voice that speaks volumes.

You are the one that has a dream that will impact many.

You are very special to someone else.

You are a leader by inspiring others to dream more.

You are no longer wearing a mask, hiding your true-self.

You are serving others when you think of them before yourself.

You are bringing joy to the hearts of many by sharing your smile.

You are a good friend that listens and does not judge.

You are a hero to a little child.

You are loved by more people than you realize.

You are happy

You are here for a reason and have a purpose in life.

You are rich with a treasure chest of values

You are that one that will make a difference in this world.

Yes, YOU ARE, all of these and much more.

Be happy... Be blessed... Be grateful... Be loved... Be yourself.

October 10

We find ourselves today pushing an empty wheelbarrow. It is well constructed and is easy to push as we start on our path. As we go along, we pick up rocks and put them in our wheelbarrow. We continue our journey, still gathering more stones and placing them in our wheelbarrow. It's becoming a little harder to push, but yet we still add more and more rocks. Our path is not smooth, even the slightest hill becomes very difficult to travel, pushing this ever increasing load of rocks. Our wheelbarrow is full and very heavy. We think we can add one more rock, and when we do, the wheelbarrow topples over, spilling our load. Our wheelbarrow has exceeded its capacity, and the axle of the front wheel is bent; the handles are splintered, and all the rocks we gathered are scattered.

These rocks are the rocks of burdens we carry. We pick them up as we go about our day, adding to our stress and mental anguish. These are the rocks of anger and resentments, of disappointments from failed expectations, of painful situations, and we continue to fill our wheelbarrow. And when we cannot stop picking them up or releasing some of these, our journey becomes very hard to travel. Why do we pick up these rocks of burden? Some of the stones we gather are not even ours to pick up, yet we reach down and pick them up and add them to our already full load.

Our wheelbarrow can only carry so much and we need it to light and easy to push on our path. There may come a time during the day to stop, evaluate the rocks in the wheelbarrow, and toss some aside. Look closely at the stones we pick up and ask ourselves, do we really need to carry this load on our journey?

October 11

*O*ur eyes begin to adjust to the morning's light, and the sleep is washed away. A good night's sleep begins our morning with a sense of serenity and contentment. Our first thoughts should be of gratitude and recognize that we are blessed with another day. We are blessed knowing we have family that loves us. We are blessed knowing we have friends we can trust and count on when the times get rough. We are blessed with the ability to serve and inspire others with the love from our heart.

We are blessed to see all the miracles and wonders that have been graciously come into our lives and into the lives of others. How precious the miracle in seeing a little boy looking out the window, watching the snow gently fall from the sky and say, "Snow Mama!" How sweet is the miracle seeing two lovers walk hand-in-hand in the park and share a little kiss? Miracles are the little smiles of the triplets that are now home with their Mom and Dad after a long stay at the hospital after they were born.

Miracles are everywhere. We simply need was away the sleep from our eyes, count our blessings, move into gratitude, and the miracles will magically appear. We will wonder how we missed seeing them before. We see them today because our eyes are now synchronized with our heart. Look for the miracles, not with skepticism, but with love.

October 12

A gentle breeze fills our sails as we steer our vessel from the safety of the harbor into the ocean ahead. This is yet another part of our journey, and we must leave the quiet cove and venture to new ones. The light wind pushes us through the calm water, and we eventually lose sight of the harbor behind us. It is just us; our vessel, the clear blue water of the ocean, and a gentle breeze. Quiet and peaceful, our journey continues.

There will not always be calms seas and following winds. We will find the ocean turn ugly and rough. Our gentle breeze is now fierce and gusty. Our vessel is tossed about like a small cork. We still have some control; we can set our sails and steer our vessel. While the storm and rough sea give us challenges, life gives us the same. We're faced with challenges in life, like the harsh ocean and gusty winds, but we cannot sit idly by, waiting for the storm to pass. We must batten down our hatches and trim our sails. We must take action and not let whatever storm we're facing deter us from our journey. The sea will once again be calm and peaceful as soon as this storm passes and when it does, we will know that we can face our next storm, rough seas and gusty winds, and get through it as well.

The challenges of life are opportunities for us to grow and learn. We learn how we can weather the rough seas of life and how to trim our sails for the uncontrollable winds. Fear not the storm and all its turbulence, but fear giving up and being washed overboard into the ocean's abyss.

October 13

I t's early morning in the forest, and the sounds of nature begin the morning's wake-up call. The light on the horizon filters through the tall trees and begins to illuminate the forest floor. There, on the top of the rise, is a small cabin. Smoke coming out of a small smoke stack and a flickering light shines through a small window from an oil lantern. The hermit begins his day. He is completely isolated from the world; no electricity, no radio, television, or phone, the hermit lives in total isolation from the rest of the world. Alone, without any other human contact, the hermit tends to his needs and serves only himself. A life void of friends and family is the life the hermit has chosen.

There may be times in our lives when we may think the hermit's life would be wonderful. The hassle of traffic, the impatient customer, the noise of construction, or the constant pressure to meet deadlines, all adding up to unbelievable stress. We want to escape into the woods and find peace and serenity. Is that the solution? Isolation? A hermit's life?

Just as the hermit serves only himself and cannot fulfill a purpose in life and when we isolate and crawl into our own little world, we stop living a life with purpose. We stop living our values and fall into a pit of self-pity, and we think being alone is a good thing and will solve our problems. Well, it won't; in fact, it makes it worse. So before we follow that path of a hermit's life, into a pit of self-pity, reach out to a friend. Grasp their hand and hold on. Whatever the situation, whatever the issues we are facing, the hand of a friend can be the best guide to the solution.

Running away and isolating is not the answer. It serves no one, including ourselves. Reach out to a friend for help, or be that friend to help someone else.

October 14

Someone's life is a little better today because we held the door for them.

Someone's life is a little better today because we simply said good morning with a smile on our face.

Someone's life is a little better today because we let them over in traffic, so they could make their exit.

Someone's life is a little better today because we made the coffee for our coworkers, even though we don't drink coffee.

Someone's life is a little better today because we sent an email to a long distant friend, just to say hello, and that we were thinking of them.

Someone's life is a little better today because we picked up an extra doughnut for a coworker.

Someone's life is a little better today because we held the hand of a friend while sad tears rolled down their cheeks.

Someone's life is a little better today because we gave them the bigger piece of the homemade pie.

Someone's life is a little better today because we shoveled the first season's snow from the widow's walkway.

Someone's life is a little better today because we took the time to read a book with a child.

Someone's life is a little better today because we told them we loved them.

We see that it doesn't take much to make someone's life a little better by a simple act of kindness. It takes little of our time, yet the reward is priceless in that we made a small difference in their lives. We touch the lives of so many, and it is through our values do we make a difference in the world and make someone's life a little better.

October 15

*D*arkness is the absence of light. Absolute darkness is not only the absence of light; it is also the absence of hope. There may come a time during our lifetime when we find ourselves in absolute darkness and by the mere fact we're there, we cannot continue on our journey, we are paralyzed. We can't see which way is up, and we won't move in any direction because we are in fear of what may harm us in the absolute darkness. This overwhelming sense of helplessness grows as each moment passes as we remain in this state of absolute darkness. When we find ourselves in this absolute darkness, we have a void of love in our heart for others, and sadly, we have a void of love for ourselves. We begin to curl up into a small ball to find comfort within our own body.

The fetal position is not the solution to our dilemma. We need to stand, reach out and feel all around us. Reach for that friend's hand. Call out their name. Reach for that light switch that will turn on a little glimmer of hope. It's time we help ourselves find a way out of this absolute darkness. And when we find that light switch, absolute darkness begins to disappear, and we are led away from the abyss of our own self-made darkness.

The light switch that takes away the absolute darkness was never far away in the first place. It was right there within our reach all the time. The light switch is the touch of a friend's hand who brings light to our darkness. The light switch is a faith within our heart that will bring that glimmer of hope. It is courage, faith, and love; all working together that makes up our light switch which brings light to our darkness. The light switch is within each of us and there isn't any reason for us to be in absolute darkness ever again.

October 16

"Well, that was easy." We probably have said this to ourselves at some point in our lives. When it comes to us easily, whatever 'it' may be, we are not so upset when we lose it. "Easy come, easy go," we may think to ourselves. When things come to us with little or no effort on our part, we take them for granted, and we don't value them like we should. So what if we lose 'it', we will get another one any time we want one. It's like the child getting an allowance each week for some small chores around the house. They are not difficult and take a little time, and the allowance of five dollars comes each Saturday. Now that same five dollars that they had to work for, mowing a lawn, raking leaves, or shoveling snow is valued so much more. It's the same five dollars, but the value is greater in the child's mind.

It's when we work for something that does not come easy, and in fact, we may fail during the process, but when we do get it, we treasure it. We value the reward at the end that took effort, our sweat equity. We find this to be true in so many aspects of our lives and the one that is in everyone's life is relationships. If we make friends easily, then we probably won't even notice when a friend no longer calls or sends us a text message once in a while. However, when we work on a relationship because we value that friendship, it is the one that will last a lifetime. It will be the one that we can't seem to get that person out of our mind. When we work on ourselves and not try to change others, this work pays off in developing a solid and long-lasting bond of two people. The work is not easy, but the reward is so worth all the effort.

"Easy come, easy go." This is for the fool who takes too much for granted. Recognize that working toward a goal or a relationship is what brings true value to our lives. Life is not about getting an allowance each week; it's about working hard and earning the reward at the end.

October 17

 $\mathcal{M}$ any of us will start the day with a cup of coffee. Some may even go to a fancy coffee shop to order, almost in a foreign language, their cup of coffee, while others take it black, right out of the pot. And still others will simply add a little milk or cream. In any case, we start our day with the cup of goodness in hand.

There is another cup we should fill each morning to start our day. We should fill this other cup with words of kindness. Kind and caring words are needed and appreciated by each life we will touch today. To add just a little sweetener to our cup of kindness, add kind and caring actions. This sweetener can last a lifetime. Our cup of kindness has a special flavor, a hidden ingredient, and that is love. Love is the magical ingredient that has brewed this cup of kindness we hold.

If we find our cup running low, simply reflect on our own life, the gifts that were so freely given to us; the memory of the kindness of others will replenish our cup of kindness. Refilled with the kind words and actions that touched our lives in the past, we can now continue our day with a full and overflowing cup.

We should not let one day go by that we speak and act with kindness and love. We should fill our cup of kindness every morning upon waking. Acts of love and kindness make a difference to everyone we will touch and if more people would start their day with this cup, the world would be a much better place. Be kind to everyone, even the stranger, for we do not know what has brought them into our lives. Be of service with our cup of kindness and love. Ready for a refill?

October 18

*T*oday is a day for new beginnings, a day to let gratitude pour from our hearts. We are all blessed with loving family and caring friends, and these are so special. We are also blessed with a roof over our head and food in the pantry. We are also blessed with miracles in our lives and one that we sometimes forget is that we are a miracle too. We are all miracles. The sooner we realize this; we find gratitude and humility.

Gratitude is not limited to a single day on the calendar. It is the attitude we should begin each morning and reflect upon each evening. An attitude of gratitude is just that... an attitude which we can do something about. We can focus on all the things wrong in our life, and in the world, dragging ourselves as well as others down, or we see the world, and in particular, our life as the miracle it is.

Some may struggle with finances, health issues, relationships, and other issues, and it's hard to be grateful at times. However, if we look within our heart, we see a twinkle, a flicker of hope and with that tiny speck of hope in all our despair, we see love. And with this little glimmer in our lives, it is worthy of our gratitude.

Be grateful today and every day when we can get up in the morning and greet the morning's sunrise. Be grateful today for the opportunity to do something nice for someone else. Be grateful for who you are, because we are grateful for who you are.

Gratitude it is an attitude, and even more; it is a way of life.

October 19

LEFT LANE CLOSED AHEAD, the flashing sign on the side of the road blinks its warning. EXIT CLOSED – DETOUR AHEAD, reads the sign as we approach our exit. Now what? We always use this exit and now, because of construction, we have to go out of our way to get to our destination. We could lash out some verbal expletives or pound our steering wheel in a tantrum. We could have those fits of anger, but did it make the detour go away? The construction and detours are necessary for improvement and eventually will make our travel better; we just need to be patient.

As in life, we may not always get to go the way we want. There will be times where construction and detours will come up without warning, and we are taken off our path, and directed to a new one. The construction of our journey is there for improving ourselves, though it may be hard to see when we're starring at the detour sign. We adapt with the new path and direction.

Our journey is not a race to see who can make it to the destination the fastest; it is measured by how well we cope with change and how we open our minds to these new paths. The detour sign is far behind us, and we are set on our new path. This new path brings new opportunities to make our life, and the lives of others better.

Don't curse the DETOUR sign; see it as an opening to new ventures.

October 20

O ur eyes begin to open early in the morning, and we look at the time; it is 7:00 AM!! We have over slept. We jump out of bed only to find the toilet is backed up. So still in our pajamas, we find the plunger and fix the problem, and we think to ourselves this is not a good sign on how the day will be. Showered and dressed, we skip the coffee pot, and rush to our car. After starting it, we see the gas gauge is near empty, we forgot to get gas last night on the way home. Yet another delay causes us to be even later. Somehow, by some miracle, traffic is not bad, and we're only a few minutes late. It's only an hour into our day, and we're exhausted, frustrated, stressed, and ready for 5:00 PM.

All this stress and anxiety are washed away in a flash, when we learn that a close friend has just lost a loved one. We may get a call, a text message, or whatever, but it hits us hard, knowing our close friend is in need. All our problems are no longer important. Our focus and all our energy is now channeled to providing comfort and support to this friend and their family. This is what is important now and nothing else matters at the moment. This is love in action.

It's a matter of perspective. We get so wrapped up in our own little world and our insignificant perceived problems; we forget that there is someone we know may be having a worse day than us. If we approach each morning with a sense of gratitude for what we have and with a sense of care and compassion of others, our day will be filled with love. The over-sleeping, toilets backed up, and empty gas tanks are really not a big deal. What is a big deal is expressing and living a life that is centered around love; love of others and love of ourselves.

October 21

*I*n our hand, we hold a large ring of keys. The keys are made up of many shapes, sizes, and obviously designed for special locks. Some of the keys have a letter or letters engraved in them. We hold this ring of mystery keys, knowing the ring and all its keys are here for a purpose.

On our journey, we come to a locked gate, blocking our progress. It has been a stressful journey today, and we don't need anything else to interrupt our travel, and yet we have this locked gate. Remembering our ring of keys we have, we examine the lock on the gate, noticing its unique design. We then search for a key with a similar design, and we find one with an "A" engraved on it. It fits; the lock opens, and the gate swings open. We walk through and are overwhelmed with peace and serenity. The key was the key of Acceptance. Acceptance of others for who they are and acceptance of who we are, and with this key, we discovered peace and serenity.

On another day, we may notice that we seem to be weighted down, like a heavy steel chain around our neck and shoulders. We can't seem to let remove it, so we can progress on our journey. The chain has a massive padlock in the links and no matter how hard we fight it; we cannot remove it. We take our ring of keys and search for one to unlock this heavy chain of resentments and anger. The key with "F" appears to fit and the lock opens, and the chain falls away. The heavy load of the massive steel chain is gone with the key of Forgiveness.

Our journey is a never ending one, and we face many challenges. We may at times feel unfulfilled, lacking an emotional connection. The lock box of our heart and soul needs to be opened. We now know, our ring of keys is the solution. We find the key with a "L," and it opens our heart. This is the key of Love and when we open this lock box and let love pour out; the emotional disconnect is now gone. When we open our heart to love ourselves, then we can learn how to love others more deeply.

The ring of keys still has many keys that we may use only once, while other keys are used many times. The keys on our ring are our values. Our values will unlock any door, any padlock, or any locked box; we simply need to use them.

October 22

*O*ne of the most influential inspirational speakers and mentors of our lifetime passed away this week, Zig Ziglar. A leader in so many ways, he touched the lives of millions, and his inspiration will live on through those he touched for many years to come. The great leaders around the world knew Zig Ziglar and Zig Ziglar was a man who cared for every man and woman he met; rich or poor, elite or common, each one he never judged, but tried to inspire with his words.

We have seen many quotes over the last few days as a tribute to Mr. Ziglar, and this one, in particular, rings the message for today's Thought of the Day.

"If you go out looking for friends, you're going to find they are very scarce. If you go out to be a friend, you'll find them everywhere." – Zig Ziglar

Many of us never met Mr. Ziglar, but very few will not know who he was and what impact he had on the world. In this quote, he inspires us to be the friend we wish we had in our lives. It's not about us, it's about them and being a friend to someone who needs someone they can count on. It's about being of service to others and sharing our heart with another human being. It's about love and friendship. While we may not be able to change the world like Mr. Ziglar, we can change the life of one person by being their friend.

Mr. Ziglar… we will honor you today by reaching out to be a friend to someone. We will seek to inspire others through our actions and our words as you did. Mr. Ziglar… you made a difference in this world, and we thank you.

October 23

We put the key in the ignition, hoping our car will start this morning. It does and we let out a sigh. The gas gauge is below a half of a tank, and payday is still four days away. So it's off to work we go. Waiting at the stop light, a shiny new Mercedes pulls up. The driver is talking on their cell phone, laughing having a great conversation. The light turns green and we go on our merry way to work. We wonder, where was the fancy Mercedes going? Who was that person? Obviously, some successful family that has few cares in the world. And now we look at ourselves, comparing them to us, as we pull into the parking lot at work.

We have the sense of being less of a person from this morning's encounter. The situation has probably happened many times in the past, but today, we felt different; we felt we were not as good, not as successful, and not as pretty as the driver in the fancy new car. We felt overwhelmed with payday being days away, needing gas to get to work, much less buy any food for the week.

We are slipping down a muddy slope headed to a pit of self-pity. So we grab a limb of a small bush to stop us from going further down this muddy slope. We are grateful for the limb being there. Holding onto the limb, we begin to think, what else are we grateful for? Perhaps we are grateful for a loving family and loving friends. Suddenly, another limb appears and we grasp it. We are grateful for a job, a home, and so much more and with each new thought of gratitude, we are no longer on the muddy slope to the pit of self-pity. We are standing in the sunshine of life.

We don't need to compare our insides to the outsides of others. We are blessed with so many riches that go beyond the shiny new Mercedes. Today let's remember how rich we really are

October 24

*I*f we spend less than we earn and take a portion of that and save, we will accumulate wealth. Wealth gives us the ability to live a good life and have everything in life we desire. It also provides for our family what they need in their lives. Accumulating wealth can add to the legacy we will leave behind when our time here has come to an end. With all this wealth, are we rich?

Rich is difficult to define. Does being rich mean, we don't have to balance the checkbook each payday? Is being rich buying expensive jewelry and fancy cars just because? Or is being rich that sense of fulfillment we feel when we do something for someone else, expecting nothing in return? Can we experience the sense of being rich with an abundance of love in our heart? When we give our love away in serving others, the dividends we receive in return far exceed anything a monetary investment we may make.

The legacy we leave is not valued on what the bank account balance is; it is how we lived our lives. Reaching out and helping others, being caring and compassionate, and serving others in helping them achieve what they want from life is the legacy we will want to be remembered by. Our bank account balance is not our legacy. Our legacy is how we enriched and inspired the lives of those we touch. We are rich even when the bank account balance dwindles to our last ten dollars.

October 25

*T*here is a crowd around the customer service counter, and we work our way to the ticket number machine and take a number. It's 56 and the electronic sign says, "Serving 41." Now we're in line. We finish there and go to the Department of Motor Vehicles to get a new driver's license, and we see a similar mass of bodies, and we work our way to the number machine, and we take number 7. Their electronic sign says serving number 88. We hope that the numbers will start over at 100. Only one more stop today and the super store parking lot is full, but we have to get some things for dinner. Again, our task is met with yet another line; even the "10 items or less" line is ten deep.

So we spent so much time in lines, waiting for someone else, we seem to accept that waiting for what we want is the norm. We wait in traffic, in shopping lines, all waiting for someone to finish ahead of us, so we can proceed. Are we putting our life on hold, because we think, we're in a line for someone to do something ahead of us before we can proceed too? Are we waiting for junior to finish high school before we go back to school ourselves? Are we waiting for the just the right time to start that exercise program? Is the waiting line an excuse line?

There is no waiting line. We don't have to wait on others to improve ourselves. There is no waiting line for us to seek serenity and peace in our lives. The number machine doesn't exist for us to wait for our number to be called to reach out and help a friend. The express line is empty to send a smiley face text to a friend. There is no waiting line;

there is the 'doing' line, for us to take control of our lives. We cannot afford to wait for this or for that to happen before we begin to live. No more waiting, let's start living; for tomorrow is never promised.

October 26

The Food and Drug Administration (FDA) requires certain products to list the ingredients that are contained in the package. It will be prominently displayed; listing each ingredient in descending order. We quickly evaluate the product on the first three on the list. This, of course is done to protect the consumer from misleading advertising and to keep the consumer aware of the true nature of what they are buying.

Another modern innovation is the barcode. While initially designed around inventory maintenance and ease of pricing at the checkout register, it has progressed to each of us having a barcode reader on our phone, and we can get product details and price comparisons in mere seconds. We, the consumer, are now given a new window to view through into where our hard-earned money is spent.

What if… what if we had to list our ingredients? What would our top three ingredients be? (Yes, some will analytically come up with water as number one.) Is our first in the list, ego or humility? Could it be resentment or forgiveness? Where does love fall on the list of our ingredients? Maybe our list changes from day to day. Our ingredient list consists of our values and defects of character. Which ones are at the beginning of the list and which ones are at the end, are based on how we live our lives? We get to choose the order.

Now, what does our barcode that is tattooed on our forearm tell the person scanning us with their cell phone scanner? Are we the real deal? Or are we some cheap imitation that has horrible reviews? Of course, we don't have a barcode tattooed on our body, nor do we have a list of ingredients for others to look at. We don't need these because our actions and the way we live our life are all that others need to see to make a decision about us.

Each of us have a list of ingredients and each of us has a barcode for others to scan, we just get the choice of what are the top three ingredients and where we rank in quality as a person.

October 27

When a friend has fallen on their journey or is weighted down carrying so many burdens, their lives seem to be at a low point. They can't see the beautiful sunrise, or the wonders of their lives because they have fallen off their path into the ditch of despair. With each passing moment, they become weaker, unable to climb out of the ditch on their own; we extend our hand and help them up.

Out of the ditch of despair, our friend is weak and disoriented. We remove the burdens that weigh them down with caring words of compassion and love. With our strength, we lift them higher, and now they can see the beautiful sunrise, and they smile.

Our good deed for the day is done; we think. If we think, we are limited to one good deed a day, how sad that would be. On our journey, we may pass several others that could use our hand, be comforted with a caring word, or simply sharing a smile in passing.

Good deeds are not rationed, and we have a huge supply stock piled. It's very doubtful we will ever run out of ways to serve others, either by extending our hand, or a simple random act of kindness, or just our smile.

October 28

*D*o you feel like you're the square peg trying to fit in the round hole world? Do you sometimes feel you're always exiting the entrance door or going the wrong way on a one-way street? If the answer is yes to either question, congratulations. Where would we be without those that thought out of the box and didn't necessarily go with the flow of the world?

When we think slightly differently than others, we are exercising our mind and imagination. Imagine the day, not so long ago, when we could not envision a telephone without one of those curly cords attached to a phone base. The round hole world needed the square peg to break through that mindset. We can come up with many more examples of how exiting out the entrance door was the breakthrough to another futuristic advance in our lives. So if we feel like we're just not fitting in, we feel out of place, we need to assure ourselves that it's okay. We are, who we are, and have no reason to feel less than anyone else, nor should we feel bad that we think a little differently than others.

Maybe we're a zebra running with a herd of horses, but when we find the herd of zebras, we suddenly fit in. We are here in this world with a purpose, and we need to discover that purpose and begin to live it. If we're a square peg, find the square holes and live a life of purpose. We should not feel ashamed for being a square peg; we should be proud of who we are, because we will make a difference in the lives of others by being who we are, not how we perceive the world wants us to be. Be yourself and be proud.

October 29

When we allow doubt to enter into our day, we have set the stage for failure. We have given that tiny little grain of doubt the power to lead us down a path where we will not succeed or achieve what we're working toward. That little thought of doubt of our own abilities or a belief in ourselves, sets off a chain reaction and we start planning for the evitable, failure and disappointment.

Why do we doubt ourselves? Aren't we working as hard as we can and doing our very best? We seldom fully recognize our abilities and the power they bring to our life. Many of those around us see it and recognize the fact that we can do so much more. They support us, coach us, and try to get us to see that we should replace that doubt and uncertainty with a faith and belief in ourselves. Once faith extinguishes that tiny flame of doubt, great things are placed before us and our life just got better.

Let's remove doubt from our mind and allow faith and belief in ourselves from our heart control our destiny. We need to believe in ourselves, so many others already do.

October 30

*D*arnn it!!! It happened again. We made a mistake. It is that little annoyance that just sometimes jumps up and takes a little fun out of our day. For instance, we think it is a casual jean's day Friday, and we soon discover, after we get to work of course, we misread the email and it's not a jean's day. It's not a life shattering mistake; no one is hurt, and we are slightly embarrassed. Now we could plead ignorance and try to get through the day by hiding behind our desk so no one sees us, or we could do the right thing and change into the proper work attire.

Few of us will not make a mistake now and then; some are minor errors, while others are huge and impact others. We need to understand; we're not perfect, and we are going to make mistakes in our lives. So if we accept the fact that we're fallible, why can't we accept the mistakes of others? We're not perfect, and we cannot hold others to a different set of standards. Sweeping it under the rug or trying to hide it from others, so we're not embarrassed, goes against what we know we should do. We need to own our mistake; fix it if we can, but don't allow our ego to stuff our mistake away and pretend it didn't happen.

Integrity is a value that stands out and one that is most admired in others. Integrity is doing the right thing when it is easy to just pass it by. We will make mistakes, but when we take ownership and admit our faults, others will not be critical of the mistake we made but will be inspired with our integrity to make it right.

October 31

*A*s we begin our journey today, we notice that there is a fog along our way. The fog is thick, and we can barely see our path. We just don't feel like ourselves as we carefully and slowly meander along our way. This fog seemed to appear from nowhere, and we wish we could escape walking through it, but our path is our path. And right now, the "fog of funk" surrounds us. We're just out of sorts and can't pinpoint why; we're just in a funk and feel yuk.

Meteorologically speaking, the sun will dissipate the fog as the morning progresses. Likewise, the fog of funk will dissipate when we allow the sunshine of gratitude to enter our day. The more we can see how good our life is and all that we have, the gratitude sun begins to shine brighter and with its power, the gratitude sun begins to make the fog of funk go away.

We are responsible for our own happiness. If we're in the fog of funk, then it's time to redirect our thoughts to all the wonderful things we have to be grateful for. Perhaps we are grateful for our family, our home, our job, and the gratitude list goes on. The more we add to the gratitude list, the brighter our gratitude sun becomes and the fog of funk disappears from our path.

If we're not happy, we must change our attitude. We cannot wait for someone else to come along and wipe away our funk feeling. It's ours, and we need to remove whatever is robbing us from our happiness. Happiness is having a perpetual smile in our heart. Happiness is a state of serenity. Happiness is loving ourselves for who we are. Why would anyone choose not to be happy? Why walk in the fog of funk any longer than necessary? It's time for some action. It's time for happiness and gratitude, and the fog of funk will disappear from our path.

November

November 1

*I*t's the holiday season for giving. We go shopping and try to find that special gift for that special someone. In some cases, we spend countless hours searching for the perfect gift, while others simply walk in, go right to the shelf, and pick it up. We then take this special gift and carefully, or in some cases not so carefully, wrap it in pretty paper and place a contrasting colored bow, slightly crushed from being at the bottom of the sack of bows. We're proud of the gift, the wrapping, and well... the bow will just have to work.

What we need to realize, it's not about the shopping. It's not about the pretty wrapping paper and the slightly crushed bow. It's about the time we spent picking out the gift. It's about thinking, and doing for someone else. Giving of ourselves... our time, our listening ear when they need to vent, or give them our hand to comfort when times get rough. It's about sharing a cup of coffee, or sending an email or text message telling that person we're thinking of them. These are the special gifts that will last longer than the gift we buy at the mall.

It is the season of forgiveness, and the season for gratitude. The gifts of care and compassion are priceless and cannot be bought or wrapped. It's the season for love, which warms the hearts of both the receiver and giver. Being a true friend is a gift that will last a lifetime, and we have that gift to give away, regardless of how much money we have or not have.

But wait! All these gifts are not just for this holiday season; these are the gifts we can give every day. Let's be generous in our special gift giving for it will make a difference in someone's life.

November 2

We get out of bed and the routine starts, but the routine is different. We're rushing through the morning and off to work. Traffic is getting worse each morning, which means we have to get up earlier in order to get to work on time. Meeting after morning meeting, and the lunch hour is here. We have to run to the post office to mail a package to Aunt Ann and Uncle Bob. As soon as we pull out of the parking lot, we're in bumper-to-bumper traffic. Finally, at the post office, the line is out the door, and we begin to wonder whether Aunt Ann and Uncle Bob will really miss the homemade cookies. We wait and wait, and the line seems never to move. We're out of there with just enough time to rush back into traffic and get back to work. The day, of course, is only one-third over, we have so much more to do today; afternoon meetings, grab dinner in the drive-through, one of the kid's Christmas Pageant this evening, and yes, it's only Thursday, and we need to get clothes ready for the morning for everyone.

Whew! What a day we think as we finally settle in bed. We go through the mental inventory of the day and try to remember if there was anything we forgot to do. Did the boss get the report we promised? Did little Sally get the cookies for the teacher ready? Did we do this ... did we do that? Our mind continues to race until we finally drift off to sleep, exhausted and drained.

Did we forget something? Yes, we did. We went through this whole day and forgot to take a minute and enjoy this life of ours. We got so bogged down and spun up like a tornado; we forgot to see the beauty of our life. We let this whole day go by, which we can never get back, without seeing the joy and happiness in our life. Did we forget to kiss our spouse and tell them we love them? Did we take a minute and share a smile with a stranger and hold the door for them? Did we think for a fleeting moment of our gratitude list? What else did we forget?

We can allow the world and others to control us, but it is our choice to take a moment and enjoy this precious life of ours. It goes by too quickly not to take a minute of it and reflect on our joy, happiness, the love in our heart. Now, get busy....

November 3

A new day, a new month and a new year has greeted us this morning. We bid the last year farewell last night and welcomed the New Year in celebration and merriment. Today is a fresh start for the rest of our lives and many will make resolutions or promises to us to improve our health, wealth, or some other aspect in our lives. Many of these self-made promises will fall by the wayside, but our intent was sincere when we make them. Whether or not we make resolutions or not, we at least think of how we can make this year better than last year. What can we do better? What can we accomplish this year we couldn't get done last year?

The last year is now behind us and we should not bring all the sadness and grief, anger and resentments it brought into the new year. We need leave those rocks of burden behind us and we do that with forgiveness and love starting today, this first day of a new year. We begin our new journey today, free from those heavy rocks, with a smile on our face and a sense of serenity in our heart. What an awesome start on our journey today!

Let's start moving forward on our path today and every day with a pledge to do our best to make a difference in the world. It can be one person at a time, and if we touch one life, the world will be just a little better. We go forward on our journey today with a caring and loving heart; more forgiveness and compassion in our soul and live a life of values. Living these values each day, we will touch the life of a friend or will make a difference to a stranger, making the world a little better.

Start the day by reaching out and sharing the love in our heart with a friend. It's a day to smile and be grateful for another day to walk our journey.

November 4

The elusive peace of mind evades us and the harder we try to find it, the further away it seems to be. We try this and we try that, but what we're doing is not working, yet, we fight on to find that magical place called serenity. We try soothing tea, a warm throw across our lap, sitting in front of a fireplace, and still our mind does not allow that overwhelming sense of serenity to find us. We become more and more frustrated because not so long ago we had that peace of mind, and now it's gone and we want it back.

So what is preventing us from that peace and serenity? The solution may be simple, yet may not be easy. If the turmoil along our journey is causing this chaos in our head, what part of it can we change? Perhaps we need to find the courage that hides deep within us and change what we can. We need to figure out that we cannot change other people and some situations. We may only have the power to change ourselves. So then, what about those people and situations, we cannot change? The answer to this question is simple, but hard to implement. It's called acceptance. When we stop fighting ourselves over things, we cannot change and accept them as they are, then peace of mind almost immediately follows. The level of acceptance is directly related to the level of serenity.

What we can change and what we must accept that we cannot change can sometimes be challenging to figure out. We find the answer in the lessons learned along our journey. These lessons made us wiser and with that wisdom, we can find acceptance and the courage to take those steps toward that elusive peace of mind called serenity.

November 5

$\mathcal{M}$any of us know what it's like to change a tire on our car. It's not terribly difficult when we have the proper tools; the lug wrench, the jack, and of course, the spare tire. It may be a little messy, and the conditions may not be the best, but the majority of us can take care of it, or watch someone do it for us.

The cause the flat tire is yet another story. There are several scenarios; a slow leak from a nail puncture, a faster leak from a road hazard, or the most extreme, a blowout at high speed. In the last situation, our tire is destroyed causing our car to swerve and possible lose control. Some of us may never experience such an event, but we all can imagine what it must be like in that situation. However, perhaps we have experienced all of these scenarios in a slightly different way.

The slow leak – we go about our life, and slowly we begin to get down in the dumps; our 'tire' is losing air. Joy and happiness are slowly leaking out. It may be caused by the 'nail' of unrealized expectations, or feelings of loneliness. We see it coming, yet we just allow it to leak out of our life until we're flat.

The faster leak – we don't see this hazard coming, and it suddenly deflates us rapidly. It could be that we're all set to set the world on fire; we're energized and then we are suddenly slapped in the face with the realities of life. It may be a job task that failed, or the death of a friend. Without warning, and little time to prepare, joy and happiness rapidly escape from our life.

The blowout – We're unprepared for this catastrophe. It the most rare of all three, but is the most extreme and most dangerous to recover. This is the loss of a job, the loss of a long-term relationship, or the death of loved one. This rips our 'tire' to shreds and everything; all the joy, happiness, and peace are ripped up and there is little left as we try to keep it together on the road.

In each of these scenarios we have the tools to get back on the road, back on our path of joy and happiness. Just like the jack, lug wrenches are the tools to change our tires; we have the tools of courage, faith, friendships, compassion, and love. We have the tools, and they are with us always to get us back on our path, because we may never know when we will need them. Our spare tire is our personal values, and we need to believe in ourselves that we can change any flat, at any time with them.

November 6

The rain has been coming down for days, and our shoes are wet and covered in mud. We walk up to our door and wipe our feet on the doormat; cleaning our shoes as best we can before we walk in our house. Satisfied our feet are clean after scuffing them on the doormat over and over, we walk through the door. The doormat has served its purpose and has served us well. And that is what doormats are supposed to do; allow us to walk on them and clean off our dirt and mud.

Is there another doormat in our lives? Are we a doormat, allowing others to walk all over us, scuffing their muddy shoes all over us? Do we simply allow it to happen, perhaps rationalizing the abuse away? We are fooling ourselves if we come up with reasons it is okay for others to walk all over us. We say, "It's okay; they're having a bad day." Or, "It's okay; they are family." Bunk! Bunk! Bunk! It is never okay to allow others to take advantage of our kind heart and generous soul. We need to find the courage to stand up for ourselves. We need to find the truth within us and stop making excuses that it's okay for others to scrape their muddy shoes all over us. It takes courage to stand up and be our authentic self.

Let's think for a moment. Are we treating someone like a doormat? Are we abusing that relationship to take advantage of them, so we can look good, or get what we want in life? Our gain should never be at someone else's pain, and we should never look down upon anyone and treat them as something to wipe our mud away.

It's about values… respect, courage, compassion, care, honesty, authenticity, and probably the most powerful value, we hold dear… love. If we live these values, the only doormat in our lives is the one at our front door, serving its intended purpose.

November 7

L ife is a great teacher. We begin learning right away, as soon as we step on our path in life, it begins to teach us. Life teaches us the wonderful feeling of love very early in life, with the love of parents and grandparents. Life teaches us that just because we fell down trying to take our first step as a baby, we try again and again, until we hold the edge of the table and walk across the room.

Life teaches us lessons that are not always good. It teaches us anger, greed, and hatred. However, life also teaches us to love, to give, and to have forgiveness in our heart. There are hard lessons at times, and sometimes we fail to learn a lesson, yet; life teach it to us in a different way by bringing in distinct people and different circumstances into our life. Life's challenges are great lessons, and as we learn them; we a little wiser. We may think life isn't fair, but perhaps we aren't seeing the lesson it's trying to teach us yet. So instead of condemning life for what we perceive as not being fair, let's be fair with life. By exercising this sense of fairness, it in itself was a lesson life taught us in the past.

Life's teachers come in so many different forms and in some respect, we are some of life's teachers, and we are also students, learning these lessons. We teach others, by the way we live our lives and we learn from observing the way others live theirs. What kind of lesson are we teaching today?

Life never stops teaching us, we're always in the classroom, learning and growing. We will never graduate from life, until we reach our destination at the end of our path. Keep an open mind and an open heart and the lessons of life will be rewarding.

November 8

*M*esmerized, we sit in our boat, looking at the wake behind us. The small waves ripple over each side the churning water in the center. We sit quietly and look back to the wake we left behind as our boat continues to move forward. But WAIT!! Who's steering our boat if we're looking at the wake behind? We jump up grab the wheel and look to see where we are.

Breathing a little easier now, we cast our eyes to the distant horizon. The sky touching the water is far away, yet we focus on the smallest things that may be awaiting us on the horizon. With our focus on the distant horizon, we miss seeing the rocks just in front of our boat, or perhaps we miss the porpoise swimming alongside of our boat. We're missing the whale spouting its plume of air and water as it gently swims nearby.

We get out of our boat (the now) when we focus our attention on the wake (the past), or look to the far horizon (the future). We miss what is right in front of us. We will miss the small obstacles, by turning our boat to avoid them, before they turn into bigger problems, like the rocks of a reef. Focusing on the wake or the horizon, we miss the beauty of our today; the beauty of friends and family. We don't enjoy the soothing sounds of the water on the hull of our boat. We miss the warm sun and peaceful sea breeze.

The wake (the past) has been churned up and is behind us, and our boat is not going in that direction any longer. The horizon (the future) holds our dreams in life. The boat (our now) is how we travel today, and today is all we need to live for.

November 9

*E*ach of us has some level of expectation of how the day will go. We also expect others to be a certain way when we meet them. These expectations are usually based on how we would act and what we would do in a similar situation. We expect people to be on time for a meeting or dinner. We set an expectation of ourselves that we will be a certain way in our actions. Expectations are that sense of feeling that things will go our way.

When the expectations are not met, for whatever reason, we then experience disappointment. We thought one thing was going to happen, and it didn't and now we're disappointed. Disappointments in life should be expected. (Did I really just say that?) We will not always get our way, and people will disappoint us once in a while, but disappointment is not the end of the world.

Warning: expectations in an extreme sense turn into a sense of entitlement. Entitlements are expectations on steroids. And when we have a sense of entitlement, and it is not fulfilled; we are not disappointed, we are angry. What we thought was ours was taken away and now someone will pay.

An exception to entitlement is when we pay for services or products, and that would be justified. We are entitled to it. It's when we think we're entitled to be treated a certain way, or be given things without earning them; this sense of entitlement is unjustified.

Expectations will part of our life because we're human. Entitlements are nothing more than our ego taking over our expectations.

November 10

Now where did we put our car keys? We remember we came in the house and laid them on the table and now where are they? We eventually find them and think to ourselves, of course I remember now. We find ourselves in similar situations, looking for a book, our purse, our cell phone, whatever, and we simply misplaced it.

More critical and more important than a lost set of keys or our cell phone is when we lose our values. We allowed negativity to dominate our day. We become critical, angry, and perhaps egotistical and when this negativity consumes our day, we have blinders on that prevent us from seeing what is truly right in front of us. Recognizing this fact we replace the crucial attitude with compassion. We can remove the anger with forgiveness, and we can deflate the ego with humility.

But there is one value that we seem to misplace that can be a huge part of our lives and that is love. Love does not disappear from our lives; we just sometimes misplace it just like the car keys, and we laid it down and can't remember where we put it. It's not really lost. It's still where it belongs. If we look deep within our heart, we will discover it was always there. Loving ourselves is the first step in loving others. And when we love ourselves just a little more than yesterday the amount and power the love, we have to offer is huge.

Misplaced cell phones, car keys, purses, will be a part of life, but we don't have to look very far to find love. It is there in our heart and soul. Accept the love we have for ourselves with grace and humility, and our values will be found again too.

November 11

*T*he winds and rain of the nor'Easter is the worst seen in decades. The rain, cold and relentless, is coming like water from a fire hose and the wind is gusting with the power of a hurricane. Weather unfit for any sort of outdoor activity, yet, there he stands, polished shoes, perfectly fitted uniform, standing with his rifle at the Tomb of the Unknown Soldier. Cold and soaking wet, the wind and water do not deter the guard from his duties in honoring this veteran who lies in this tomb. The changing of the guard ceremony does not change because of the weather. Each move is precise, perfectly performed by each member of the guard. The nor'Easter's wind and rain do not leave the tomb unattended.

While we cannot stand guard at the Tomb of the Unknown Soldier, we can fly our flag today. We can say a prayer for the families that lost a husband, brother, wife, sister, aunt, uncle, mother or father. We can thank our veterans by simply saying 'Thank You.' We need to remember those veterans that sat in wet, water-filled foxholes from World War I and II; that fought on the cold snow-covered hills in Korea, in the jungles and rice paddies of Vietnam, and the relentless blowing sand storms of Iran, Iraq, Kuwait, and Afghanistan. It's a day where we honor those that served this country and put their lives on the line many times, while we sat home resting comfortably in our homes.

'Thank You' seems inadequate for showing our appreciation for all the sacrifices of our veterans. If it is all, we can do, then do it. If we can show appreciation in other ways, take the time to do that too. The 'time' we have is because of a veteran, and we need to find a small way to give back.

Happy Veteran's Day to all that served and are serving today. God Bless our service men and women, and God Bless America.

November 12

We have all seen, or at least heard of schemes where we are enticed with one thing, and then it turns into something else; the preverbal, bait and switch. Our gullible nature sets us up for this easy con, and we fall prey to their deception. Is it because we are trusting people that think that others will not intentionally harm us or do us wrong? For sure, that is the definition of gullible, but still, how sad we find ourselves victims of such deception.

Has society changed? Are there less people in this world playing the bait and switch game? Perhaps we are becoming a society where honesty, integrity, and authenticity are real values and mean something. With that mindset are we being gullible? Perhaps we are. What is best, a life not trusting anyone in what they are offering and not believing what they say? Or is trusting and believing in others a best way to live our life? Will we get burned by letting our guard down? Maybe, but living a life where we believe in our fellows is a much more pleasant way of living than distrusting all that come into our life.

We also have some responsibility in this game of bait and switch. We need to be real in the way we live our lives. We need to make sure we're not hiding behind a mask and pretending to be one person, while the real person hides. Being authentic takes courage. Being authentic is telling the truth to others about who we really are and not someone we want them to think we are. By pretending or wearing a mask, we're playing the bait and switch game, causing others not to trust us when they discover our ploy.

Be honest. Be authentic. Just be yourself.

November 13

URGENT!!! Our smart phone just chimed, and we have new mail! The email is from a friend. We must stop whatever we're doing to see what it is. As we're stopped to check our email, we notice a friend request, a new follower, and a new connection request on our social media apps. We must respond to those too as soon as we check our email.

We find ourselves allowing technology, and the perceived urgency of others take us off our path. For whatever reason, we think we must stop whatever we're doing to answer emails, respond to text messages, or click "Accept" on friend requests. Isn't what we're doing right now important too? Why do we allow the self-perceived emergency chimes on our smart phone take us away from our life, and what is important to us? The reasons are many, but few are good reasons.

We have a life, and we must give it some priority. Most, probably ninety-eight percent of messages and emails can wait to be answered on our time, not someone else's time. We control our reactions to these interruptions in our day. We can continue the conversation with a friend and not respond to an email right away. Nor do we have to answer the phone just because it's ringing. We need to give some priority to our time and not let these little interruptions control us. The voicemail will pick up and deliver us a message later; the email will still be in our inbox later.

It's time we give our life priority and not allow the urgency of others, and technology rob us of our life. Our life is important; we need to treat it as such.

November 14

The matriarch of the family sits in her rocker, slowly going back and forth. The fabric on the arms of the chair is worn and is covered in intricate lace doilies. Our grandmother sits quietly in her chair knitting an afghan for an elderly neighbor. We watch her thin feeble hands, wrinkled with age, work the needles like an expert while she shares stories with us of when she was young. She tells us of the days of courtship with our grandfather, long passed now. She tells us of the silly things our parent did as young child, and the mischief they got into when they were knee high to a grasshopper. We sit on the footstool and listen intently to each word of her soft voice and the wonderful stories.

Each story our sweet grandmother tells is another part of the legacy she will leave us. Each little cinnamon pinwheel she baked with the dough left over from the apple pie will be a memory, we will treasure. We recall one time when we laughed together when she put the Jell-O in the freezer to harden and forgot about it. A new frozen dessert was now a part of our memory, and this simple little event is etched in our memory.

Sadly, grandmothers do not live forever, and they must join our grandfather, and their parents. We find it hard to accept this, and we grieve when they come to the end of their journey with us. Their path in this life has come to its end, and they start a new path the loved ones that have passed before us. In all the years, our grandmother walked her path, she left us so many tidbits of wisdom, so many funny memories of Jell-O in the freezer, and many more.

This is the legacy she leaves behind. This legacy is wrapped, like the intricate lace doilies on the arms of the rocker, in love.

The memories of the sweet smell of our grandmother's perfume, and wonderful stories will always live in our heart. While she doesn't walk with us on our journey any longer, her love and kindness are always with us in our heart.

November 15

Things don't always go our way, and we get ourselves stressed out over them, and we lose our serenity. It can be any number of things; we have to stop to get gas on the way to work because we forgot the night before to fill up, and now we're late to work. We get out of routine in the morning, and we get angry at others, though they really had no part in it. We allow the little things to become so magnified they consume each minute and every thought.

Well, it's time to get over it, and we need to get over it right now before it takes another precious minute of our day. Bringing this big deal down to its real size is not something we always want to do. We want to let it be bigger than life, so we can let it fester, and we can complain to others about our dilemma. Do others want to hear us complain? No. So why do we do it? We seek sympathy to feed our ego.

The solution in finding the right way to make things right-sized is by acknowledging the things we are grateful for. We should be thankful for the car that has little gas, and appreciative for having the money to put into the gas tank. We should be grateful for a job and for friends who listen to us complain about the smallest things.

Being grateful for what we have; the little things in life that come our way will be set to their actual size and not magnified by the lens of our ego. When we find ourselves in a state of gratitude, the lives that we will touch today, will see and feel that sense of peace and serenity. They too will want what we have… gratitude.

November 16

$\mathcal{A}$ time machine has been invented, and we have been chosen to take a trip, either into our future, or revisit our past. We must choose one or the other, and we will never have this offer again; it a once in a lifetime opportunity. Which we will choose?

What if we decide to go back in time? At what point will we select? Will that time be the revisit the missed opportunity for that kiss to our first crush in school? Will we want to go back to make an amends to someone who is no longer with us? If we change our actions of the past, will these new actions cause a new history? Will changing our past change the life of someone else, or change our life too? There are so many questions to consider before making a choice to back into our past.

Well, that leaves us the other choice… to go into our future. This option comes with one small restriction; we can only go as an observer and can only communicate with our future-self. So will we want to go and see what our life will be like in ten years? If this is our decision, we should be prepared with some questions as our stay is limited. Pretend we are just outside the place our future-self lives… what does it look like? We knock on the door and our future-self greets us… what do we look like? How are we dressed? Do we appear to be successful? But more importantly, do we appear happy?

So we have time for a couple of questions… we ask our future-self, "What stands out most in your memory of the last ten years?" And we listen intently to the answer. Our next question is, "Future-self, what do I need to be most aware of to get me from where I am now, to where you are?" Again, we listen carefully to their response. What other questions would we ask our future-self? Now, listen to the answer.

Our past is the past, and we cannot change it. Our past has brought us to this place and time; making us who we are today. Our future-self has given us wisdom, and now we need to take those answers and start living our life today in a way we will be who we imagined we would be in ten years.

November 17

S ometimes gradually, the light in our life slowly disappears, and we find ourselves in darkness. While other time darkness comes into our life suddenly; in either case, we find ourselves in darkness. We are on this journey, and now our path is dark and frightening. It could be the loss of a parent or grandparent who we held so close in our heart; or a relationship that has turned against us, and now we feel alone. What will bring us away from this dark path and back onto our journey?

We remember we have a flashlight, and we turn it on. Now the darkness is partially replaced by a beam of light. The beam shines forward and lights up our path before us. Our flashlight is now our guide, and we shine it to light the way.

Our flashlight also gives us more than just light; it gives us hope. It forgives the darkness and brings to light the good; not only, the good in our lives, but the good in others. We shine our light on others on this journey, and it shines beyond the darkness and sees the beauty in others. Our flashlight is there to take us from our dark path and lead us to the joy and happiness that lie ahead.

Our guiding light is powered by our values. Faith, hope, care, compassion, integrity, respect, and love all give our flashlight its power. Darkness envelopes us for many reasons, and we have the tools to walk out of our darkness, and into the light of peace and serenity with the flashlight powered by our values. We need to turn on our light so others can find their way out of their darkness too. We make a difference by living our values.

November 18

UN!!! LAUGH!!! SMILE!!! PARTY!!! EXCITED!!! HAPPY!!! Isn't it a great start to our day with these words? Aren't these great words to be part of our afternoon snack? If these are so great, why aren't they thought of more often?

We roll out of bed and start our day. The likelihood a smile is on our face is rare, and we moan about getting up and dread the drive to work, or taking the kids to school. We have set the stage for the day, and it is BLAH! We will carry BLAH all day because that is what latched onto us the very first thing this morning and getting rid of it will take a lot of effort, and we're, frankly, not interested in that work because BLAH has drained our energy. So, we're stuck with BLAH. Now BLAH is not anger, painful, or agony; it's just BLAH. When we have BLAH, we don't smile; we don't laugh or spread joy and happiness. We merely get through each minute, each hour as best we can.

On the other hand, we have the option to think of the words at the beginning, FUN, SMILE, PARTY, EXCITED. When we start our day with those in mind, BLAH can't attach itself to us. Starting our day with these words in our thoughts, we may smile a little more, laugh at the silly things that happen, and are a better person to be around. We kiss our kids, our spouse, hug a coworker, and smile as we hold the door open for someone else. We attract others to join and share in our happiness and great feeling.

"We are responsible for our own happiness today." is the sticky note we should put on our mirror and read it the first thing each morning. The BLAH has no business in our life, and we need to focus on smiles, joy, happiness, and laughter.

BLAH Humbug! Let's PARTY!!! Let's SMILE!!! Be HAPPY!!!

November 19

The day is warm, and the occasional white puffy cloud blocks the mid-morning sun. The park is filled with children running from here to there; kicking a ball or sliding down the tall slide. There is one child who is swinging on the swing. Back and forth, the child kicks their legs to go higher and higher. Swinging alone, this child hasn't a care in the world. Their only responsibility is to make sure they kick forward and fold back their legs to maintain their momentum.

Is it really their only responsibility? Shouldn't they be mindful of other children playing around them? Shouldn't they be considerate and let someone else swing on the swing? A sense of responsibility comes with some maturity and the foundation of values. Learning responsibility is witnessing it on others.

Some may think they are only responsible to take care of ourselves and let others take care of themselves. This shirking of true responsibility is selfish and self-centered. In reality, we are responsible for much more.

We are responsible for our actions and the impact they might have on others. We are responsible to live our personal values so that we will make a positive difference in the lives we touch. We are responsible for our own happiness and success and should not rely on something or someone else to give it to us. We are responsible and accepting that responsibility; we become living examples for others to look up to and to learn the value of responsibility.

We should pledge each morning, "I am responsible." Responsibility – the grown-up thing to do.

November 20

*W*e snap on our tool belt and head out to our work site. We have our basic tools; hammer, screwdriver, wrench, level, and a few others. We begin where we left off from yesterday. We seem to have a problem today... the screwdriver we were using yesterday is not working on the bolt of today. No matter how hard we try, we can't seem to make any progress on securing that bolt to our master project. Perhaps we need to look at the blueprints again. For some unknown reason, it does not occur to us to put the screwdriver down and use our wrench.

Using tools for their unintended purpose is like trying to be someone else in our life. We need to stop pretending to be a 'screwdriver', when we're really a 'wrench'. We are who we are, and we bring great tools to this world. We carry the basic tools of our values; love, care, compassion, and faith. We also bring with us special tools, unique to us. These unique tools are our talents which we bring to the job site of life.

We develop these special tools over time. It's like we begin our journey as an apprentice and with time become a journeyman. Our skills and tools become more sophisticated, and we become a master craftsman; working on the master project. A master craftsman does not need to borrow tools from someone else to complete their project, and we do not need to 'borrow' someone else's tools either. We don't need to act like someone else (a screwdriver), when we can be ourselves (a wrench) to turn the bolt. We have the tools on our tool belt; we simply need to use and master them.

Our master project is our purpose in life, and we have the tools; basic (our values) and special (our talents), to complete this beautiful project. It will be a masterpiece once completed; one that the master craftsman would be proud to show off.

CAUTION: CONSTRUCTION ZONE AHEAD

November 21

The path on our journey is not always smooth and level. We will find hills and valleys, soft green grass and rocky, treacherous, and narrow walkways. Sometimes our path gets rough and our footing becomes uncertain, yet we continue our journey. It would be easy to turn around and go back to the easy path, but deep within our heart, we know that turning around is not the answer. We carefully take each step on this treacherous path with some fear of slipping off the edge and into the cavern below. Our next step, the rocks on the edge break away, and we fall to our knees. One leg dangles over the edge; the other leg begins to slip too, so we reach up and grab a branch of a small bush on the side of our path.

The blackness of the cavern below us seems to envelope us with the blackness of fear and hopelessness. We hold on to the branch, not moving a muscle for fear the branch will break and our journey will now come to an end. We gather our thoughts and try to dismiss the fear. We must not give up trying to find our way back to better footing. Looking down is not where the answer lies; it is the branch above that holds our hope, and our focus must be on it. The branch is sturdy and holds our weight, and we gradually pull ourselves off the ledge and onto safe ground.

The branch can represent the hand of a friend who pulls us off the ledge and onto safe ground. The branch is our courage not to allow the darkness of fear overcomes us when we find ourselves in precarious situations. Our branch is merely a symbol of our internal values of hope and faith. So we question, "How strong is our branch?" Our branch is sturdy and can bring us off any ledge, if we hold on to it. We just need to hold on to it and never give up.

November 22

*T*aken for granted is that sense of unimportance, expected, or just the norm. We take our life for granted and don't appreciate all that we have. When we are blessed with so many things in our lives, we find ourselves not giving full credit to all that we have.

Today we should celebrate our freedom. We take it for granted because we have not lived in a place where our freedom was taken away. We may not fully appreciate the freedom we have to speak our peace and opinions, even though they may be contrary to the majority. Today we have the freedom of expression; to wear a red shirt on a "red shirt" Friday or put glitter on our face, if that strikes our fancy. We have the freedom to travel from one end of this country to the next. We have the freedom to disagree with others. We enjoy the freedom of sharing our voice in electing our government officials. How many other freedoms do we have? The list may be endless.

Freedom wasn't free though. Freedom was fought for by many great Americans, many whose life was taken away. Freedom was very costly, and yet we take it for granted. Today, even for just the few minutes, let's remember that all the freedoms we enjoy today and not take them for granted. Today, remember the service men and women all over the world that are fighting for, not only our freedom, but for the freedom of others. We fight these battles for freedom because we know how precious freedom is, yet we forget sometimes. It's time we move into gratitude for the life we have and the freedoms that come with it.

November 23

illions of dollars are spent on short thirty-second commercials during huge sporting events on television. Some will be silly, some provocative, while others will tug at your heart and bring a tear to your eye. The purpose is for us to remember their brand. Marketing experts spend countless hours preparing this short segment to be seen by millions. Some commercials miss the mark completely with some and yet others will think it was the best they have seen. Good or bad, patriotic or provocative, funny or emotional, they are there to sell something.

Most of us do not have millions to spend on a commercial to sell our brand. We don't have huge marketing firms laboring over a thirty-second segment to get some word out for us. Our 'commercial' will have much more impact; maybe not to millions, and may only be to a few hundred, yet it will make a difference. Television commercials sell brands, and we sell a brand too… ourselves. We are a living commercial with each action we take and with each word we speak. Our commercial is when we do the right thing when no one is watching… our brand is integrity. Our commercial is when we care more deeply about someone else than ourselves… our brand is love. Our commercial when our heart aches when someone else suffers pain… our brand is compassion. Our brand is our values.

We are unique; one of a kind and no one else is exactly like us. Our brand is special, and we need to protect it and not let it be tarnished by our commercials showing anger, selfishness, fear, and greed. We are our own marketing staff and create our own commercials to sell our brand. How will others see our commercial today?

November 24

*F*our fingers and a thumb; attached to our wrist, it is an extension of our arm. From the shoulder, it is attached to our torso. There is an invisible attachment that we cannot see. It's not a blood vessel below the skin, nor is it a nerve, tendon, or muscle.

Our hand wipes away a friend's tear and comforts with the light touch on their shoulder. Our hand welcomes a stranger into our lives with a handshake and may become our best friend. Our hands hold a new-born baby with care and gentleness. Our hand writes a personal note to a friend far away, sharing from the heart that we miss them. Our inter-twining fingers wrap around another person's fingers giving them a sense of security and affection.

That invisible attachment links our hand to our heart and soul. The energy that flows from our heart to our hand is love. Our hand is a beautiful instrument of our love in action.

We should never miss an opportunity to extend our hand in friendship or to comfort and relieve someone's pain. We shouldn't miss the chance to gently touch the shoulder of a friend, letting them know we are there for them.

Our hand... what a wonderful gift and instrument of love.

November 25

$\mathcal{M}$ any of us can recall a dot-matrix printer. Each dot was clearly visible; making up each letter. Obviously, technology improved printing with fine inkjet and laser printers. The dots are invisible to the naked eye and are quite intricate. Our high-definition television is millions of small dots giving a crystal clear picture for us to enjoy. It's almost life-like and hard to imagine it is just a group of dots, millions of dots making up the picture.

Each dot plays a role in all the examples just given. Without one dot, the difference would probably not be visible. However, if more and more dots were not there, we would see less quality in the printing or in the picture on the screen, and it will begin to make a difference. High quality means every dot plays a role in the overall quality, and each dot serves a purpose.

Like one less grain of sand on the beach, the beach would not be as big as it was before. The loss of one drop in the ocean, it would be less massive. Without that one dot on the HD TV, the picture will not be as clear. We are that one dot; that one grain of sand or drop of the ocean and we add quality to this world. While we may not think our existence is important, we do make a difference. We make the beach bigger, the ocean fuller, and the picture clearer.

We should never doubt our existence and the importance we play in this world. We touch many lives each day, directly and indirectly as we are that 'dot' that made a difference to them. We should be proud we're playing such an important role, because the truth is, we are. And without each of us doing our part, the universe would be less than it was.

November 26

We stand in front of our full-length mirror and look at ourselves. We make minor adjustments to our hair, make sure our clothes hang correctly, the jewelry we selected accents appropriately, and our belt buckle is in alignment with the row of buttons on our shirt or blouse. Satisfied with our appearance, we go out to meet the world. However, there was something missing in the reflection.

What if our full-length mirror we just stood before was a two-way mirror, and our best friend was on the other side. Who would they see? Will it be the same person that is reflected back to ourselves, or will they see something we're missing? Perhaps one scenario may be that our best friend sees through the mirror a person that is giving and loving, with a heart of gold. We see a reflection of low self-esteem and inadequacy in the mirror. Another scenario is we feel good about ourselves; our life and our heart are filled with gratitude. Our friend on the other side of the mirror sees a face without a smile and sadness in our eyes.

The two-way mirror sees two people. The reflection side sees our exterior, our outer shell; the way we want people to see us. The see-through part sees our inner self and what is really going on in our lives. We try to hide this from others to see. Should there be two different images? Shouldn't our inner self be reflected in our exterior? Sadly, we hold our true self within, not wanting the mirror to see it. In reality, our close friends can see through that reflection and into our heart and soul. These friends accept us for who they see in the see-through mirror and not the reflection.

So as we look into the mirror again, let the smile come across our face and let's see that reflection in the mirror. Let's remind ourselves with that smile, we are special, and we are as beautiful inside as the reflection in the mirror.

November 27

We all have something in common; we all have opinions. Each of us usually has one on any particular topic and so many times we give our opinion without being asked for it. We will interrupt conversations just making sure we get our opinion into the conversation. We will even go out of our way to start conversations solely to voice our opinion on something that the other person has little or no interest.

Why do we act this way? It is our ego ruffling its feathers to see if we can make ourselves look smart in front of others. It's boasting and antagonistic in some cases. We give our opinions on politics, religion, and whatever may be the hot topic, yet we probably really don't have the facts correct. We taint our wordy opinion, and spin what little facts we may have, into an emotional exchange of words. Typically, we will look more like an idiot, a babbling buffoon with our ramble. And now the person we are 'sharing' our opinion with, now has a new opinion of their own…, and it's about us and our babble.

We will still have opinions on many topics and if asked for them, we should voice our thoughts with honesty. We also need to respect others in that they may have a different opinion. We can keep our ego in check, and not allow it to flap its feathers when we don't force our opinions onto others. It really boils down to respecting others.

Just my opinion…

November 28

*L*ooming on the horizon on our path appears to be a huge mountain. With each step, we get closer and instead of the mountain getting bigger, it gets smaller. How is that possible? As it turns out, the mountain we saw first was really just a mole hill. We started our day making something we saw in the future a big deal, when, in fact, it wasn't as big of a deal as we initially made it to be. It was an obstacle we needed to overcome, but it wasn't that big of a deal; it was just a deal.

So what other facets of our life do we over or under estimate? Our ego will make us believe we are a big deal. We are a big deal because we have an expensive car, or by the position, we hold in an organization. The mere thought that we are a big deal eliminates any ounce of humility we may have had at one time. We also may think just the opposite, and that we are a little deal. We are not worthy because we drive a clunker, or we wear clothes from a thrift store. Our self-worth suffers when we think we are a little deal.

The truth of the matter is, there are no big deals, or little deals; there are only deals, and it is the way we manifest them in our mind that makes them seem one way or the other. The mountain on the horizon is not a big deal; it is just an obstacle we will face later in life and there isn't any reason to make a big deal of it now. And we need to stop pretending to be a big deal or think we're a little deal either.

We are who we are. We only need to be the real deal. If we can just be ourselves, live life as best we can, serving others, living our personal values and principles, we will be the real deal. Those around us want honesty and authenticity. No one can ask us to be anyone else other than our true self; never doubt we are the real deal.

November 29

Today...

Smile with your eyes

Be gentle in your touch

Let your words be filled with love

Laugh a little

Don't judge others

Give Mr./Ms. Ego the day off

Be inspired

Get some fresh air, take a walk

Just whisper

Look in the mirror and love that person

Have some ice cream

Send a text to a friend just to say "hi"

Say, "I can"

Be a friend

Remove your mask and be <u>yourself</u>

November 30

W hat if... two simple words that begin a question, we may ask. What if I had finished college; where would I be today? What if I hadn't met this person; would I have a different family? What if I had turned the other way instead of the way; would I have missed being in an accident? What if this and what if that is a mental mind game that we play and try to change the past. We relive decision and events, wondering the outcome had the circumstances been a little different, or if we had made some different choices. The "What if's" serve no purpose in our life today.

Trying to live in the past and predict the different outcomes will not change the present. The present is where we are and the decisions we make today could be the "What if's" of tomorrow. So living in today, as best we can; realizing our decisions today are just that, choices made today. If our choices we make today are self-serving and based on greed or acting out in vengeance, we will suffer through the "What if's" soon. However, if these choices are made with a sense of living our life's purpose, guided by our personal values, we will have few "What if's" tomorrow.

Today we will make decisions that will impact our lives. Some of these decisions may be mistakes, but as long as we learn from those choices, we continue to grow. As we grow we become a better person, a better friend, a better spouse, or better parent. We needn't look back and try to relive the past with the "What if's" because our past has taught us great lessons, and we are a better person today.

So as soon as the "What if" creeps into our mind, think for a moment before reliving that scenario, did we learn a lesson and are we a little better? If yes, then there is no reason to complete the question... "What if...?"

Thanksgiving

*I*t's the "Big Feast" at Grandma's house. We can expect the whole family this time, and it will be so great to see brothers, sisters, aunts, uncles, and all the cousins. We look forward to the feast that will be prepared except for one small side dish… the Brussels sprouts. That tiny little cabbage vegetable, that no one really likes, is prepared each year. Who grows these teeny round cabbages? Are they insane?

As the great day approaches, we commit to ourselves that we will once again, take our customary three tiny Brussels sprouts as they are passed around the table, and we will eat them. We, of course, will quickly take a large fork full of the mashed potatoes to wash it down. We will complement the cook for the fabulous feast and how well everything tasted. The Brussels sprouts weren't all that bad after seeing the smile on Grandma's face.

As we go through life, we will face challenges we don't like doing, yet we do them anyway. We work through these difficult times and do those things we would rather not do. By doing these, we grow as a person, and we may, just may, make someone else happy. We need to recognize the easy way, or our way, is not the only way, and we may find ourselves having to eat a Brussels sprout or two along our journey. It's part of life, and if we think for just a moment… what an awesome life it is.

Seconds on the Brussels sprouts?

December

December 1

The little boy walks onto the ball field again this season to try out for the team. He hasn't grown much from when he tried out last season and wasn't picked, but he hopes practicing with his dad will make the difference this year. Glove in hand, ball cap straight, he waits for his turn to bat and throw the ball. He sees there is a new coach this season; so maybe, just maybe he will be picked this year.

All the other boys have had their turn, and he was the last one to bat. He swings the bat as the ball comes toward him. He misses. The next pitch, he thinks, he will hit the ball; he swings and misses again. Only one more pitch and he will strike out. Focused on the ball as it comes toward him, he hits it with his bat. It flies just over the pitcher, and lands near second base. "I hit it" he thinks to himself and almost forgets to run toward first base. His smile is as wide as the brim of his ball cap.

The new coach calls all the players into a circle and tells them he will be picking this year's team based on throwing, running, and batting. The little boy, smaller than his other teammates, thinks he won't make the cut again. He didn't throw well, but he did the best he could. He didn't run as fast as some of the others, and he only hit the ball once. He was certain, he would not be chosen this year either. He listened as the coach read off his clipboard the names of the team. The coach was about to read off the last name; the little guy sighed feeling rejected again. The coach reads his name. In total disbelief, he made the team!

There are times when we try our best, yet we feel we're not qualified. We question our skills and abilities, though we're doing the best we can. Feeling somewhat "less-than", we find ourselves being chosen to be part of something big. Why us? The simple answer is that someone else sees our capabilities when we can't. We all have special qualities. Sometimes it takes another person to show us our true value. We will always miss the ball we never swing at, so it's time we step up to the plate. We can hit that home run, as long as we take that swing.

December 2

The young surfer walks over the sand dune and looks out over the ocean. It's early in the morning, and the sun is just about to break over the eastern horizon. The ocean is smooth and waves roll in, one after another. The young surfer thinks to himself, today he will ride the perfect wave. The young surfer sees another surfer has already paddled out and is riding some of the waves.

After waxing his board down, the young man begins to paddle out. Paddling over the gentle swells of each wave he faces, he finds himself in the perfect spot to wait for the perfect wave. He greets the other surfer and notices that he is an older man, mid-forties. "What is this old man doing out here?" the young man thinks, but he is polite as he waits for his wave. He sits on his board, facing the beach and looks over his shoulder as each swell rises. At the crest of the swell, he can look out to see another set of waves coming. Surely, one will be the perfect wave he waits for.

He looks around the old surfer is paddling back out from riding a wave. The old man rides one after another. But the young surfer is going to wait for that perfect swell to give him the best ride. Again, the old surfer catches another wave and rides it toward the beach. Kicking out at the peak, he begins to paddle back out. One wave after another, the old man rides another wave. The young surfer sees a possibility. He lays on his board, begins to paddle, but then stops and lets the wave pass by... it wasn't as good as he thought. Yet the old surfer gladly takes this wave to the beach.

The old man is now sitting on his board on the sand as the young surfer makes his way up the beach. "Pretty awesome day," the old surfer says to the young man. "You didn't catch too many rides. How come?" he asks. The young surfer merely said, "I was waiting for that primo wave."

The experienced surfer says, "Yea, I know what you mean, but I found riding a lot of waves is more fun than not riding any. We can wait for that perfect wave, but what if it never rolls in? Or worse yet, it comes and we miss riding it? What then?"

So, are we waiting for that perfect wave too? Are we letting one opportunity roll by, one after the other, like the young surfer? Life is more fun when we live it to the fullest; riding as many waves as we can. The perfect wave may come tomorrow, but tomorrow is never promised, nor is that primo wave. Enjoy life today, don't wait.

December 3

"Jack of all trades, master at none" is a well-known phrase where the person is claiming they know a little about everything but isn't honestly good at anything. While we know that this philosophy is not one we should adopt as our lifestyle, many of us tend to take on a similar concept; we try to be a different person than who we truly are.

We, sometimes, tend to take on a role in life that is based on what we perceive others want us to be, and we play that part. As soon as we are with another person, we feel we must assume another role. We soon become as "Jack of all roles" and never who we really are. We put on a mask, and we play this part when we're home with family; another mask to play another role when we're at work, another yet another mask for the role when we are with friends. The roles and masks we wear and play become overwhelming, and we can barely remember who we're supposed to be at any one given time.

It's time assume only one role, and that is one that we play ourselves. We need to remove all the masks of all the other roles we tried to play before and only let the real, authentic self be the character we assume in all aspects of our life, regardless where or who we are with. When we can just be ourselves, not hide our flaws with masks, but just be our authentic self, it's then the weight of the world is lifted from our shoulders.

Let others play their roles, and we will just be ourselves. We are unique and bring such value to the world when we simply be who we are and not try to be someone we're not. Today we will make a difference in someone's life today, make sure they see the real us.

December 4

Are we really this lucky to have what we have? Are we really this lucky to have the friends and family we have and love? Are we really this lucky to be who we are and be where we are on our journey in life? Are we?

Some may say we are lucky to have the wonderful things in life. But some may say luck had nothing to do with it. In some cases we worked hard to be where we are in our job, or that we worked hard with a relationship to have the family we have and love. Luck had nothing to do with those in our lives. We took action to study and learn new things to better our lives. Luck had nothing to do with it either.

So why do we feel lucky? Perhaps it's as simple as replacing 'lucky' with 'grateful'. When we say we're lucky to have this or that, aren't we really saying we are grateful to have this or that. Luck is random, a simple chance of an occurrence. Luck is winning the lottery. Our lives are not random or simple. Most of our lives should not be filled with feeling lucky, but filled with the feeling of gratitude.

Be lucky in the lottery, but grateful in life.

December 5

I t is early in the morning, and we are about to set foot on our journey today. We recall that at the end of the day yesterday we were exhausted. So before we start today, imagine we have the ability to look into a mirror before we start. What do we see? We see we're wearing a heavy coat made up of guilt and shame. We have a backpack full of resentments. On one shoulder, we have a shoulder bag bursting with anger and hatred. On the other shoulder, we carry a sack filled with selfishness. Suitcase in one hand is filled with past hurts, secrets, and bad habits. Lastly, our other free hand pulls a wagon filled to the brim with ego. It's no wonder we were exhausted at the end of yesterday's journey. Do we really want to start today with the same load and perhaps add even more along the way?

Of course not, but how do we rid ourselves of all this excess baggage; all this negativity that burdens us? We find the solution within. We drop the wagon handle of ego when we think of others first and find ways to be of service to them. We find the sack of selfishness falls away too. The suitcase filled with hurts, and secrets is dropped when we tell the truth and are honest in our actions. The backpack full of resentments drops to the ground when we find forgiveness in our heart. And the heavy coat of guilt and shame is shed when we seek our own forgiveness and make amends for our wrongdoings.

Our load is lighter when we look within our heart and soul to see our values. Our values will take away all that weighs us down; keeping us from our journey. We have a purpose in life, and that purpose is not to carry all that weighed us down before, but to move forward in living our values. Our values are not merely words; they are the way we act and live each day. When we live our values, the weights of burden cannot attach themselves to us and slow us down. We make a difference in this world, and our life's purpose is our guiding light, fueled by our values.

Are we prepared to venture forward on our path now? Are we eager to make a difference? Yes, we are.

December 6

Our path leads us to a foot bridge crossing over a small stream. We pause for a moment on the bridge and lean over the rail, looking at the clear water that passes under it. We take a few minutes and simply watch the ripples of water pass below us. Smooth river rocks line the stream bed and crystal-clear water flows over the rocks, giving a shimmer and twinkle from the sunlight above. Mesmerizing, we watch the glistening ripples of the water pass under the foot bridge.

Our trance is broken when we see an orange leaf floating on the surface of the water come towards the bridge. We intently watch it float under the bridge, and we look over the other railing, and watch it disappear downstream. That leaf is now out of sight.

Just like the leaf and the water that carried it away, it represents our past and has now gone downstream too. We cannot reverse the stream to bring it back, nor should we try. We need to accept the past as what it was and look for the lesson it taught us. We can over analyze and speculate about why things happened the way they did, but that effort is like trying to reverse the stream, so we can see the leaf again. It will only add frustration to our journey. Each day of our journey is precious, and if we spend even a minute worrying about the leaf, that lost minute robs us of a minute we could spend in our present. It robs us of a minute where we could share a smile, give a hug, or be of service to someone in need.

Water passes under our bridge each day, and each ripple can hold a lesson to be learned. We shouldn't dwell on the leaf that passes below, but the focus on the glistening sun on the ripples of water below our feet. Look into the water and we see our reflection... now smile. We are loved by the person we see in the water.

December 7

A sheen on the water gives light to small rainbows glistening in the sunlight on the surface of the water below. Some say we will even see a bubble slowly float to the surface; a solemn reminder of the ship, its crew remains in their watery grave at our feet. We stand above the USS Arizona as it lies in the floor of Pearl Harbor in eerie silence. Hawaiian flowers are cast over the bay, honoring those that died here. Today we honor them with prayers, by flying our great flag, and by simply knowing this is a day in history that reminds us of the horrors of war.

The brave men and women on that Sunday morning, living in a topical paradise would soon know the evil that can arise from nowhere. These brave Americans were fighting with all their might against this horrible attack, are the ones we honor today. There are few survivors of the attack on Pearl Harbor today, and if they were here with us in person, we would salute them, shake their hand and thank them for their service.

We should do no less for every other service man and woman who served or is serving today in our armed forces. Today is a reminder, and it is a sad day. Today we should all try to find some way to honor the memory of the attack on Pearl Harbor. The tiny bubble of oil floats to the surface as if the USS Arizona weeps. The oily sheen with its small beautiful rainbows are the beauty of each soul lost in Pearl Harbor.

December 8

*I*t's our treasure. It's our pride and joy. We have worked hard for this, and now it is ours. This treasure of ours is very special, and we take care of it; making sure it remains as beautiful and pristine as it was the day we got it. We find a special place for our treasure, to show it off and let others enjoy its beauty too. There, we found a perfect place.

Without warning, a friend accidentally bumps the treasure, causing it to fall and break. We watch, as if in slow motion, our treasure falling, and there is nothing we can do to catch it in mid-air. Our friend is devastated by the accident and looks over to us. They see our anguish and sadness, as we stare at our treasure lying on the floor. Apology, after apology does not mend our broken treasure.

We begin to blame them and then ourselves. What could we have done to prevent this accident? Why did they bump against our treasure? Is it our fault our treasure lays shattered on the ground? We begin to pick up the pieces and realize it is only an object. We may be able to fix it, but it won't be the same, and we know that. What is most important is that we mend the other treasure that is bruised, our friend's guilt. We need to find forgiveness, and heal the hurt our friend feels in their heart.

The treasure of friendship is truly priceless. This treasure is not to be placed on a pedestal or locked in a cabinet behind glass doors. The treasure of friendship needs to be held, cuddled, touched, forgiven, cherished, and most of all, be fed with love. Our true, priceless treasures are not objects on a pedestal, but are the ones that hold our hand and comfort us in sadness. Our treasures laugh with us and cry with us. Our friends make our life special and there is no better treasure than a true friend.

December 9

$\mathcal{D}$ ebtors are a part of the business world, where an individual is under some sort of financial obligation to an institution or another individual. There is a repayment plan in place usually. At some point in our life we may be a debtor too, and there is nothing wrong with that. What we see today is there is a twist to this concept.

In some people's mind if they do someone a favor, that other person now owes them something in return. They may not owe money, but they 'owe' the person doing the favor, some sort of repayment. This is not always clear to the person receiving the favor, but most assuredly it is in the mind of the person doing the favor. In fact, this person has a running tally of all the favors owed to them by the countless others they have done favors for. This sense of entitlement of repayment can ruin relationships.

The concept of the world owing us goes far beyond doing favors for others. Some think the world owes them a life. Some teenagers think their parents owe them a car when they turn sixteen. While others think, with their mere presence and sharing their company with us, we owe them something. BUNK!

The perception of entitlement has spread throughout our society. Whatever happened to the concept of earning a living, saving our money to buy a car, and being responsible? We repay our parents, teachers, and whoever else influenced us, by living our values. We cannot go around this world thinking it owes us a living. We need to give to the world our very best in making it better, expecting nothing in return. The world doesn't owe us anything, but it has provided us huge opportunities to make our own life. Make a payment to the world today by making a difference in someone's life with no expectation of repayment.

December 10

Imagine...

Imagine the split second the sun crests the eastern horizon and casts its rays to the high clouds above; filling the sky with a swath of color.

Imagine a moment in our life where we are fully at peace and are enveloped in a sphere of serenity.

Imagine the beautiful rainbow, arching across the sky on a cloudy and rainy day.

Imagine the sounds of a baby laughing and giggling when we can't seem to find much happiness in our life.

Imagine inhaling courage and exhaling fear.

Imagine a life where there is no anger and hatred; only compassion, forgiveness and love.

Imagine looking in the mirror and loving the person looking back at you.

Imagination is a powerful thought process. It is the beginning of a dream we may have, or it may be the start of changing our life. Our imagination is as vast as the universe. We are our own roadblocks from allowing our imagination to build our dreams and our dreams from becoming reality. There is a whole new world out there, limited by our lack of imagination. Remove the roadblocks and let's imagine.

Imagine the very best life we could possibly conceive of having... now... start living it today.

Imagine...

December 11

We begin today's journey with a little emptiness and lack of spirit. We're uneasy and wonder what lessons need to be learned today to allow this void to be filled. It's not long walking on our path, when we see a large, leather-bound book along the side of our path. We pick it up and on the front of the book, the title, Today's Lesson, written in gold across the brown leather cover.

We open the book, to the first page. The paper is old and has been yellowed in age. Written on the first page, in beautiful script, Today's lesson is not hard, but is essential for your growth. Today, look at the beauty around you and see the wonders of nature. The words almost come alive as we read them, as if we hear a soft deep voice sharing these words of wisdom. We continue to read: Be gentle in your words and actions today and not cause others around you to feel less than or unimportant. Again, we hear the words come off the yellowed paper as we read, as if the book is talking to us in this deep, wisdom-filled, fatherly voice.

The voice in our head reads on: Your greatness is not of things or position in this life; it is your love, humility, and serving others. Your greatness is you living your values. Your values will fuel your passion and lead you to your life's purpose. When you discover why you are here, and why you're on this path, your journey will become clear. The emptiness and lack of spirit we started the day with is slowly becoming filled with the wisdom of each word.

We turn the page, and it simply reads: One final lesson for today; be thankful for those that serve you today and have gratitude in your heart for all that you have, as your travel this journey.

We close the book and feel a sense of purpose as we continue our journey, remembering each word we read. The book merely reminds us of what we already know. The book, in reality, are our heart and soul shining through, with a small reminder of what is important in our lives.

December 12

There are only twenty-four hours in a day, no more and no less. It seems each hour is filled with some sort of activity; working, sleeping, eating, playing, driving, exercising, or something else. While each twenty-four hours may vary with the amount of time dedicated to each activity, we will fill our day and wonder, where did the day go? Soon it will be, where did the week, month, or year go? Like a metronome keeping time for the musician, our twenty-four hours continue to tick off with each minute, with each second; it does not stop.

We know we only have twenty-four hours in our day, and we know that we control most of the time we allocate to those hours. There is one hour, perhaps even just a half-hour we seldom allocate any time; that is time for reflection. If we chose to take this time just before bed, we can reflect on the previous hours of the day to see how our day went. Did we harm anyone? Were we of service when given the opportunity? What could we have done better today? We take these answers and not dwell on them, but simply acknowledge them.

Some of us may want to take the morning to be our time of reflection. Perhaps we will read a little, and reflect on the words. Some may take this quiet time and formulate the day's activities. Maybe we can ask ourselves during this brief reflection time, how can we help someone today? How can we more positive in our words and actions? How can we live a day we can be proud of? What can we do today to make it the very best day for someone else? Answers to these questions will probably not come right away, but they set the tone for all the activities the next twenty-four hours will consume.

Quiet time, reflection time, meditation, whatever we may call it is an important part of our twenty-four hours, and yet, too many of us let it pass by because we have too much to do today. Do we really? Try to reflect fifteen minutes today on the day and see if our day isn't just a little better. Remember the metronome is ticking.

December 13

As we walk into work, we see a notice on the bulletin board, "THE CEO WILL BE MAKING A BIG ANNOUNCEMENT TOMORROW." We wonder... what could this be? We get to our desk and the first email we see, in the Subject line is, "CEO WILL MAKE BIG ANNOUNCEMENT." We open the email and it simply restates the subject line and adds that the announcement will be tomorrow in an email. Wow! This must be really big and now our creative mind takes over.

So we begin to think, could it be layoffs? Could the CEO be moving on and this big announcement is to name her replacement? Our mind kicks in and now we start thinking of all the worst-case scenarios possible. The more creative we get, the more worried we become. We can barely work today, fretting over the "BIG ANNOUNCEMENT." During breaks, we discuss with coworkers what they think and their creativity adds to our concerns and worries. It's like a tornado, spinning out of control, sucking up everything in its path. With the added fuel of negativity from our coworkers, we feed upon each other. The break room is a buzz of whispers and conjecture. What is our fate?

The day arrives for the "BIG ANNOUNCEMENT." We check our email, nothing. We look at the bulletin board, nothing. This is insane; WE NEED TO KNOW! The morning coffee only adds to our jitters. The morning goes by and now lunch. It's mid-afternoon; an email pops up on the computers with the subject line, BIG ANNOUNCEMENT. We're afraid to open it, what will it say? Just open it, we say to ourselves, and we click the email and it opens.

"As CEO, I want to thank everyone for all their hard work and dedication in serving our customers. You have made me proud to lead this company to where it is today. I am honored to serve with such a fine group of men and women. So, I am happy to announce, Friday will be an unscheduled, fully paid, day off. Enjoy! We will see you on Monday."

Why can't we see the beautiful sunrise in the morning and not focus on the clouds? It's time we focus on the positive and not allow our minds to run crazy with doom and gloom. Stay focused on the present and our present looks pretty darn good. Enjoy!

December 14

The self-move truck's rear door slides down and closes. All the worldly possessions are packed away in boxes and fill the bed of the truck. Their cat is in a small crate on the front set. A car trailer is attached to the rear bumper, and their small red car is secured in place. Cooler filled with water, soda, and snacks sit on the floor board on the passenger side. It's time to say good-bye to our best friend. Moving thousands of miles away, our heart is filled with sadness as our friend prepares to drive away.

We've been dreading this day ever since they told us they were moving away. We tried to cram so much in the time remaining with them; it was a whirlwind few weeks. The late evenings of playing board games, laughing at silly things, and being there to hold our hand or comfort us with a hug when things were not so good. Our friend has walked many miles with us, and has touched our life in more ways than we can speak.

The truck pulls away, turns right at the stop sign, and we see their arm waving. It will be the last time we will see them for a long time. A tear rolls down our cheek as we wave, hoping they will see us too. We wait, staring at the intersection, hoping for whatever reason; we would see the truck come back. We wait, and wait. Soon we realize the truck is not coming back, and we sadly retreat into our home.

Our friend has gone, and we are very sad. We are selfishly thinking of ourselves, and not the positive aspect of their new life. Our sadness should be replaced with joy and happiness. Joy, because our departed friend has a new and wonderful life ahead in their next chapter in life. We should feel happiness, because we were touched by their lives; their companionship, and mostly with their love. While they may not be physically with us, they are, and will always be, in our heart. Friends are never truly gone. The memories, their laughter, their smile, their voice, are the sounds and images that will be locked away in our heart, and the key to that lock is called love.

December 15

ourteous behavior is taught to us by our parents and grandparents. We say, "Yes Sir and Yes Mam." We're taught to say please and thank you. These are basic manners we learn in early childhood. When a child or adolescent demonstrates these simple courtesies, we return the courtesy and we also immediately give credit to their parents for teaching them to respect others. Some will take these simple, basic courtesies into their teenage years and young adulthood, while others will simply dismiss them from their lives.

Courtesy is a kindness we can share with everyone. A handshake when meeting a stranger or an old friend is a courteous act. A smile, and perhaps a simple greeting as we hold the door for the person walking in is courtesy in action. Our parents and grandparents taught us the basics of manners early in life, but it is the actions of others that will reinforce them. When someone is rude, impolite, or ungracious, we are taken aback, and we are reminded of our value of respect.

So we make a difference in this world in many ways. We can make a difference by leading a life of disrespect, selfishness, and just plain rudeness; teaching others how valuable their values are. Or we can make a difference in this world by living a life of courtesy, respect, and kindness; demonstrating to others living their values is a life worth living. Which method will we demonstrate today?

December 16

*G*raduating from high school was the best day of our life, or perhaps graduating from college was the best day of our life. Others may see the day they met their true love, soul mate as the best day of their lives. The wedding day was surely the best day of our life, right? How can we not include the birth of our first child, seeing them graduate, or get married as not being the best days of our lives?

We all have "good days," but it's that special event, that milestone in our life, that we label it as the "best day of our life." We hold that label close and do not freely give it away. As we look back on our lives, we see how blessed we are to have so many 'best days of our lives." Our heart fills with gratitude, as each chapter in our lives, so far has some good days and some chapters are rewarded with the gold seal of "The Best Day of My Life."

The best days of our lives are measured and evaluated from our past. These days are very special. However, our journey is not over. The book of our life has not reached its final page. We look at the journey that lies ahead of us today and see that this could be the best day of our life. We don't know what is around the corner, or whose life will be changed because we were there. We make a difference and our actions today may cause someone else to have the best day of their lives.

The best day of our life is not in the yesterdays, but is what is ahead of us on our path. As we move forward on our journey, along the way we will touch another's life and will make a difference. For that instant, we may experience another "best day of our life." Enjoy the journey today.

December 17

The sand is cool and damp from the ocean's waves that have subsided with the tide. This is a perfect place to build our dream sand castle. The sand feels good on our feet and knees as we begin with our base. Wet sand is only a few feet away, and the supply is endless. Our friend, however, has picked a different spot. It's further up on the beach where the sand is hot and dry. They must walk across yards and yards of hot sand to get their buckets of wet sand to build their sand castle.

Hours and hours go by and our dream sand castle is approaching completion, but our friend still has a way to go before it is close to what ours looks like. We guess it's because of the distance from where they chose to build, and the wet sand needed to make a sand castle. Our castle spires are intricate, as the wet sand was drizzled over each one. A delicate sculpture of sand and sea, we admire our dream. The castle walls, etched with detailed design, it is a prize-winning sand castle.

Hours later, our friend has finely finished. We go to see his work. His sand castle is equally elaborate and detailed. We think to ourselves, how many trips he must have made to the wet sand to create this masterpiece. We admire his work, but think to ourselves; we were smarter by not having to make so many long trips to the wet sand.

We turn to walk back to our sand castle to see if there are any little extras we could add. Just as we begin to walk back, we see an ocean wave washing up to our sand castle with great speed. It crashes over our wall and washes away all the details of our work. A second wave follows, larger than the first, and soon our sand castle returns to the ocean. The tide has come in and all our work, our sand castle, our dream, has washed away. Our friend's sand castle will remain, because we now see theirs was built beyond the tide line.

Dreams, just like sand castles, built by taking shortcuts, and not long-term planning and hard work, are many times washed away and never fulfilled. Our efforts in working towards our dreams will pay off, and no tide or wave will wash it away when we don't take shortcuts or the easy way. Our dreams are worth our hard work.

December 18

The early-morning dew rests on the pedals of the new blossoms greeting the dawn's light. A bird chirps in the not too far distance, singing its morning song. A small waterfall close by adds yet another peaceful sound to the beginning of the day. We don't hear the sounds of the engines of cars in traffic, or the honking of horns. We are not listening to loud music or the banter of conversations; we have found peace and serenity.

This solitude can easily be interrupted, and we're pushed back into the hustle and bustle of life. Peaceful nature is replaced by the calamity of a tornado. The quietness of our serenity bubble is burst with the demands of others. Our serenity is lost in the madness, and once it's gone, getting it back is a challenge.

Peace and serenity should be more than the occasional, once a week, or once a month life experience. Most would agree a few minutes of peace, and serenity is relaxing and enjoyable. This quietness of the mind amidst the chaos that surrounds us is achievable. Relaxing our mind, releasing all the stress and tension is waiting for us; we simply need to make it a priority. Peace and serenity are an inside job, and we can get there, virtually any time we wish.

December 19

W here are we today? Not in the sense of our physical location of a city, but where are we on our journey? Do we have some vision of where we would like to be today? Tomorrow? Our path will take us to our destination; however, the route in which we get there may be a little round about.

So why are we here? What brought us to this place on our journey? The answer may seem difficult to answer, but in reality, the answer is quite simple; it was our past that had led us to where we stand today. Our past, or decisions, the good and the bad ones are what have brought us to this point in time and place. We made decisions along our way as we faced various forks on our journey and some of these decisions were not the best. Some of our decisions were the lucky; while others we just knew the right one to make. Our journey is making one decision after another on this path we face each day.

Are we happy with where we are on our journey? If not, what can we do today, what decisions can we make to get onto the path that we want and believe we should travel? If we are happy with where we are, then we need to be grateful for our past and how it has brought us to this place on our journey.

So we step forward today on our journey. We will make some decisions today, some good, and maybe some not so good. Decisions made to serve others unselfishly and help make a difference in the world, will be good ones. Decisions made thinking of ourselves first; allowing our ego to make these decisions may not be the best choice.

Decisions, decisions… in any case, we're moving forward and hopefully on the right path for our intended journey.

December 20

From darkness, we can celebrate the light of day. If we had not experienced the solitude of darkness in our life, the joys and happiness of the light in our life would be less appreciated. Likewise, a sense of sadness today will make the overwhelming bliss of tomorrow much more powerful. Each valley we travel is made up of two peaks. The peaks are joy, freedom, happiness, love, and many others. The valleys are sadness, pain, anger, and more.

When we find ourselves in the valley of our journey, we will come to a fork on our path. One way leads further down, deeper into the dark and foreboding valley. The other way leads upward, toward the peak. Certainly, the path down deeper into the valley is the easier way to travel. While the path upward to the peak of joy is steep and will be difficult at times to walk. So here we are, in the valley of despair. It's dark, wet, cold and lonely. We have a choice to make, and only we can make that choice.

Choosing the difficult path upward, toward the peak is the answer, and as soon as we begin, we soon discover we have guides along the way to help us. Like the Himalayan guides, the Sherpa's, we have friends who will reach out their hand to help us to the peak. At the peak, we find the beautiful sun, the clouds at our feet, and joy back into our heart.

Our focus should be on the peaks and understand the valleys in life are there to make the peaks more impressive and meaningful.

December 21

We may have a beautiful voice that sings the pretty songs, sharing messages of hope and faith. Others of us may have the gift of writing a wonderful message that enlightens and inspires. Still others may have the gift of a listening ear and words of comfort and compassion. However, so many times we think we don't have much to give, and that we have no special talents to share with others. We place ourselves into the role of "taker" and not one as of a "giver."

We see others sharing their special talents and the differences they are making in the world, while we sit idly by and take. We simply don't feel we matter. So what if we can't carry a tune, write well, or have a hard time putting the right words together. That doesn't matter. What matters is that we discover that special gift we have and then put it to use. We may sew well and can teach someone else to sew. We may have some free time and a vehicle to deliver meals to those that are housebound. We can volunteer in a hospital, serving others in so many ways. The one special gift we have is our smile and sharing it takes little talent; it simply takes a willingness to smile.

We don't have to be just a taker; we can be a giver too. Each of us has special talents, and this incredible force within us can make a huge difference in someone's life. Let's see what we can give today that will make a difference. It may be just our smile, and that is a beautiful gift for sure.

December 22

There isn't a band playing crazy wild music of celebration. There aren't cheerleaders screaming at the top of their lungs waving pom-poms either. Streamers and confetti don't fill the air either. However, today is a special day.

Today is special because we may have reached a milestone, accomplished a goal we have been working hard toward, or it may be that we simply see a glimmer in a child's eye that they now 'get it'. The celebration needs not to be so obvious to all around us; we merely need to feel that glow in our heart; knowing our life has gotten better because we made a difference in someone else's life.

We don't look for the fanfare; we just want to use the gifts we have to see how we can make a difference. Each of us has talents we can use, not only to accomplish the goals we set, but some the same talents can be used to help others achieve their dreams too.

So instead of looking for the cheerleaders and band, let's look to see how we can serve others. Let's look within and give thanks for what we have and for the gifts and talents we bring to the world. Let's look into the eyes of a child or friend and see that we helped give them a glimmer of hope. Let's serve others as best we can; inspire others by living our values, and make a difference in the world in some small way. The band, cheerleaders, and streamers can wait; we have more work to do.

December 23

As we begin our day, believe today will be the very best day of our life. Today everything will fall into place, and great joy and happiness shine on us like the sun. Believe that we can make a difference in someone's life by sharing a smile, reaching out our hand to help, or simply be there with a caring soul.

Believe we are on this journey called 'life' with a purpose. Our purpose may be to teach our youth, and one may grow up to find a cure for cancer. Our purpose may simply be to touch one person's life in such a way that moves them out of the self-imposed darkness and helps them find their way into the sunlight of their journey.

We need to believe in ourselves and have confidence that we are worthy travelers on this journey. We need to believe in love. We need to believe in others and not judge them.

Believing in all these things is not easy sometimes. We must find the strength and faith deep within our heart and soul to allow ourselves to believe. Believing in ourselves, in others, and the fact we are here with a purpose, is far better than the darkness of doubt and disbelief.

Believing, truly believing is a huge step forward in changing the world to be a better place for everyone.

December 24

T hings don't always go the way we want them. We don't live in a perfect world and there are times when the bumps in our road seem bigger than normal. People don't act like we expect them to, and we get upset with them. We didn't get this or that like we thought we should, and now we're disappointed or if it's really big, we're developing a resentment that will eat away at us until we let it go.

So we complain to anyone that will listen about all our troubles. Some will listen politely and may even give a small suggestion, but it comes back to us to take action to resolve our issues. If we're not willing to take some action to help resolve the issues that are bothering us, we have no business complaining. If it is something that we have no control over, then we need to let it go and move on with our life. We should stop complaining. Complaining is a sign of weakness. We want to cast off our troubles and complain to someone else, hoping they will agree with us and give us sympathy, and solve our problems. These are our problems, not theirs. They have problems of their own. We need to take the action necessary and not rely on someone else to bail us out.

So before we open our mouth to complain out loud, when others can hear us, we should ask ourselves first, "Have I taken any action to resolve the issue myself?" If the answer is no, then we should keep our complaints to the only complaint department that can do something about it. That complaint department is our self.

December 25

*T*he gift under the Christmas tree is not wrapped; it's actually invisible to some, yet very visible to me. The gift under the tree is not a gadget, pair of socks, or flannel pajamas. It is the gift of inspiration. Inspiration is that power within our heart and soul to reach out and make a difference in the world in whatever small way we can. To inspire others is giving an invisible gift, which can be repaid only by paying it forward and inspiring others.

Another gift under my tree is the abundance of blessings of so many friends, both physical and virtual. I am inspired by the number of people that like what I share in my Thoughts of the Day, my social media postings, and my professional speaking/coaching. I am blessed.

The gifts under my tree are priceless, and I am so very grateful. I hope the gift of inspiration finds its way into your life, and that you discover your life's purpose. The two combined will make a difference in the world, and they can contribute that change to you.

If your faith celebrates a different holiday this time of the year, I wish you and your family the very best and joyous holiday. We all don't celebrate Christmas, but most of us will have a celebration during this time of the year. We naturally will be grateful and blessed by whatever our faith leads us. So Merry Christmas, or a belated Happy Hanukah or whatever you may celebrate.

Inspire!

December 26

Whether our car has an automatic transmission or a standard one, each one has basically the same concept, neutral, reverse and varying forms of drive. Each one has its purpose and some are used more than others.

Just like our car, we have the same internal transmission concept as we travel on our path, with the exception of reverse. We cannot go backwards on the part of our journey we have already travelled, so reverse is not an option. But the question is, are we in neutral on our journey? Are we waiting, idling in neutral for something or someone to come along and give us direction?

It's time for us to put 'it' in gear and get moving on our own. We cannot sit in neutral, with our engine running at idle, and think we're going to get somewhere in life. We need to get it in 'drive', stomp on the gas, and get moving forward on our journey.

So, are we in neutral? Or are we ready to take some control of our lives and put our life in drive? We're behind the wheel, we have control, and we can make it happen. Drive On!

December 27

We walk along a path that meanders through the woods. The autumn colored leaves gently float to the ground as the branches of the tree gently sway in the cool wind. The sun's rays are clearly visible as they stream through the woods and reflect the wonderful colors of each leaf as it gently falls to the ground. Silence fills the cool brisk air as we continue to slowly walk along the path.

Our path brings us to a slow moving stream. The water is crystal clear as it flows over and around the rocks that fill the stream bed. We pause for a moment to watch the water, mesmerizing and soothing this form of beautiful nature. We become so relaxed as we just lean against a tree and watch the water follow its appointed path. Just as the stream has its path, we have ours and it has brought us here, to this place, in this time.

The water flows over the rocks in the stream and one catches our eye, a special rock that stands out from the others. We slowly kneel, reach into the cold water and take the rock from the bed of the stream. The rock is beautiful. The patterns of various colors that nature has woven appear to be a word. As we look closer we see a word and that word is 'Believe'.

We are that stone, unique from all the others in the stream. We are the stone that has 'Believe' woven into ourselves through all the beautiful patterns and colors that makes us who we are. It's time we look at our stone and put it in our pocket to carry from now on, as we travel on our journey. Believe.

December 28

*V*ery few of us enjoy having stress in our life. While there are a few that feed on this energy, sometimes gut wrenching emotion, most of us try to avoid it. Stress leads to medical issues; high blood pressure, strokes, and possibly psychological problems. Yet, we find ourselves in these situations from time to time, and upon close examination, the stress is driven by some sort of self-imposed pressure. We have found a way to increase our stress level by trying to be better than the best. We are trying to live up to the expectations of others, and we place ourselves into a boiling pot of stress. We put ourselves there; now what do we do?

Striving to do the very best we can at our job, or some other task at hand is one thing, but placing ourselves into a stressful lifestyle is a different story. So many times when we wrap ourselves up so tight with pleasing others, or trying to be the person, they want us to be; we forget who is in control. We are the ones that will suffer the strain of this self-imposed stress.

Stress in life is just sometimes part of life. We can reduce some of it by setting our own expectations and deciding to please ourselves with our efforts. What others think of us is really none of our business, as long as we're honest with ourselves. Stressing over what others think about us is our ego fluffing its feathers. Release the self-imposed stress and live your life. It's your life, not theirs.

December 29

You made a difference to someone. You made a difference to the waitress that served you lunch. When she brought you the bill, you simply looked at her, thanked her for her service and then commented on how good the meal was and that you would be back. You left a good tip as well. You made a difference to her because she now feels better about herself and the fifty-cent tip from the previous customer is just a memory. You made a difference.

You made a difference to someone. It was a cold blustery winter day, cold, but not cold enough to snow, just a miserable wet rain. Your spouse asked you to pick something up at the grocery store on the way home. Still all dressed you your business attire, you wanted to get in and out of the store quickly. Well, everyone else was there at the store after work too and the parking lot was full. Then all of a sudden a parking spot opens up, just 3 slots down from the closest one to the door. You see an old mini-van coming up the lane and you rush, put your blinker on and quickly pull in. A smile comes across your face, and you whisper "YES!" You rush in and get what you needed and go home. What difference did you make you ask? The mini-van was a single mom with three children she just picked up from daycare. She parked many rows over and walked her children into the store, now wet, cold and crying. Yes, you made a difference in not such a good way.

We just need to be aware that we touch the lives of so many, and we may never know how many, but we do. As we go about our day, just remember that our actions and words will make a difference. What kind of difference will you make today?

December 30

*L*ittle does the farmer know how much of a difference, he will make to one person as he plants the seeds of his crop. Months later, the crop is ready to harvest. He looks over his farm and sees a sea of white cotton balls. The slight roll of the land looks like waves of white snow. He starts his machine and begins his harvesting. One cotton ball after another, it soon becomes a bail of cotton to be sent to the processing plant.

The engineer of the processing plant doesn't realize how he will make a difference in one person's life today either. He oversees the cotton process, making sure the dye is the right, and that the yarn is void of defects. The finished yarn is packed into boxes and shipped to the distributor.

The driver of the delivery truck is completely unaware of the life that will be a little better because of his delivery route today. He unloads the boxes of yarn to the destination store and then leaves to make more deliveries. The stock boy, fresh out of high school, unpacks the boxes of yarn and places them on the shelves of the store. He too doesn't know how he is making a difference.

The daughter of an elderly mother comes to the store and selects several skeins of beautifully colored yarn and goes home. Knitting for days, now weeks, the afghan is finished, and she takes it to her mother who is living in an assisted-living facility. "It is beautiful." the elderly parent says as her daughter hands her the labor of love. "You have made my day very special. Thank you." she says.

The afghan is a labor of love from the time the farmer plants the cotton seed, through all the other hands who made it to what it is today; a beautifully knitted afghan that now is draped over the elderly woman's lap. Each person made a difference in the life of this lady.

Sometimes we don't realize the impact we have on others. We make a difference each day, though it may not be apparent. Let's hope that our actions today are a labor of love.

December 31

The last day of the year has arrived. Some may be glad this year is over, while others will cherish each of the 365 days this year brought us. Regardless, it's the last day of the year, and a new year will begin soon.

Each day this year we were greeted with a gift of another day. Each gift was wrapped in a beautiful sunrise on some days, while other days were in a cloak of clouds. The meteorological phenomena is not the wrapping, it is how we viewed the start of the day. It could be cold and rainy, yet we saw this day as another gift for us to travel our path with joy and happiness in our heart. Others will not see the beautiful sunrise because they only look at the ground and feel their journey is one of drudgery, and their heart is heavy with rocks of anger and resentments. It's about how we choose to see this gift of another day.

So today, the last day of the year, are we viewing it as a gift and see the beauty of what it beholds? Or do we view it as just another day in which we must trudge on, continuing to be weighed down with those heavy rocks?

It's time; it's time to commit to changing the way we see each day as we will begin a new year tomorrow. Regardless of the weather, clear or cloudy, see each day as a gift filled with joy, happiness, care, compassion, and love. See each day as another day to serve others and make a difference in their lives, and by doing so, we will make the world a little better.

This year brought us to where we are today, and we should give thanks. We have grown and become a little wiser, so we should not regret a single day of this year.

Thank you this year for all the gifts you brought us.

Afterword
&
About the Author

Afterword

O nce again, we have come to end of the year, but certainly not the end of our journey together. I hope that some of the messages helped you along your journey and perhaps made a small difference in your life.

By being inspired and enriched with our lives, we can inspire others to find the same sense of peace and serenity. We will meet many people on our journey and maybe one of the messages in this book will be shared with them so their journey is not quite as difficult to travel. Our paths will cross again, and I am honored to walk with you along yours. Safe travels my good friend.

About the Author

*I*nspirational Speaker and Author, Doug Petersen is a decorated Vietnam veteran and having served more than twenty years as an aviator in the United States Army, Doug continued to serve others by working in the financial services industry, helping families with their financial security.

Like many, his journey has not always been smooth sailing. An addiction to alcohol for many years took over his life and the defects of character consumed him, pushing aside the personal values that are so important. This changed on July 11, 2001, when he placed recovery as his first priority and the reawakening his personal values within his heart and soul.

Today he continues to take deep-seated passion in making a difference in the lives of others through his life-affirming messages, and is fulfilling his life's purpose by inspiring people into action. Author of five enlightening, thought-provoking books, Doug's words reaffirm the good in all of us.

You can contact Doug at doug@inspirevalues.com or visit his web site, www.inspirevalues.com.

Other books by Doug Petersen include:

Inspire: A Collection of Thoughts of the Day
(ISBN 978-1-60264-404-5)

Inspire: Collection II of Thoughts of the Day
(ISBN 978-1-60264-477-9)

Inspire: Collection III of Thoughts of the Day
(ISBN 978-1-60264-601-8)

Inspire: A Year of Daily Inspirational Thoughts
(ISBN 978-1-60264-872-2 (softcover))
(ISBN 978-1-60264-874-6 (electronic))

Books are available at www.Amazon.com,
www.Barnes&Noble.com, and
www.VirtualBookWorm.com

CPSIA information can be obtained
at www.ICGtesting.com
Printed in the USA
FFHW021527111118
49312555-53563FF